THIS DATE IN
CHICAGO
WHITE SOX
HISTORY

THIS DATE IN
CHICAGO
WHITE SOX
HISTORY

The complete story in text, charts, statistics, and photos—since 1901

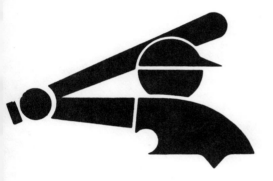

Art Berke and Paul Schmitt

A SCARBOROUGH BOOK
STEIN AND DAY/*Publishers*/New York

First published in 1982
Copyright © 1982 by Art Berke
All rights reserved
Designed by Louis A. Ditizio
Printed in the United States of America
STEIN AND DAY/ *Publishers*
Scarborough House
Briarcliff Manor, N.Y. 10510

Library of Congress Cataloging in Publication Data

Berke, Art.
  This date in Chicago White Sox history.

  "A Scarborough book."
  1. Chicago White Sox (Baseball team)—History.
2. Chicago White Sox (Baseball team)—Records.
I. Schmitt, Paul, 1952– . II. Title.
GV875.C58B47   796.357′64′0977311   81-40804
ISBN 0-8128-6132-9 (pbk.)   AACR2

ACKNOWLEDGMENTS

The authors would like to thank Chuck Shriver, Ken Valdiserri, and Dan Evans of the White Sox; Barbara Kane, Susan Aglietti, Helen Stone, Pam Norman and the rest of the staff at the Baseball Commissioner's Office; Tony Rezza of ABC Public Relations; and the writers and editors who contributed to the wealth of material contained in *The Sporting News*.

Photos courtesy of the Chicago White Sox and the Baseball Hall of Fame, Cooperstown, New York.

CONTENTS

Photos between pages 81 and 82

FOREWORD

"If I was going to storm a pillbox, going to sheer utter, certain death, and the colonel said, 'Shepherd, pick six guys,' I'd pick six White Sox fans, because they have known death every day of their lives and it holds no terror for them."

—Humorist Jean Shepherd

Jean Shepherd is one who knows. In fact, you'd have to be a Sox diehard like the popular humorist to really, I mean really, understand the full meaning of his observation.

To be a White Sox fan is to have suffered—to have experienced few winners, several near misses and numerous total collapses. Through the years the Sox have tested the strongest will of their faithful. Since 1919 when the notorious "Black Sox" lost to the Cincinnati Redlegs in the World Series, only the 1959 "Go-Go White Sox" have been able to win a pennant. Generations of White Sox fans have literally come and gone without a championship flag.

Why, then, would fan loyalties remain so intense despite this persistent failure to win? It is, in essence, the real magic of this franchise, a charter member of the American League.

To evaluate the attractiveness of Chicago's South Side major league baseball team one first must take into account more than a mere tally of won and lost ball games. To White Sox fans that has never been the determinant of their enthusiasm. They have found that there is more to cheer for at the ballpark than a winning team.

This philosophy may be difficult for young Yankee, Red and Dodger fans to comprehend, but the game of baseball does lend itself to appreciation through more than just the won-lost column. White Sox fans, by necessity, have adopted this philosophy. But if you think about it, that is really what rooting for your favorite team is all about—and not deciding how much of a fan you'll be by looking at the daily standings. Sox fans go to the ballpark hoping to win, but never really expecting it.

This shouldn't paint an altogether dismal picture. It is wonderful rooting for the White Sox. I feel sorry for those Yankee fans in the 1950s who didn't have Nellie Fox, Minnie Minoso, Luis Aparicio, Jungle Jim Rivera and Billy Pierce to cheer for. The Yanks won year after year in those days, often at the Sox expense, but their fans didn't enjoy the game any more. These players and their accomplishments on the diamond were truly extraordinary.

Through the years there have been good teams, good players, and excitement. During the Bill Veeck years, both in the '50s and '70s, Comiskey Park—the most underrated of all parks—was like the midway of a carnival. Win or lose, it is hard not to have a good time at a Sox game.

What this book attempts to do is to bring you the White Sox on their own terms. If you compare their history with that of teams possessing impressive winning traditions you have missed the point. Accept them for what they are. I have, for 34 years, and have never—well, rarely—been sorry.

Need anybody to storm a pillbox?

ART BERKE

THIS DATE IN
CHICAGO
WHITE SOX
HISTORY

INTRODUCTION

The Chicago White Sox were founded by Charles A. Comiskey, who gained the nickname of the "Old Roman" while managing and playing first base for the old St. Louis Browns. He was instrumental in bringing both the Sox and the American League into existence in 1900.

When the league itself began play in 1901, the team became known as the White Stockings, the exact name used by the Chicago National League team years earlier.

During Comiskey's reign with the White Sox the club won four AL flags and proved to be one of the truly great teams in the early years of the league.

The 1906 team, which upset the crosstown Cubs four games to two in the only all-Chicago World Series in history, was affectionately known as the "Hitless Wonders." The team had the lowest batting average in the league at .228 and clouted only seven homers, but combined great pitching—led by Hall of Famer Ed Walsh, Nick Altrock, Frank Owen and Doc White—and speed (209 stolen bases).

Another powerful Sox team, paced by future Hall of Famers Ray Schalk, Eddie Collins and Red Faber along with "Shoeless Joe" Jackson, brought Chicago a second world title in 1917. The Sox defeated John McGraw's New York Giants in six games.

The Sox won the American League crown in 1919. But they lost the Series that year to Cincinnati, five games to three, after which eight Sox players were banned from baseball for conspiring with gamblers.

It was 40 years later before the club won another flag as the "Go Go Sox" of 1959 sat atop the AL standings. The team's strengths were pitching, defense and speed, as they led the league in stolen bases. Nellie Fox won the league MVP award that year, Early Wynn was the Cy Young Award winner as the loop's top pitcher and Luis Aparicio led the circuit in steals.

Even though late-season acquisition Ted Kluszewski powered three homers, drove in 10 runs and compiled a .391 average, the Sox lost the Series to Los Angeles, four games to two.

During the lean years before the 1959 title—with stars like Hall of Fame shortstop Luke Appling in the 1930s and 1940s—and since—with standouts like Dick Allen in the 1970s—the Sox have still given their fans much to cheer about.

The current White Sox outlook is as promising as ever as new ownership, headed by Jerry Reinsdorf and Eddie Einhorn, is committed to bring a winner to the South Side of Chicago. They, and Sox fans everywhere, are hoping the present club with a nucleus of Carlton Fisk, Greg Luzinski, Steve Kemp and Tom Paciorek and outstanding young pitching, led by Britt Burns, can accomplish that goal before very long.

THIS DATE IN CHICAGO WHITE SOX HISTORY CALENDAR SECTION

The following chronological table lists White Sox players and managers of the past and present (through 1981) by their birth dates. Following each name are the years each played with this team. The next symbol indicates the position the individual played: *P* = pitcher, *C* = catcher, *1B* = first base, *2B* = second base, *3B* = third base, *SS* = shortstop, *IF* = infield, *OF* = outfield, *PH* = pinchhitter, *DH* = designated hitter; *MGR* = manager.

The number following the letter *G* indicates the number of games the individual played for the White Sox as of the end of the 1982 season.

Highlights of White Sox history are also recorded by date. The symbol (H) following comments about a game indicates that it was a home game.

JANUARY 1

1874 — Ned Garvin — 1902, P G-23

1924 — Earl Torgeson — 1957–61, 1B G-397

1955 — Lamarr Hoyt — 1979–82, P G-109

January 2

1907 — Red Kress — 1932–34, IF–OF G-272

1951 — Jim Essian — 1976–77, 81, C G-219

      Royle Stillman — 1977, OF G-56

January 3

1904 — Bill Cissell — 1928–32, SS–2B G-539

1912 — Frenchy Bordagaray — 1934, OF G-29

1950 — Bart Johnson — 1969–74, 1976–77, P G-185

January 4

1903 — Alex Metzler — 1927–30, OF G-475

1906 — Blondy Ryan — 1930, 3B G-28

1930 — Don McMahon — 1967–68, P G-77

1941 — Bought pitcher Joe Haynes from Washington.

January 5

1879 — Erwin Harvey — 1901, P G-17

1899 — Bill Hunnefield — 1926–30, SS–2B G-415

1901 — Luke Sewell — 1935–38, C G-433

1914 — Jack Salveson—1935, P G-20

1924 — Freddie Marsh — 1953–54, 3B–SS G-129

1935 — Earl Battey — 1955–59, C G-151

1958 — Ron Kittle — 1982, OF G-20

January 6

1878 — Jack Slattery — 1903, C G-63

1882 — Willis Cole — 1909–10, OF G-68

3

1886 — Billy Purtell — 1908–10, 3B G-231

1895 — Foster Blackburn — 1921, P G-1

1897 — Buck Crouse — 1923–30, C G-470

1902 — Bob Barnes — 1924, P G-2

1903 — Fred Eichrodt — 1931, OF G-34

1917 — Phil Masi — 1950–52, C G-236

1920 — Early Wynn — 1958–62, P G-157

January 7

1900 — Johnny Grabowski — 1924–26, C G-89

1905 — Frank Grube — 1931–33, 1935–36, C G-308

1920 — Dixie Howell — 1955–58, P G-112

1921 — Ted Beard — 1957–58, OF G-57

1946 — Joe Keough — 1973, PH G-5

January 8

1921 — Marv Rickert — 1950, OF G-84

1927 — Jim Busby — 1950–52, OF G-276

1934 — Gene Freese — 1960, 1965–66, 3B G-192

January 9

1897 — Ray French — 1924, SS G-37

January 10

1908 — Bill Swift — 1943, P G-18

1937 — Jim O'Toole — 1967, P G-15

1959 — Dick Dotson — 1979–82, P G-102

January 11

1922 — Neil Berry — 1953, 2B G-5

1929 — Don Mossi — 1964, P G-34

1949 — Sold catcher Mike Tresh to Cleveland.

January 12

1876 — George Browne — 1910, OF G-30

January 13

1918 — Emmett O'Neill — 1946, P G-2

January 14

1892 — Billy Meyer — 1913, C G-1

1902 — Smead Jolley — 1930–32, OF G-218

1952 — Terry Forster — 1971–76, P G-266

1963 — Traded shortstop Luis Aparicio and outfielder Al Smith to Baltimore for pitcher Hoyt Wilhelm, shortstop Ron Hansen, third baseman Pete Ward, and outfielder Dave Nicholson.

January 15

1885 — Grover Lowdermilk — 1919–20, P G-23

1915 — Dick Culler — 1943, 3B–2B G-53

1937 — Bob Sadowski — 1962, 3B–2B G-79

1949 — Luis Alvarado — 1971–74, SS–2B G-289

January 16

1891 — Erskine Mayer — 1919, P G-6

      Ferdie Schupp — 1922, P G-18

1892 — Fred Bratschi — 1921, OF G-16

1904 — Jo-Jo Morrissey — 1936, 3B–SS G-17

January 17

1889 — Pete Johns — 1915, 3B G-28

1935 — Dick Brown — 1960, C G-16

1954 — Jerry Turner — 1981, OF G-10

January 18

1930 — Brief boxing career of Art "Whataman" Shires, including fights against baseball players, football players and soft touches, plus a proposed match against Cub outfielding great Hack Wilson, inspires Commissioner Landis to ban boxing for all players in Organized Baseball.

5

1932 — Mike Fornieles — 1953–56, P G-89

1950 — Bill Sharp — 1973–75, OF G-194

January 19

1888 — Chick Gandil — 1910, 1917–19, 1B G-455

1906 — Rip Radcliff — 1934–39, OF G-684

1948 — Ken Frailing — 1972–73, P G-14

January 20

1888 — Bill James — 1919, P G-5

1917 — Joe Dobson — 1951–53, P G-80

1933 — Gene Stephens — 1963–64, OF G-88

1965 — Traded outfielders Jim Landis and Mike Hershberger to Athletics for outfielder Rocky Colavito, then traded Colavito to Cleveland with catcher Camilio Carreon for catcher John Romano, pitcher Tommy John, and outfielder Tommie Agee. (White Sox sent pitcher Fred Talbot to Athletics to complete deal, February 10, 1965.)

1969 — Traded outfielder Bill Voss and pitcher Andy Rubilotta to Angels for pitcher Sammy Ellis.

January 21

1886 — Joe Benz — 1911–19, P G-250

1899 — Lew Fonseca — 1931–34, OF–IF–MGR G-162

1923 — Sam Mele — 1952–53, OF G-263

1947 — Bill Stein — 1974–76, 3B–2B G-206

1953 — Infielder Fred Marsh acquired from Browns for minor league infielder Roy Upright.

January 22

1880 — William O'Neill — 1906, OF G-94

January 23

1914 — Merv Connors — 1937–38, 3B–1B G-52

1918 — Randy Gumpert — 1948–51, P G-128

1928 — Chico Carrasquel — 1950–55, SS G-837

January 24

1879 — Dave Brain — 1901, 2B G-5

1903 — Clay Touchstone — 1945, P G-6

1910 — Johnny Dickshot — 1944–45, OF G-192

1953 — Tim Stoddard — 1975, P G-1

January 25

1943 — Brian McCall — 1962–63, OF G-7

1953 — Junior Moore — 1978–80, OF–3B G-157

1957 — John Flannery — 1977, SS–3B G-7

January 26

1886 — Frank Owens — 1909, C G-64

1927 — Bob Nieman — 1955–56, OF G-113

January 27

1896 — Milt Gaston — 1932–34, P G-87

1899 — Bibb Falk — 1920–28, OF G-1067

1913 — Floyd Speer — 1943–44, P G-3

1943 — Doug Adams — 1969, C G-8

1948 — Traded outfielder Thurman Tucker to Cleveland for catcher Ralph Weigel.

January 28

1869 — James Holmes — 1903–5, OF G-246

1904 — Clarence Hoffman — 1929, OF G-103

1920 — Sam Hairston — 1951, C G-4

1953 — Traded infielder Joe DeMaestri, first baseman Eddie Robinson, and outfielder Ed McGhee to Athletics for first baseman Ferris Fain and infielder Robert Wilson.

January 29

1880 — Bill Burns — 1909–10, P G-23

1900 — Charles A. Comiskey gets permission to move St. Paul franchise to Chicago—renames club the White Sox.

January 29 (continued)

1919 — Hank Edwards — 1952, OF G-8

1931 — Jim Baumer — 1949, SS G-7

1981 — American League owners approve the sale of White Sox to a group headed by Jerry Reinsdorf and Eddie Einhorn. Twice in the previous four months, AL owners turned down the sale of the White Sox by Bill Veeck's group to Edward DeBartolo.

January 30

1923 — Walt Dropo — 1955–58, 1B G-387

January 31

1897 — Charlie Robertson — 1919, 1922–25, P G-117

1898 — Webb Schultz — 1924, P G-1

1949 — Jim Willoughby — 1978, P G-59

FEBRUARY 1

1875 — Billy Sullivan, Sr. — 1901–12, 1914, C–MGR G-1051

1892 — Thomas McGuire — 1919, P G-1

1903 — Carl Reynolds — 1927–31, OF G-485

1914 — The world-touring White Sox and Giants play their first African game in Cairo, Egypt, battling to a 3–3 tie after 10 innings.

February 2

1878 — James Hart — 1905–7, C G-56

1884 — Ray Demmitt — 1914–15, OF G-155

      Walter Kuhn — 1912–14, C G-118

1895 — George Lees — 1921, C G-20

1900 — Willie Kamm — 1923–31, 3B G-1170

      Frank Mack — 1922–23, 1925, P G-28

1907 — Gerald Byrne — 1929, P G-3

1937 — Don Buford — 1963–67, 3B–2B G-621

1952 — Warren Brusstar — 1982, P G-10

1982 — After losing free agent pitcher Ed Farmer to the Phillies, White Sox become first team to select a player from the new compensation pool — part of the 1981 season strike settlement. Selected was catcher Joel Skinner from the Pirates organization.

February 3

1915 — Buck Ross — 1941–45, P G-96

1925 — Harry Byrd — 1955–56, P G-28

February 4

1898 — Johnny Mann — 1928, 3B G-6

1908 — Hank Garrity — 1931, C G-8

1955 — Rusty Kuntz — 1979–82, OF G-129

February 5

1891 — Roger Peckinpaugh — 1927, SS G-68

1929 — Al Worthington — 1960, P G-4

1954 — Traded outfielder Sam Mele and infielder Neil Berry to Baltimore for infielder Johnny Lipon and outfielder John Groth.

February 6

1901 — Glenn Wright — 1935, 2B G-9

1927 — Smoky Burgess — 1964–67, C–PH G-243

1949 — Richie Zisk — 1977, OF G-141

February 7

1866 — Thomas P. Daly — 1902–3, 2B G-180

1884 — Barney Reilly — 1909, 2B G-12

1894 — Charlie Jackson — 1915, PH G-1

1928 — Al Smith — 1958–62, OF–3B G-699

1938 — Juan Pizarro — 1961–66, P G-195

1939 — Frank Kreutzer — 1962–64, P G-19

1941 — Traded pitcher Clint Brown to Cleveland for pitcher John Humphries.

February 8

1914 — Bert Haas — 1951, 1B–OF G-25

1921 — Willard Marshall — 1954–55, OF G-69

February 9

1934 — Ted Wills — 1965, P G-15

February 9 (continued)

1950 — Bought catcher Phil Masi from Pittsburgh.

1951 — Eddie Solomon — 1982, P G-6

1953 — Traded pitchers Marv Grissom, Bill Kennedy, and Hal Brown to Red Sox for infielder Vern Stephens.

1971 — Traded pitcher Gerry Janeski to Washington for outfielder Rick Reichardt.

February 10

1904 — Harold Anderson — 1932, OF G-9

1913 — Bill Adair — 1970, MGR

1916 — Ralph Hodgin — 1943–44, 1946–48, OF–3B G-498

1946 — Bob Spence — 1969–71, 1B G-72

February 11

1905 — Ed Walsh, Jr. — 1928–32, P G-82

1941 — Sammy Ellis — 1969, P G-10

February 12

1879 — Clarence "Pants" Rowland — 1915–18, MGR

1893 — Earl Sheely — 1921–27, 1B G-948

1937 — Stan Johnson — 1960, OF G-5

1941 — Mike Joyce — 1962–63, P G-31

1943 — Paul Edmondson — 1969, P G-14

1955 — Chet Lemon — 1975–81, OF G-785

February 13

1883 — Hal Chase — 1913–14, 1B G-160

1919 — Bobby Rhawn — 1949, 3B–SS G-24

1927 — Jim Brideweser — 1955–56, IF G-34

1968 — Traded pitchers Dennis Higgins and Steve Jones and shortstop Ron Hansen to Washington for pitchers Bob Priddy and Buster Narum and infielder Tim Cullen.

February 14

1880 — Claude Berry — 1904, C G-3

February 15

1900 — George Earnshaw — 1934–35, P G-36

1951 — Tommy Cruz — 1977, OF G-4

February 16

1897 — Paul Castner — 1923, P G-6

1926 — Howie Judson — 1948–52, P G-161

1942 — Tim Cullen — 1968, 2B G-72

1952 — Jerry Hairston — 1973–77, 1981–82, OF G-325

February 17

1892 — Nemo Leibold — 1915–20, OF G-552

1897 — Ike Boone — 1927, OF G-29

1909 — Work on Comiskey Park begins.

1924 — Recently appointed manager Frank Chance resigns due to illness. Owner Charles Comiskey names coach Johnny Evers to be acting manager with Chance to return when he recovered. Chance never managed a White Sox game and died September 14, 1924.

1959 — Bill Veeck buys majority ownership of the White Sox from Mrs. Dorothy Rigney, granddaughter of Charles A. Comiskey and wife of former White Sox pitcher Johnny Rigney.

February 18

1889 — George Mogridge — 1911–12, P G-21

1923 — Joe Tipton — 1949, C G-67

1939 — Bob Miller — 1970, P G-16

1952 — Marc Hill — 1981–82, C G-69

February 19

1890 — Larry Chappell — 1913–15, OF G-82

1894 — Ernest Cox — 1922, P G-1

1900 — John Kane — 1925, SS-2B G-14

1941 — Gail Hopkins — 1968–70, 1B G-269

11

February 20

1896 — Muddy Ruel — 1934, C G-22

1900 — Al Williamson — 1928, P G-1

1922 — Jim Wilson — 1956–58, P G-87

February 21

1896 — Richard McCabe — 1922, P G-3

February 22

1895 — Roy Graham — 1922–23, C G-41

1907 — Dan Dugan — 1928–29, P G-20

      Marty Hopkins — 1934–35, 3B G-126

February 23

1908 — Bob Boken — 1934, 2B–SS G-81

1914 — Mike Tresh — 1938–48, C G-989

1958 — Juan Agosto — 1981–82, P G-3

February 24

1907 — Bob Seeds — 1932, OF G-116

1930 — Bubba Phillips — 1956–59, 3B–OF G-389

1948 — Traded pitcher Ed Lopat to Yankees for pitchers Bill Wight and Fred Bradley and catcher Aaron Robinson.

February 25

1900 — Joe Burns — 1924, C G-8

1908 — Al Hollingsworth — 1946, P G-21

1940 — Danny Cater — 1965–66, OF G-163

      Ron Santo — 1974, 2B–3B G-117

1957 — Kevin Hickey — 1981–82, P G-101

February 26

1898 — Lee Thompson — 1921, P G-4

1914 — Playing before King George of England, the White Sox and Giants finished their world tour, having played in every inhabited continent except South America. Tied 2–2 after 9 innings, both teams scored two runs in the tenth before Tom Daly's leadoff home run won the game for the White Sox in the eleventh. The White Sox won the series 24–20–2.

1945 — Don Secrist — 1969–70, P G-28

1950 — Jack Brohamer — 1976–77, 2B–3B G-178

February 27

1916 — Don Hanski — 1943–44, 1B–P G-11

1920 — Connie Ryan — 1953, 2B–3B G-17

1952 — Henry Cruz — 1977–78, OF G-69

February 28

1887 — Joseph Fautsch — 1916, P G-1

1898 — Jake Miller — 1933, P G-30

1906 — Pete Daglia — 1932, P G-12

1929 — Traded outfielder Bibb Falk to Cleveland for catcher Martin Autry.

1951 — Tom Spencer — 1978, OF G-29

February 29

1940 — Court ruling allows Mrs. Grace Comiskey to retain ownership of White Sox, ending battle with bank over estate of J. Louis Comiskey.

MARCH 1

1888 — Howard Baker — 1914–15, 3B G-17

1896 — Roy Elsh — 1923–25, OF G-173

1917 — Ike Pearson — 1948, P G-23

1932 — Dom Zanni — 1962–63, P G-49

March 2

1902 — Moe Berg — 1926–30, C G-278

1907 — Jack Knott — 1938–40, P G-70

1924 — Cal Abrams — 1956, OF G-4

March 3

1919 — Steve Souchock — 1949, OF G-84

1950 — Jesse Jefferson — 1975–76, P G-41

March 4

1876 — Charles Hickman — 1907, 1B–OF G-21

1894 — Jose Acosta — 1922, P G-5

1921 — Traded first baseman-outfielder Shano Collins and outfielder Nemo Leibold to Red Sox for outfielder Harry Hooper.

1926 — Cass Michaels — 1943–50, '54, IF G-795

1939 — Jack Fisher — 1968, P G-35

1958 — Lorenzo Gray — 1982, 3B G-17

March 5

1897 — Lu Blue — 1932–32, 1B G-267

1903 — Martin Autry — 1929–30, C G-77

Lou Rosenberg — 1923, 2B G-3

1941 — Phil Roof — 1976, C G-4

1952 — Mike Squires — 1977–82, 1B G-530

March 6

1953 — Bought pitcher Earl Harrist from Browns.

March 7

1890 — Dave Danforth — 1916–19, P G-132

1929 — Red Wilson — 1951–54, C G-85

1954 — Nyls Nyman — 1974–77, OF G-120

March 8

1882 — Harry Lord — 1911–14, 3B G-463

1917 — Bill Salkeld — 1950, C G-1

1942 — Dick Allen — 1972–74, 1B G-348

March 9

1893 — Claude "Lefty" Williams — 1916–20, P G-183

14

1908 — Myril Hoag — 1941–42, '44, OF G-236

1934 — Jim Landis — 1957–64, OF G-1063

1948 — Dan Neumeier — 1972, P G-3

1981 — Free agent catcher Carlton Fisk reaches contract agreement with White Sox. He had been declared a free agent following arbitration of a contract dispute with the Red Sox. Fisk was formally signed on March 18.

March 10

1894 — Jack Weineke — 1921, P G-10

1907 — Art Herring — 1939, P G-7

1924 — John Perkovich — 1950, P G-1

1939 — Bill Heath — 1965, PH G-1

March 11

1870 — Herm McFarland — 1901–2, OF G-141

1900 — Russell Pence — 1921, P G-4

1918 — Ed Fernandes — 1946, C G-14

March 12

1880 — Babe Towne — 1906, C G-13

1882 — John Beall — 1913, OF G-17

1887 — Wally Mattick — 1912–13, OF G-156

1939 — Johnny Callison — 1958–59, OF G-67

March 13

1889 — Byrd Lynn — 1916–20, C G-116

1942 — Marv Staehle — 1964–67, 2B G-53

1949 — Denny O'Toole — 1969–73, P G-15

1952 — Bought pitcher Bill Kennedy from Browns.

March 14

1885 — Jimmy Block — 1910–12, C G-140

1905 — Jack Rothrock — 1932, OF G-39

1921 — Bill Kennedy — 1952, P G-47

March 15

1876 — Bill Hallman — 1903, OF G-63

1886 — Rube Peters — 1912, P G-28

1890 — Charlie Mullen — 1910–11, 1B G-61

1938 — Bob Locker — 1965–69, P G-271

1944 — Wayne Granger — 1974, P G-5

1946 — Bobby Bonds — 1978, OF G-26

1949 — Jim Kern — 1982, P G-13

1959 — Harold Baines — 1980–82, OF G-384

March 16

1910 — Bob Poser — 1932, P G-5

1927 — Clint Courtney — 1955, C G-19

1943 — Rick Reichardt — 1971–73, OF G-285

1947 — Tom Bradley — 1971–72, P G-91

March 17

1888 — Ed Klepfer — 1915, P G-2

1923 — Pat Seerey — 1948–49, OF G-99

March 18

1874 — Nixey Callahan — 1901–5, 11–14, OF–3B–P–MGR G-698

1888 — Cecil Coombs — 1914, OF G-7

Wiley Taylor — 1912, P G-3

1916 — Hi Bithorn — 1947, P G-2

1925 — Fred Hatfield — 1956–57, 3B G-175

1926 — Dick Littlefield — 1951, P G-4

1938 — Traded first baseman Zeke Bonura to Washington for first baseman Joe Kuhel.

March 19

1884 — Bobby Messenger — 1909–11, OF G-53

1908 — Gee Walker — 1938–39, OF G-269

March 20

1879 — Rube Vinson — 1906, OF G-7

1883 — Harry Clark — 1903, 3B G-15

1890 — Mellie Wolfgang — 1914–18, P G-79

1907 — Vern Kennedy — 1934–37, P G-102

1912 — Clyde Shoun — 1949, P G-16

1925 — Al Widmar — 1952, P G-1

March 21

1904 — Frank Sigafoos — 1929, PH G-7

1918 — Eddie "Babe" Klieman — 1949, P G-18

1923 — Jim Hughes — 1957, P G-4

1939 — Tommy Davis — 1968, OF G-132

1982 — Traded pitchers Ross Baumgarten and Butch Edge to Pittsburgh for infielder Vance Law and pitcher Ernie Camacho.

March 22

1906 — Moose Solters — 1940–41, 43, OF G-334

1908 — Marv Owen — 1938–39, 3B G-199

1913 — Hank Steinbacher — 1937–39, OF G-203

1926 — Billy Goodman — 1958–61, 3B G-291

March 23

1881 — Cliff Cravath — 1909, OF G-19

1928 — Jim Lemon — 1963, 1B–OF G-36

1943 — Bruce Howard — 1963–67, P G-97

1949 — Jim Geddes — 1972–73, P G-12

1977 — Traded pitcher Clay Carroll to Cardinals for pitcher Lerrin LaGrow.

March 24

1906 — Art Veltman — 1926, SS G-5

March 25

1891 — Polly McLarry — 1912, PH G-2

March 25 (continued)

1919 — Bill Evans — 1949, P G-4

1923 — Grover Bowers — 1949, OF G-26

1932 — Woodie Held — 1968–69, OF–IF G-96

March 26

1901 — Jim Battle — 1927, 3B–SS G-6

March 27

1906 — Fred Tauby — 1935, OF G-13

1932 — Wes Covington — 1961, OF G-22

1938 — Shortstop Luke Appling breaks a leg sliding in an exhibition game versus the Cubs and misses half of the 1938 season.

1950 — Lynn McGlothen — 1981, P G-11

March 28

1920 — Fred Hancock — 1949, SS G-39

1981 — Traded pitcher Ken Kravec to the Cubs for pitcher Dennis Lamp.

March 29

1894 — Dixie Leverett — 1922–24, P G-98

1910 — Bill Dietrich — 1936–46, P G-235

1921 — Ferris Fain — 1953–54, P G-193

1971 — Reacquired outfielder Ed Stroud from Washington for first baseman-outfielder Tom McCraw.

March 30

1899 — Harold Rhyne — 1933, 2B–3B G-39

1919 — Bud Sketchley — 1942, OF G-13

1938 — Dave Baldwin — 1973, P G-3

1970 — Traded pitcher Gerry Nyman to San Diego for pitcher Tommie Sisk.

1978 — Traded pitcher Steve Renko and catcher Jim Essian to Oakland for pitcher Pablo Torrealba.

1981 — Bought outfielder Greg Luzinski from Phillies.

1982 — Acquired outfielder Rudy Law from Dodgers for two minor leaguers, outfielder Cecil Espy and pitcher Burt Geiger.

March 31

1918 — Marv Grisson — 1952, P G-28

1971 — Traded catcher Duane Josephson and pitcher Danny Murphy to Red Sox for first baseman Tony Muser and pitcher Vincente Romo.

APRIL 1

1912 — Jake Wade — 1942–44, P G-55

1935 — Tom Qualters — 1958, P G-26

1941 — Dick Kenworthy — 1962, 64–68, 3B G-125

1943 — Mike DeGerick — 1961–62, P G-2

1956 — Mark Esser — 1979, P G-2

1981 — Traded pitcher Mike Proly to Phillies for infielder Jay Loviglio.

April 2

1906 — Robert Way — 1927 — 2B G-5

1907 — Luke Appling — 1930–43, SS G-2422

1927 — Billy Pierce — 1949–61, P G-487

1938 — Al Weis — 1962–67, 2B G-521

1982 — Traded outfielder Wayne Nordhagen to Toronto for third baseman Aurelio Rodriguez.

April 3

1931 — Bought first baseman Lu Blue from Browns.

1943 — Barry Moore — 1970, P G-24

April 4

1900 — Julius Mallonee — 1925, OF G-2

1903 — Les Bartholomew — 1932, P G-3

1960 — Traded catcher Earl Battey and first baseman Don Mincher to Washington for first baseman Roy Sievers.

April 5

1907 — Merritt "Sugar" Cain — 1936–38, P G-53

John Godell — 1928, P G-2

1936 — Jimmie Schaffer — 1965, C G-17

1938 — Ron Hansen — 1963–69, SS G-769

1977 — Traded shortstop Bucky Dent to Yankees for outfielder Oscar Gamble and pitchers Lamarr Hoyt and Bob Polinsky.

1978 — Bought pitcher Jim Willoughby from Red Sox.

April 6

1926 — Ed White — 1955, OF G-3

1937 — Phil Regan — 1972, P G-10

1958 — Leo Sutherland — 1980–81, OF G-45

April 7

1879 — Art Weaver — 1908, C G-15

1902 — Buck Redfern — 1928–29, 2B–SS G-107

1933 — Joe Hicks — 1959–60, OF G-42

April 8

1878 — Clarence Foster — 1901, OF G-12

1910 — Charlie English — 1932–33, 3B–2B G-27

1975 — Signed first baseman Deron Johnson as a free agent after release by Red Sox.

April 9

1879 — Doc White — 1903–13, P–OF G-455

1905 — Earl Caldwell — 1945–48, P G-131

1949 — Sam Ewing — 1973, '76, 1B G-30

April 10

1900 — Edward Corey — 1918, P G-1

1930 — Frank Lary — 1965, P G-14

1937 — Fritz Ackley — 1963–64, P G-5

1949 — Pete Varney — 1973–76, C G-64

1962 — Catcher Sherm Lollar tied major league record by catching six fouls in one game during season opener versus Angels.

1981 — Carlton Fisk made a memorable White Sox debut with a 3-run, game-winning, eighth-inning home run against his former teammates, winning the season opener in Boston, 5-3.

April 11

1875 — Ossee Schreckengost — 1908, C G-6

1936 — Bought pitcher Clint Brown from Cleveland.

1959 — Early Wynn achieved his 250th career victory with a 7-hitter over Detroit, 5–3.

1975 — Signed pitcher Claude Osteen as a free agent after release by Cardinals.

1982 — After first four scheduled games of season were lost to the effects of a freak spring blizzard, White Sox swept doubleheader from Yankees in New York, 7–6 and 2–0.

April 12

1889 — Reb Russell — 1913–19, P G-263

1909 — Eric McNair — 1939–40, 3B–2B G-195

1922 — Bill Wight — 1948–50, P G-99

1942 — Tommie Sisk — 1970, P G-17

1943 — Vicente Romo — 1971–72, P G-73

1966 — Eventual Rookie of the Year, Tommie Agee, hits game-tying, two-run, seventh inning home run as White Sox go on to beat Angels, 3-2, in the season opener.

April 13

1967 — After losing nine straight at Fenway Park, White Sox score five unearned runs in the ninth to beat the Red Sox, 8–5.

April 14

1917 — Ed Cicotte pitches no-hitter as White Sox pound the Browns, 11–0.

1927 — Don Mueller — 1958–59, OF G-74

1928 — Herb Adams — 1948–50, OF G-95

1981 — White Sox win their home opener, 9–3, over Milwaukee, highlighted by Carlton Fisk's grand slam and hometown Greg Luzinski's two-run single in his Comiskey Park debut. Crowd of 51,560 is largest at Comiskey Park for single day game and opening day.

April 15

1915 — White Sox swamp Browns, 16–0.

21

1940 — Every White Sox batter ends the game with the same average as when he entered. Cleveland's Bob Feller pitches the only opening day no-hitter in major league history.

April 17

1959 — Rookie Rudy Arias gains his first major league victory and rookie Norm Cash hits key three-run home run as White Sox defeat Tigers, 6–5, in Detroit.

April 18

1934 — Deacon Jones — 1962–63, '66, 1B G-40

1946 — Gerry Janeski — 1970, P G-35

1948 — Ron Schueler — 1978–79, P G-39

1954 — Traded infielder Johnny Lipon to Cincinnati for infielder Grady Hatton.

1960 — Traded pitcher Barry Latman to Cleveland for pitcher Herb Score.

1972 — Carlos May knocks in 6 runs versus Texas as Wilbur Wood breezes to 14–0 win. (H)

1982 — Sox open season 8–0, best start in their history, beating Baltimore, 6–4. Salome Barojas recorded his fifth save of the season, coming in his first five major league appearances. (H)

April 19

1885 — Roy Mitchell — 1918, P G-2

1889 — Otto Jacobs — 1918, C G-29

1892 — Joseph Morris — 1921, P G-4

1901 — Bernie DeViveiros — 1924, SS G-1

1907 — Pitcher Ed Walsh ties two major league fielding records with 13 chances accepted and 11 assists.

1955 — Mike Colbern — 1978–79, C G-80

1960 — Minnie Minoso celebrates his return to the Sox by knocking in 6 runs versus Kansas City, including 4th inning grand slam and 9th inning solo shot to break 9–9 tie. (H)

1966 — White Sox beat California, 3–1, in first major league game played at Anaheim Stadium, Tommy John beating Marcelino Lopez.

April 20

1886 — Ted Easterly — 1912–13, C–PH G-90

1973 — White Sox pound Royals, 16–2, at Kansas City.

April 21

1900 — The revived White Stockings make their Chicago and American League debut, losing to Milwaukee, 5–4, in ten innings. Chicago was considered the key franchise in changing the league name from Western to American. The league was still not considered major until the addition of larger Eastern cities and the raiding of National League teams for players in 1901.

1909 — Bill Chamberlain — 1932, P G-12

1937 — Gary Peters — 1959–69, P G-327

April 22

1908 — Fabian Kowalik — 1932, P G-6

1941 — Steve Jones — 1967, P G-11

1959 — White Sox scored 11 runs with only one hit in the 7th inning of a 20–6 win in Kansas City. The following is a play-by-play of the strange inning: Ray Boone reached first base on shortstop Joe DeMaestri's error; Al Smith was safe at first on third baseman Hal Smith's error; John Callison singled, Boone scoring, then Smith scoring and Callison going to third when right fielder Roger Maris made an error on the play; Luis Aparicio walked and stole second base; Bob Shaw walked, loading the bases; Mark Freeman relieved Tom Gorman with a 2–0 count on Earl Torgeson, who walked, forcing in Callison; Nellie Fox walked, Aparicio scoring; Jim Landis grounded into a force play at the plate; Sherm Lollar walked, forcing in Torgeson; George Brunet replaced Freeman on the mound for the Athletics and walked Boone, forcing in Fox; Smith walked, Landis scoring; Callison was hit by a pitch, forcing in Lollar; Aparicio walked, Boone scoring; Shaw struck out; Bubba Phillips batted for Torgeson and walked, forcing in Smith; Fox walked scoring Lou Skizas who had pinch-run for Callison; Jim Landis then had the distinction of making two of the three outs in the inning, ending the debacle for Kansas City.

April 23

1888 — Jim Scott — 1909–17, P G-315

1917 — Tony Lupien — 1948, 1B G-154

1919 — White Sox beat Browns, 13–4, on opening day in St. Louis, collecting 21 hits.

1925 — Buddy Peterson — 1955, SS G-6

1939 — White Sox beat Browns, 17–4, as Marvin Owen hits four doubles. (H)

1947 — Pat Jacquez — 1971, P G-2

1955 — White Sox beat Athletics in Kansas City, 29–6, tying American League and modern major league records for most runs scored in one game. Sox also collected 29 hits, one short of the AL record, including 7 home runs (2 by Bob Nieman and Sherm Lollar, others by Minnie Minoso, Walt Dropo and Jack Harshman). Lollar also had three singles in the game and hit safely twice in the

April 23 (continued)

2nd and 6th innings. Bob Nieman had 7 RBIs while Chico Carrasquel and Minnie Minoso each scored 5 runs.

1981 — White Sox pound Oriole pitchers for 26 hits, most ever given up by Oriole pitching, to beat Baltimore, 18–5, in the first game of a doubleheader. White Sox scored in each of the first six innings, including 7 runs in both the 4th and the 6th. Sox also took the nightcap, 5–3. (H)

April 24

1901 — The first game in official American League history as a major league is played at Chicago as Roy Patterson beats Cleveland, 8–2.

1903 — James W. Moore — 1930, OF G-16

April 25

1868 — Fred Hartman — 1901, 3B G-120

1900 — Jake Freeze — 1925, P G-2

1944 — Ken Tatum — 1974, P G-10

1951 — Twenty-four years after outfield grandstand roof had been added to Comiskey Park, Eddie Robinson becomes the first White Sox player to hit one over the structure with a blast off Al Widmar. Visiting players had managed the feat seven times before Robinson connected.

April 26

1919 — Virgil Trucks — 1953–55, P G-96

1920 — Ron Northey — 1955–57, OF–PH G-107

1922 — Sam Dente — 1952–53, IF–OF G-64

1968 — White Sox win their first game of season after losing 10 straight, beating Twins at Minnesota, 3–2.

April 27

1902 — Sam Strang draws five walks in one game.

1909 — White Sox post third consecutive 1–0 victory.

John Whitehead — 1935–39, P G-127

1910 — Bernard Uhalt — 1934, OF G-57

1925 — White Sox score nine runs in the 8th inning, overcoming 4–3 deficit to beat Cleveland, 12–4. (H)

Bill Higdon — 1949, OF G-11

1930 — In St. Louis, Bud Clancy becomes the first 1st baseman since 1900 to play nine innings without a fielding chance.

1932 — Traded pitcher Bump Hadley and outfielder Bruce Campbell to Browns for infielder Red Kress.

1974 — Traded infielder Luis Alvarado to Cardinals for pitcher Ken Tatum.

April 28

1927 — Charlie Maxwell — 1962–64, OF–1B G-142

1949 — Pablo Torrealba — 1978–79, P G-28

1955 — Dewey Robinson — 1979–81, P G-30

April 29

1877 — Frank Dupee — 1901, P G-1

1883 — Amby McConnell — 1910–11, 2B G-136

1888 — Ernie Johnson — 1912, 1921–23, SS G-317

1932 — Traded outfielders Smead Jolley and Johnny Watwood and catcher Bennie Tate to Red Sox for catcher Charlie Berry.

1966 — Gary Peters pitches and hits home run to lead White Sox to victory in Cleveland, 4–1, snapping Indians' 10-game winning streak.

April 30

1922 — Charlie Robertson pitches a perfect game, beating the Tigers in Detroit, 2–0. Johnny Mostil saved the gem with a long running catch in the 2nd inning and fell into the crowd making the final putout. Ironically, it was the only time that Mostil, a regular centerfielder, played left field in his major league career.

1934 — White Sox outslug Cleveland, 20–10. (H)

1941 — Bought outfielder Myril Hoag from Browns and pitcher Buck Ross from Athletics.

1951 — Traded outfielders Gus Zernial and Dave Philley to Athletics and acquired outfielder Minnie Minoso from Cleveland and outfielder Paul Lehner from Athletics in a three-team deal. (Pitcher Lou Brissie went from Athletics to Cleveland, and pitcher Sam Zoldak and catcher Ray Murray went from Cleveland to Athletics.) Minoso thus becomes the first black player in Sox history.

MAY 1

1901 — White Sox not only hit American League's first grand slam, they also become the first AL team to hit two in one game when Herm McFarland and Dummy Hoy connect.

May 1 (continued)

1919 — Al Zarilla — 1951–52, OF G-159

1924 — Bill Barrett steals home twice in one game.

1945 — Joe Haynes pitches one-hitter against Detroit, 5–0. Skeeter Webb's third-inning single deprives Haynes of a perfect game.

1951 — Minnie Minoso hits a two-run homer vs. New York in his first time at bat at Comisky Park.

1959 — Early Wynn tosses one-hitter and breaks up pitching duel with eighth-inning home run to beat Red Sox, 1–0. (H)

Traded pitcher Don Rudolph and outfielder Lou Skizas to Cincinnati for outfielder Del Ennis.

May 2

1887 — Eddie Collins — 1915–26, 2B–MGR G-1670

1901 — American League's first forfeit is awarded to Detroit when manager Clark Griffith's stall tactics are punished by umpire Tom Connolly. Detroit had taken the lead with outburst in the top of the ninth and when rain started to fall, Griffith hoped the game would be called so the score would revert to the White Sox lead after eight innings.

1941 — Clay Carroll — 1976–77, P G-37

1959 — Traded first baseman Ray Boone to Athletics for outfielder Harry Simpson.

May 3

1904 — Red Ruffing — 1947, P G-14

1916 — Ken Silvestri — 1939–40, C G-50

1918 — White Sox collect 25 hits against Detroit.

1922 — Ernie Groth — 1949, P G-3

1926 — Stan Jok — 1954–55, 3B–OF G-9

1952 — Traded outfielder Jim Busby and infielder Mel Hoderlein to Washington for outfielder Sam Mele.

1954 — White Sox pitchers surrender 5 hits in 3 days as Sox trounce Athletics, 14–3, behind Sandy Consuegra's two-hitter. Connie Johnson two-hit the Athletics on May 2, 4–0, and Virgil Trucks one-hit Boston on May 1, 3–0.

1969 — Al Lopez resigns second stint as manager and is replaced by long-time coach, Don Gutteridge.

May 4

1927 — Hal Hudson — 1952–53, P G-3

1941 — Outfielder Taft Wright makes his first start of the season and singles in one run in four trips against Athletics, starting American League record streak of 13 consecutive RBI games.

1980 — Mike Squires becomes the first lefthanded catcher in the major leagues since 1958 in the 9th inning of a game in Milwaukee.

May 5

1882 — Lee Quillin — 1906–7, 3B G-53

1883 — Chief Bender — 1925, P G-1

1962 — Arthur Allyn buys 46% of White Sox, making him first sole owner of club in 23 years.

1963 — Traded pitcher Dom Zanni to Cincinnati for pitcher Jim Brosnan.

1968 — Pitcher Gary Peters hits fourth inning grand slam off of Al Downing of the Yankees.

May 6

1903 — White Sox commit 12 errors and Tigers commit 6 to establish American League record for errors in one game by both teams.

1917 — En route to AL pennant and world championship, White Sox become the only team to be no-hit on consecutive days. Seventh-place Browns who won 57 games all year (White Sox won 100) turn the trick. Bob Groom pitched a 3–0 no-hitter in the second game of a doubleheader, so there was one game in between Groom's no-hitter and the no-hitter fashioned by Ernie Koob on May 5.

Mike McCormick — 1950, OF G-55

May 7

1919 — White Sox steal 7 bases against the Browns.

Al Papai — 1955, P G-7

1937 — Claude Raymond — 1959, P G-3

1948 — Ken Hottman — 1971, OF G-6

1949 — Traded infielder Don Kolloway to Detroit for outfielder Earl Rapp.

May 8

1880 — John Skopec — 1901, P G-10

May 8 (continued)

1893 — Edd Roush — 1913, OF G-9

1894 — Roy Wilkinson — 1919–22, P G-79

1934 — Third baseman Jimmy Dykes named as player-manager to replace Lew Fonseca, who resigned under pressure.

1950 — Lloyd Allen — 1974–75, P G-9

1975 — Traded outfielder Bill Sharp to Brewers for outfielder Bob Coluccio.

May 9

1882 — Buck O'Brien — 1913, P G-7

1901 — White Sox are victims of American League's first 9-inning no-hitter (by Earl Moore of Cleveland) but are still victors when they break the no-hitter in the tenth inning and win, 4–2, in Cleveland. Sam Mertes's single was the first of two hits in the inning for the White Sox.

Wally Dashiell — 1924, SS G-1

1934 — Traded infielder Red Kress to Washington for infielder Bob Boken.

1935 — Joe Shipley — 1963, P G-3

1936 — Floyd Robinson — 1960–66, OF G-880

1954 — George Enright — 1976, C G-1

1975 — Jim Kaat establishes new club record with twelfth straight victory (over two seasons).

May 10

1896 — Pat Hargrove — 1918, PH G-2

1901 — Ted Blankenship — 1922–30, P G-241

1910 — Joe Chamberlin — 1934, SS–3B G-43

1925 — Johnny Mostil's 12th-inning home run beats Washington, 10–8. (H)

1941 — Ken Berry — 1962–70, OF G-894

1959 — Comiskey family sells Sox to Bill Veeck, Hank Greenberg and Arthur Allyn.

May 11

1898 — Robert Ostergard — 1921, PH G-12

1917 — John Gerlach — 1938–39, SS G-12

1957 — Fran Mullins — 1980, 3B G-21

28

David Short — 1940–41, OF G-7

1925 — Catcher Ray Schalk catches a baseball dropped a distance of 460 feet from the Chicago Tribune tower.

1929 — After 25 straight completed starts, Tommy Thomas is removed after the 5th inning. Washington beat the Sox, 9–2, in 7 innings. Thomas still led the league with 24 complete games that year, his third straight year with 24. (H)

1930 — Bibb Falk gathers five hits, five RBIs and scores five runs in first five innings vs. Athletics.

1949 — White Sox score in each inning (did not bat in 9th) while beating Red Sox, 12–8. (H)

May 12

1902 — Dutch Henry — 1929–30, P G-37

1941 — Floyd Weaver — 1970, P G-31

1953 — Two tenth-inning walks issued by Red Sox reliever Ellis Kinder eventually came around to score as White Sox beat the Red Sox, 9–7, in Boston. Defeat charged to Kinder snapped his 18-game win streak over Chicago.

Bought pitcher Sandy Consuegra from Washington.

1954 — Connie Johnson tosses second two-hitter in 10 days, beating Boston, 1–0.

May 13

1878 — Frank Hemphill — 1906, OF G-13

1886 — Frank Miller — 1913, P G-1

1901 — Leo Taylor — 1923, PH G-1

1910 — Boze Berger — 1937–38, IF G-170

1934 — Leon Wagner — 1968, OF G-69

1947 — Steve Kealey — 1971–73, P G-101

1982 — Utilizing 20 hits, White Sox trounce Brewers, 13–2. Lamarr Hoyt raised his season record to 7-and-0. (H)

May 14

1881 — Ed Walsh, Sr. — 1904–16, P G-456

1914 — Jim Scott no-hits Washington through nine innings, but gives up hit in tenth and loses, 1–0, in Washington.

1925 — Les Moss — 1955–58, '68, C–MGR G-132

1940 — Jimmy Foxx hits a home run over the Comiskey Park roof for the third time. No other player has ever equalled this feat. Johnny Rigney surrendered the blast.

29

May 14 (continued)

1967 — Traded to Angels eight days earlier, Bill Skowron's second-inning home run is the only hit off Gary Peters as the White Sox beat the Angels, 3–1, in the second game of a doubleheader.

1969 — Traded pitcher Bob Priddy and infielder Sandy Alomar to Angels for second baseman Bobby Knoop.

1977 — Jim Spencer ties White Sox record with 8 RBIs in one game as White Sox trounce Cleveland, 18–2. (H)

May 15

1918 — Washington scores run on a wild pitch to beat White Sox, 1–0, in 18 innings. Walter Johnson outdueled Lefty Williams as both went the distance.

1941 — White Sox beat the Yankees, 13–1, in New York, but Joe DiMaggio's single off Edgar Smith starts his record-setting 56-game hitting streak.

1956 — Traded infielder Jim Brideweser and outfielder-third baseman Bob Kennedy to Detroit for infielder Fred Hatfield and outfielder Jim Delsing.

1968 — Having shifted nine regular season games there, White Sox lose first AL game played at Milwaukee's County Stadium, 4–2, to Angels. The game was shortened to five innings by rain.

1975 — Acquired catcher Jim Essian from Braves, completing deal in which first baseman Dick Allen eventually wound up with Phillies.

May 16

1909 — Traded pitcher Nick Altrock, first baseman Jiggs Donahue, and outfielder Cliff Cravath to Washington for pitcher Bill Burns.

1920 — Dave Philley — 1941, 1946–51, 1956–57, OF G-721

1944 — White Sox snap Hank Borowy's 11-game winning streak (over two seasons) beating Yankees, 10–-4.

1951 — Traded pitcher Bob Cain to Detroit for pitcher Saul Rogovin.

Bought third baseman Bob Dillinger from Pittsburgh.

1953 — Pitcher Tommy Byrne batted for Vern Stephens and smacked a ninth inning grand slam off Ewell Blackwell of the Yankees to give the White Sox a 5–3 win. Stephens had ten career grand slams at the time.

1978 — Traded outfielder Bobby Bonds to Texas for outfielders Claudell Washington and Rusty Torres.

May 17

1888 — Irving Porter — 1914, OF G-1

30

1894 — Frank Woodward — 1923, P G-2

1912 — White Sox win first game ever played at Fenway Park, beating Red Sox, 5–2.

1927 — James McDonald — 1956–58, P G-21

1931 — Traded third baseman Willie Kamm to Cleveland for outfielder-infielder Lew Fonseca.

1932 — Pitcher Milt Gaston takes part in four double plays in one game, establishing major league record.

1948 — Carlos May — 1968–76, OF–1B, G-1002

1960 — Bought pitcher Russ Kemmerer from Washington.

May 18

1901 — John Happenny — 1923, 2B–SS G-32

1906 — Fielder Jones connects for two doubles, a triple, and a home run versus Washington.

1922 — Gil Coan — 1955, OF G-17

1932 — In Boston, Carey Selph struck out for his ninth and last time of the season. Selph's string without a strikeout totalled 89 games, establishing a major league record.

1940 — Jim Hicks — 1964–66, OF G-33

1976 — Traded outfielder-first baseman Carlos May to Yankees for pitcher Ken Brett and outfielder Rich Coggins.

1982 — White Sox trounced Texas, 10–2, as Lamarr Hoyt broke Jim Kaat's club record for consecutive victories (over two seasons) with 13. Hoyt also extended his Comiskey Park career record to 15-and-0.

May 19

1910 — Rupert Thompson — 1938–39, OF–1B G-20

1929 — Outfielder Johnny Mostil fractures his ankle, ending his major league career.

May 20

1893 — Fritz Von Kolnitz — 1916, 3B G-24

1900 — Claral Gillenwater — 1923, P G-5

1904 — Pete Appleton — 1940–42, P G-42

1920 — White Sox score eight runs in the 16th inning versus Washington on two triples, a double, two singles, and four errors, winning 13–5. Both teams scored twice in the 15th inning.

May 20 (continued)

1921 — Earl Rapp — 1949, OF G-19

1925 — White Sox and Red Sox pitchers combine for twenty walks as White Sox win, 10-7. (H)

1931 — Ken Boyer — 1967-68, 3B-1B G-67

1941 — In Washington, Taft Wright doubles in a run in two trips, setting American League record for consecutive RBI games at 13. (Stopped the next day in Philadelphia.)

1946 — Jim Lyttle — 1972, OF G-44

1973 — Sunday doubleheader with Minnesota draws all-time Comiskey Park attendance record of 55,555.

May 21

1905 — Frank Smith one-hits Washington. (H)

1912 — Larry Rosenthal — 1936-41, OF G-438

Monty Stratton — 1934-38, P G-71

1918 — Stanley Goletz — 1941, PH G-5

1926 — Earl Sheely hits 3 doubles and home run at Boston in four consecutive times at bat. Three doubles in his last three times at bat the day before helped tie major league record of 7 consecutive extra-base hits. Six doubles in two consecutive games also tied a major league record.

1936 — Barry Latman — 1957-59, P G-57

1940 — Joe Kuhel hits two singles, two doubles, and a home run against Washington as White Sox win, 9-8. (H)

1943 — White Sox beat Washington, 1-0, in a snappy 1 hour and 29 minutes—fastest 9-inning night game in AL history.

1950 — Bob Molinaro — 1977-78, 1980-81, OF G-272

1956 — Traded pitchers Mike Fornieles and Connie Johnson, third baseman George Kell and outfielder Bob Nieman to Baltimore for pitcher Jim Wilson and outfielder Dave Philley.

May 22

1902 — Al Simmons — 1933-35, OF G-412

1928 — Johnny Mostil ties Happy Felsch's record of 12 errorless chances in the outfield in one game (both played centerfield).

1938 — Ted Lyons beats Senators, 9-2, for 200th big league victory.

1943 — Tommy John — 1965–71, P G-238

1947 — Rich Hinton — 1971, '75, 1978–79, P G-78

1949 — Mike Eden — 1978, SS–2B G-10

1977 — Richie Zisk becomes the fourth player in Comiskey Park to hit a home run in the centerfield bleachers (off Dave Rozema of Detroit).

May 23

1862 — Dummy Hoy — 1901, OF G-132

1892 — Clarence Smith — 1913, P G-15

1893 — Elmer Leifer — 1921, OF–3B G-9

1894 — George Payne — 1920, P G-12

1954 — Traded third baseman Grady Hatton plus $100,000 to Red Sox for third baseman George Kell.

1981 — White Sox pound Angels, 15–4, in middle game of three-game sweep in Anaheim, during which they collected 34 runs on 45 hits.

May 24

1898 — Leo Mangum — 1924–25, P G-20

1926 — Willie Miranda — 1952, SS G-70

1929 — Ted Lyons pitches a 21-inning game, losing to Detroit. It was the longest game ever at Comiskey Park.

1939 — Playing in their first night game ever, White Sox beat Athletics in Philadelphia, 4–1.

1954 — Signed first baseman Phil Cavaretta as a free agent. (Had been released by Cubs as player-manager in March.)

1967 — Tom McCraw hits 3 home runs and drives in 8 runs as White Sox beat Twins, 14–1, in Minnesota.

1982 — Lamarr Hoyt stretched his season record to 9-and-0, his two-year win streak to 14, and his Comiskey Park record to 16-and-0 with a 3–1 defeat of the Royals.

May 25

1946 — Ted Lyons replaces Jimmie Dykes as manager. When dismissed, Dykes had served as manager for over twelve years, longer than any other White Sox pilot. Lyons' former star pitching mate, Red Faber, was signed as a coach.

1950 — Glenn Borgmann — 1980, C G-32

May 26

1900 — Milt Steengrafe — 1924, '26, P G-16

May 26 (continued)

1904 — William Shores — 1936, P G-9

1950 — Jack Onslow fired as manager. Coach Red Corriden named interim manager the next day.

1973 — White Sox score four runs in the 21st inning to beat Cleveland, 6–3, at Cleveland.

1982 — Greg Luzinski leads Sox to 7–5 victory over Royals with two homers and 6 RBIs. (H)

May 27

1875 — George Magoon — 1903, 2B G-94

1938 — Hank Greenberg becomes the first player to hit a home run into Comiskey Park's centerfield bleachers when the Tiger slugger blasts one off of Frank Gabler.

1955 — Ross Baumgarten — 1978–81, P G-80

1966 — Traded infielder-outfielder Danny Cater to Athletics for infielder Wayne Causey.

1979 — Bought catcher Milt May from Detroit.

May 28

1900 — Bill Barrett — 1923–29, OF–SS–2B G-579

1923 — Bob Kuzava — 1949–50, P G-39

1942 — Buddy Booker — 1968, C G-5

1949 — Outfielder Gus Zernial is out for two months of his rookie season with broken collarbone suffered while making catch in Cleveland.

1954 — Oriole (18) and White Sox (14) pitchers combine for 32 walks in a doubleheader.

1956 — Bought pitcher Gerry Staley from Yankees.

May 29

1907 — Phil Gallivan — 1932, '34, P G-48

1945 — John "Blue Moon" Odom — 1976, P G-8

1950 — Bought outfielder Marv Rickert from Pittsburgh.

1954 — Traded catcher Red Wilson to Detroit for catcher Matt Batts.

May 30

1881 — Tom Dougherty — 1904, P G-1

1908 — Hugh Willingham — 1931, 2B G-3

1924 — Turk Lown — 1958–62, P G-234

1932 — Three players and manager Lew Fonseca fined in free-for-all with umpire George Moriarty.

1951 — Sox sweep Senators to extend win skein to 14.

1955 — Bought outfielder-third baseman Bob Kennedy from Baltimore.

1956 — Jay Loviglio — 1981–82, 2B–3B G-29

1966 — After John Buzhardt outdueled Boston, 1–0, on five hits, in the first game, Jack Lamabe beats the Red Sox, 11–0, in the second game. Joe Foy's eighth-inning single was the only hit off Lamabe. It was also the third straight shutout for the White Sox, Tommy John having blanked the Yankees in New York the day before. (H)

May 31

1894 — John Sullivan — 1919, P G-4

1912 — John Fehring — 1934, C G-1

1914 — Joe Benz no-hits Cleveland, 6–1, at Comiskey Park.

1950 — Traded second baseman Cass Michaels, pitcher Bob Kuzava, and outfielder John Ostrowski to Washington for first baseman Eddie Robinson, infielder Al Kozar, and pitcher Ray Scarborough.

1970 — Luis Aparicio and Walt Williams each stroke five hits and White Sox collect 24 hits as White Sox beat Red Sox in Boston 20–13. Williams also scored five runs.

1972 — Tom Bradley strikes out six consecutive Angels.

1978 — White Sox collect 22 hits in 17–2 romp over the Angels, scoring 11 runs in the fifth inning. (H)

JUNE 1

1896 — Johnny Mostil — 1918, 1921–29, OF G-972

1910 — Traded infielder Rollie Zeider and first baseman Babe Borton to the New York Highlanders for first baseman Hal Chase.

1926 — Ray Moore — 1958–60, P G-75

1937 — Bill Dietrich no-hits St. Louis, 8–0, at Comiskey Park.

June 2

1876 — Charles Jones — 1904, OF G-5

1899 — Sloppy Thurston — 1923–26, P G-178

June 2 (continued)

1925 — White Sox overcome 10-run deficit after five innings to forge a 15–15 tie with Tigers, but lost in ninth inning when Ty Cobb homers on a 3–2 count (at Detroit).

1932 — Lou Skizas — 1959, OF G-8

1939 — Traded pitcher John Whitehead to Browns for pitcher John Marcum.

1948 — Traded outfielder Bob Kennedy to Cleveland for outfielder Pat Seerey and pitcher Al Gettel.

1951 — Athletics snap White Sox 14–game win streak.

1958 — Luis Aparicio string of 26 consecutive steals is stopped by Yogi Berra of the Yankees on a missed hit-and-run play at Yankee Stadium.

1967 — Traded infielder Jerry Adair to Red Sox for pitchers Don McMahon and Bob Snow.

June 3

1888 — Jesse Baker — 1911, P G-22

1925 — Eddie Collins singles off Rip Collins of Detroit for his 3,000th career base hit.

1929 — Yankees nip White Sox, 1–0, in one hour and 20 minutes at Yankee Stadium.

1942 — Duane Josephson — 1965–70, C G-353

June 4

1922 — Ray Coleman — 1951–52, OF G-136

Ross Grimsley — 1951, P G-7

1965 — Eddie Fisher hurls six innings of one-hit relief, and Danny Cater and Floyd Robinson hit home runs to beat Yankees, 2–0, in 15 innings at Yankee Stadium.

1966 — John Buzhardt pitches a four-hit shutout over Washington at Comiskey Park, 6–0. It is the second straight time Buzhardt and hurler Jack Lamabe tossed back-to-back shutouts. Lamabe beat the Senators, 8–0, the previous day.

June 5

1874 — Frank Huelsman — 1904, OF G-4

1933 — The Sox collect 23 hits vs. the Browns—at least two hits by each player.

1966 — Holding Washington hitless until the seventh inning, Gary Peters settles for a two-hit, 12–0 victory over the Senators in the second game of doubleheader, giving the Sox a four-game sweep at Comiskey Park. It was the sixth shutout in 10 games for the Sox.

1931 — Rudy Arias — 1959, P G-34

1955 — Traded pitcher Harry Dorish to Baltimore for catcher Les Moss.

Chris Nyman — 1982, 1B G-28

June 7

1907 — Sloane Washington — 1935–36, OF G-128

1908 — Nick Altrock records 12 assists in one game (10 innings), most ever by a pitcher in an extra-inning game.

1933 — Herb Score — 1960–62, P G-35

1944 — Roger Nelson — 1967, P G-5

1950 — Rich Moloney — 1970, P G-1

June 8

1887 — Del Paddock — 1912, PH G-1

1901 — Leo Tankersley — 1925, C G-1

1908 — En route to a 13-game winning streak, White Sox climb from sixth place to first place in one week, despite being only three games over .500.

1925 — Del Ennis — 1959, OF G-26

1930 — Joe Dahlke — 1956, P G-5

1947 — For the second time in history of both clubs, Washington and Chicago battle until the 18th inning before Senators push over a run and win, 1–0.

1949 — Bought first baseman Charles Kress from Cincinnati.

1951 — Game with Yankees draws 53, 940, largest night game attendance in Comiskey Park history.

1953 — Jack Kucek — 1974–79, P G-32

1959 — Britt Burns — 1978–82, P G-94

1969 — Traded pitcher Bob Locker to Seattle Pilots for pitcher Gary Bell.

June 9

1893 — Charles Kavanagh — 1914, PH G-5

1908 — Paul Gregory — 1932–33, P G-56

1946 — Tom Egan — 1971–72, C G-135

1948 — Traded pitcher Earl Harrist to Washington for Marino Pieretti.

June 10

1900 — Garland Braxton — 1930–31, P G-36

1908 — Mike Kreevich — 1935–41, OF G-826

1938 — Pitcher Monty Stratton hits a second-inning homer vs. Red Sox at Boston as White Sox win, 15–2.

1952 — Sam Mele hits a three-run home run and a three-run triple in fourth inning against the Athletics in Philadelphia, accounting for six of the 12 runs scored that inning.

1953 — Francisco Barrios — 1974, 1976–81, P G-129

1961 — Bill Veeck sells controlling interest in club to Arthur Allyn, Jr. Traded pitchers Bob Shaw and Gerry Staley and outfielders Wes Covington and Stan Johnson to Athletics for pitchers Ray Herbert and Don Larsen, third baseman Andy Carey, and outfielder Al Pilarcik.

1979 — White Sox beat Brewers, 13–3, on 21 hits at Milwaukee.

June 11

1938 — Traded pitcher Bill Cox to Browns for pitcher Jack Knott.

1939 — Jimmy Stewart — 1967, OF-2B G-24

Ted Lyons pitches last four innings without a walk, starting string of 42 consecutive innings without a walk (ending June 23 in first inning). (H)

1959 — Billy Pierce pitches fourth career one-hitter, beating Washington, 3–1.

1967 — Despite eventual .225 team batting average this year, White Sox move into first place until August 12, with doubleheader win over Yankees, 2–1 and 3–2, at Yankee Stadium.

1981 — White Sox stop Doug Bird's 18-game winning streak (12 majors, six minors), nipping Yankees, 3–2, at Comiskey Park. Baseball came to a halt following the game with the major league's first mid-season baseball strike. The Sox had a record of 31–22, tied with Texas for the fewest defeats in the Western Division, but were in third place, 2½ games behind. Because of the "split season" created by the strike settlement, those 2½ games stood between the White Sox and post-season play.

June 12

1880 — Matty McIntyre — 1911–12, OF G-191

1900 — Charlie Barnabe — 1921–28, P G-29

1941 — Jerry Arrigo — 1970, P G-5

1952 — Nellie Fox ties an AL record of 17 chances in one game without an error.

38

1967 — White Sox and Senators battle for six hours and thirty-eight minutes in Washington before home team wins, 6–5. The 22-inning game is the longest in White Sox history and it continued into the following A.M. It was the longest night game in the AL for both time and innings.

1980 — Traded Randy Scarbery to Angels for shortstop Todd Cruz.

June 13

1920 — Hec Rodriguez — 1952, 3B G-124

1926 — Tommy Thomas two-hits Washington, 3-0, at Comiskey Park.

1930 — Traded outfielder Dave Harris to Washington for outfielder Red Barnes.

1933 — Whitlow Wyatt one-hits Browns, 6–1, at Chicago.

1957 — Traded outfielder Dave Philley to Detroit for first baseman Earl Torgeson.

1966 — Traded pitcher Eddie Fisher to Baltimore for second baseman Jerry Adair and outfielder John Riddle.

1968 — Traded outfielder Russ Snyder to Cleveland for outfielder Leon Wagner.

June 14

1895 — Ike Davis — 1924–25, SS G-156

1900 — Dave Harris — 1930, OF G-33

1953 — Traded pitcher Lou Kretlow and catcher Darrell Johnson to Browns for pitcher Virgil Trucks and third baseman Bob Elliott.

1980 — Traded infielder-outfielder Alan Bannister to Cleveland for catcher Ron Pruitt.

1982 — Traded third baseman Jim Morrison to Pittsburgh for pitcher Eddie Solomon.

June 15

1897 — Cy Twombly — 1921, P G-7

1904 — Everett Purdy — 1926, OF G-11

1912 — Merritt Lovett — 1933, PH G-1

1916 — Bud Stewart — 1951–54, OF G-258

1942 — Bruce Dal Canton — 1977, P G-8

1946 — Ken Henderson — 1973–75, OF G-375

1952 — Traded infielder Willie Miranda and outfielder Al Zarilla to St. Louis Browns for infielder Leo Thomas and outfielder Tom Wright.

June 15 (continued)

1955 — Bought pitcher Harry Byrd from Orioles

1958 — Traded pitcher Bill Fischer and outfielder Tito Francona to Detroit for pitcher Bob Shaw and infielder Ray Boone.

Dick Donovan and Jim Wilson whitewash Baltimore in both games of a doubleheader, 4–0 and 3–0.

1967 — Traded outfielder Ed Stroud to Washington for outfielder Jim King.

1970 — Traded outfielder Buddy Bradford to Cleveland for pitchers Barry Moore and Bob Miller.

1975 — Traded pitchers Stan Bahnsen and Skip Pitlock to Oakland for pitcher Dave Hamilton and outfielder Chet Lemon.

Traded first baseman Tony Muser to Baltimore for pitcher Jesse Jefferson.

1977 — Traded pitcher Ken Brett to Angels for pitchers Don Kirkwood and John Verhoeven and infielder John Flannery.

1979 — Traded third baseman Eric Soderholm to Texas for pitcher Ed Farmer and first baseman Gary Holle.

June 16

1889 — Wynn Noyes — 1919, P G-1

1920 — Eddie Malone — 1949–50, C G-86

1922 — Max Surkont — 1949, P G-44

1923 — Allie Clark — 1953, OF G-9

1930 — Traded first baseman Art Shires to Washington for pitcher Garland Braxton and catcher Bennie Tate.

1948 — Ron LeFlore — 1981–82, OF G-173

1957 — While pitching 3⅔ innings of relief, Dixie Howell smashes two home runs in second game of doubleheader against Washington. Sox won game, 8–6, and opener as well (4–2).

Salome Barojas — 1982, P G-61

1969 — Reversing the previous year's 1–8 in Milwaukee, for a series of "home" games, White Sox win fifth straight home game at County Stadium. Seattle transferred to Milwaukee just before the start of the 1970 season.

June 17

1890 — Phil Douglas — 1912, P G-3

1968 — In third try as home team, White Sox finally win in Milwaukee as Jack Fisher beats Cleveland, 2–1.

June 18

1888 — Marty Berghammer — 1911, 2B G-2

1933 — Taylor Phillips — 1963, P G-9

Then-largest day-game attendance at Comiskey Park watches White Sox split doubleheader with Yankees.

1938 — Pitcher Ted Lyons makes his first error since August 5, 1934. The errorless streak covered 84 games, 32 putouts and 140 assists.

1974 — Dick Allen and Jorge Orta each hit two homers and Carlos May and Ken Henderson hit one apiece as Sox beat Indians in Cleveland, 7–3. All, plus two by Cleveland, came with none on base.

June 19

1871 — George Leitner — 1902, P G-1

1884 — Eddie Cicotte — 1912–20, P G-354

1912 — Don Gutteridge — 1969–70, MGR

1923 — Luis Aloma — 1950–53, P G-116

1929 — Don Ferrarese — 1960, P G-5

1946 — Danny Osborn — 1975, P G-24

June 20

1901 — Pryor McBee — 1926, P G-1

1928 — Bob Mahoney — 1951, P G-3

1940 — White Sox beat Yankees, 1–0, in 11 innings at Comiskey Park, but New Yorkers' protest is upheld and game is replayed. Even though the contest did not count in the season standings, all individual and team records counted, including winning and losing pitchers (Johnny Rigney and Monte Pearson, respectively).

1948 — Luke Appling, playing his only year at both third base and shortstop, ties AL record for assists by a third baseman with 10.

1956 — Larry Monroe — 1976, P G-8

1971 — White Sox outslug Twins, 18–8, score 9 runs in the sixth inning at Minnesota.

June 21

1905 — Randy Moore — 1927–28, OF G-30

1906 — Arthur Smith — 1932, P G-3

1918 — Eddie Lopat — 1944–47, P G-127

1956 — Jack Harshman one-hits Baltimore in 1–0 nail-biter as White Sox manage only one hit against Oriole pitching.

1959 — White Sox, in first place as recently as June 4, fall into fifth place with loss of first game of twin bill in Boston. Billy Pierce halts five-game losing streak with 3-2 defeat of Red Sox in second game.

1961 — Roy Sievers hits two home runs in first game and Al Smith repeats the feat in the nightcap of doubleheader against Cleveland in Comiskey Park. Sievers did not even start the first game, but entered in the fourth inning to pinch-hit a grand slam home run off Johnny Antonelli.

1973 — Stan Bahnsen surrenders 12 hits, but shuts out Oakland, 2–0.

1974 — Ken Henderson knocks in six runs and White Sox get 21 hits against Twins in Minnesota for 11–7 victory. Ironically, another Henderson—Joe—got credit for the White Sox victory.

June 22

1913 — James Scott strikes out 15, including a club record of six straight.

1922 — Catcher Ray Schalk becomes first White Sox player to hit for the cycle against the Tigers in Detroit.

1926 — Manager Eddie Collins's 10th-inning double beats Indians in Cleveland, 4–3.

1934 — Russ Snyder — 1968, OF G-38

1938 — Henry Steinbacher gets six consecutive hits as White Sox beat Washington, 16–3, at Comiskey Park.

1952 — Randy Scarbery — 1979–80, P G-60

1956 — Bought pitcher Paul LaPalme from Cincinnati.

June 23

1912 — Gene Ford — 1938, P G-4

1913 — William Cox — 1937–38, P G-10

1915 — John Humphries — 1941–45, P G-122

Aaron Robinson — 1948, C G-98

1919 — Happy Felsch records 12 outfield chances against Cleveland without an error in centerfield for an AL record for outfielders.

1958 — Acquired pitcher Turk Lown from Cincinnati, sending first baseman Walt Dropo to the Redlegs the next day.

1963 — J. C. Martin takes part in three double plays from his catching position in the first game of a doubleheader (ties major league record).

June 24

1875 — John Katoll — 1901-2, P G-28

1915 — Chicago beats Cleveland, 5-4, in 19 innings.

1969 — Bill Melton slams three home runs and Carlos May and Ed Herrmann hit one apiece as White Sox beat Pilots, 7-6, in Seattle. It was the second time that season the Sox hit five home runs in one game at Sicks Stadium, the park's only season in majors.

1973 — Ed Herrmann knocks in seven runs vs. Oakland in second game of doubleheader in Chicago. Sox romp, 11-1.

June 25

1903 — Chicago and New York battle to 6-6 in 18 innings.

1905 — John Pasek — 1934, C G-4

1906 — Joe Kuhel — 1938-43, '46-47; 1B G-900

1947 — Jose Ortiz — 1969-70, OF G-31

1951 — Bought outfielder Don Lenhardt from St. Louis Browns.

1962 — Traded pitcher Russ Kemmerer to Houston for pitcher Dean Stone.

Traded first baseman Bob Farley to Detroit for outfielder Charley Maxwell.

June 26

1921 — Howie Pollet — 1956, P G-12

1975 — Bill Melton becomes most recent of six White Sox players to hit four career grand slam homers with the club. The others are Happy Felsch, Walt Dropo, Al Smith, Pete Ward, and Sherm Lollar.

June 27

1900 — Lum Davenport — 1921-24, P G-30

1923 — Lou Kretlow — 1950-53, P G-65

43

Gus Zernial — 1949–51, OF G-220

1927 — Dick Marlowe — 1956, P G-1

1950 — Bought catcher Gus Niarhos from Yankees

1958 — Billy Pierce retires 26 straight Senators before pinch-hitter Ed Fitzgerald spoils the perfect game with a looping hit just inside the first base line. Pierce ends up with a 3–0, one-hitter.

1961 — White Sox win twinbill; winning streak is extended to 12.

June 28

1927 — Dick Lane — 1949, OF G-12

1941 — Fred Talbot — 1963–64, P G-19

1952 — Bought infielder Willie Miranda from St. Louis Browns.

1973 — During a 2–0 defeat of Angels, slugger Dick Allen injures ankle in first base collision and is limited to five at-bats the rest of the season. The Sox were in first place at the time but fell to fifth in the West at the end of the season.

June 29

1876 — Patrick Flaherty — 1903–4, P G-44

1897 — Grady Adkins — 1928–29, P G-76

1898 — Jim Long — 1922, G C-3

1925 — Bill Connelly — 1950, P G-2

1933 — Bob Shaw — 1958–61, P G-126

1951 — Bruce Kimm — 1980, C G-100

1958 — Senator pitchers issue five intentional walks to White Sox in an 11-inning game.

June 30

1880 — Davy Jones — 1913, OF G-10

1921 — Joseph Stephenson — 1947, C G-16

1978 — Bob Lemon is fired as manager. Coach Larry Doby named interim manager for the remainder of the season.

JULY 1

1879 — Jake Atz — 1907–9, 2B G-205

1898 — Bert Cole — 1927, P G-27

1900 — Mel Simons — 1931–32, OF G-75

1905 — Frank Owen becomes the first American League pitcher to notch complete game victories in both games of a doubleheader (3–2 and 2–0). Owen surrendered only seven hits over both games.

1910 — Sox lose, 2–0, in Comiskey Park opener.

1920 — Paul Lehner — 1951, OF G-23

1924 — Jack Bruner — 1949–50, P G-13

1933 — Frank Baumann — 1960–64, P G-188

1937 — White Sox wallop Detroit, 15–8, at Comiskey Park

1951 — Jim Otten — 1974–76, P G-9

1962 — In second game of twin bill, White Sox hit three sacrifice flies (Juan Pizarro, Nellie Fox, Al Smith) in fifth inning against Cleveland. Sox scored six runs in the frame for a 7–6 triumph.

July 2

1909 — White Sox steal home three times in a game against the St. Louis Browns.

1929 — Chuck Stobbs — 1952, P G-38

1930 — Carl Reynolds hits three home runs (the first Sox player to accomplish the feat) and ties club record of eight RBI in one game against Yankees in New York.

1932 — White Sox bomb the Browns in St. Louis, 15–5.

1940 — Sox and Tigers each score runs in seven different innings.

1943 — Rookie outfielder Guy Curtwright's hitting streak is stopped at 26 games in Chicago. Washington pitching foils his attempt to tie Luke Appling for all-time club record.

1977 — Jim Spencer hits two home runs and ties club record of eight RBI in one game, both for second time in two months (against Minnesota at Comiskey Park).

1980 — Ross Baumgarten one-hits Angels, 1–0, at Comiskey Park. Rod Carew's leadoff seventh-inning single breaks up the no-hit bid. It is the second straight year that Baumgarten has one-hit California.

July 3

1881 — Fred Olmstead — 1908–11, P G-66

1892 — Anthony (Bunny) Brief — 1915, 1B G-48

1893 — Dickie Kerr — 1919–21, 25; P G-143

1901 — Joseph Brown — 1927, P G-1

1919 — White Sox score 10 runs in fourth inning against Indians in Cleveland, winning 17–1. Chick Gandil knocks in five of those 10 fourth-inning tallies.

1930 — Al Pilarcik — 1961, OF G-47

1940 — Taft Wright hits first-ever pinch grand slam home run by a White Sox player (off Lynn Nelson of pennant-winning Tigers).

1953 — John Verhoeven — 1977, P G-6

1973 — Tony Muser draws five walks in a game against Texas.

1976 — Sox lose 3–0 to Rangers in first "morning" game ever played at Comiskey Park.

July 4

1901 — Frank Naleway — 1924, SS G-1

1928 — Ray Schalk resigns as manager under pressure following doubleheader. Coach "Lena" Blackburne is named the new skipper.

1929 — Chuck Tanner — 1970–75 MGR

1946 — Joe Henderson — 1974, P G-5

1948 — Wayne Nordhagen — 1976 –81, OF G-408

1949 — Tim Nordbrook — 1977, SS G-15

1972 — Catcher Ed Herrmann takes part in three double plays in one game to tie a major league record.

1979 — Chicago wallops Indians, 16–4, in Cleveland. Wayne Nordhagen, Rusty Torres, and Claudell Washington each homer in a 10-run fifth inning. Nordhagen's blow is a grand slam.

July 5

1884 — Jack Quinn — 1918, P G-6

1904 — Bump Hadley — 1932, P G-3

1922 — Al Kozar — 1950, 2B G-10

1948 — Dave Lemonds — 1972, P G-34

1951 — Rich Gossage — 1972–76, P G-189

July 6

1893 — Clarence "Shovel" Hodge — 1920–22, P G-75

1933 — Baseball's first major league midsummer All-Star Game is played at Comiskey Park, with the AL defeating the NL, 4–2. After a second-inning walk, White Sox third baseman Jimmie Dykes scores the first run ever in an All-Star contest on a Lefty Gomez single. Babe Ruth clouts first All-Star homer for AL.

1954 — Virgil Trucks pitches his second one-hitter of season, beating Detroit, 4–0. The first one came on May 1 vs. Boston.

1980 — Lamar Johnson and Greg Pryor hit pinch-hit homers in same game in Sox victory over Oakland.

July 7

1884 — George Moriarty — 1916, 1B–3B G-7

1896 — John Jenkins — 1922, 2B–SS G-5

1915 — Sox buy outfielder Nemo Leibold from Cleveland

1923 — Joe Smaza — 1946, OF G-2

1945 — Bill Melton — 1968–75, 3B G-976

1982 — Harold Baines smacked 3 HRs, including a grand slam, driving in 6 runs to lead Sox to 7–0 win over Detroit as Dennis Lamp spun a 5-hit shutout. (H)

July 8

1903 — Clint Brown — 1936–40, P G-197

1928 — Sox collect 20 hits vs. Senators in Washington en route to 13–7 win.

1943 — At Comiskey Park, Orval Grove has no-hitter with two out in ninth, but Joe Gordon doubles and Grove settles for a one-hitter.

1947 — Across town at Wrigley Field, Luke Appling hits a sixth inning pinch single and scores tying run to help AL to 2–1 victory in All-Star Game.

1948 — Lerrin LaGrow — 1977–79, P G-197

July 9

1943 — Mike Andrews — 1971–73, 2B G-310

1956 — Guy Hoffman — 1979–80, P G-47

1957 — Minnie Minoso's fine running catch of a line drive off the bat of Gil Hodges ends three-run ninth-inning rally and preserves 6-5 AL victory at All-Star Game in St. Louis.

1961 — Sherm Lollar pinch-hits a grand slam homer off of Cleveland's Frank Funk. It is the second time the Sox pinch-hit a grand slam this season.

July 10

1875 — Gus Dundon — 1904–06, 2B G-247

1906 — Harold McKain — 1929–32, P G-107

1912 — Pitcher Ed Cicotte is purchased from Red Sox.

1915 — George Dickey — 1941–42, 1946–47, C G-211

1916 — White Sox pitchers hurl shutouts in both ends of a doubleheader for the second time this season. Lefty Williams and Red Russell blank pennant-winning Red Sox, 4–0 and 3–0.

1919 — White Sox move into first place to stay, passing the Yankees with doubleheader win against Athletics in Philadelphia.

1926 — White Sox and Athletics combine for 34 hits as host A's win, 17–14.

1932 — White Sox collect 25 hits against Cleveland.

1934 — After being No. 4 in Carl Hubbell's dramatic strikeout string of five (Babe Ruth, Lou Gehrig, Joe Cronin, and Bill Dickey were the others), Sox outfielder Al Simmons scores three runs and knocks one on two doubles and a single to lead the American League to a come-from-behind 9–7 victory in the All-Star classic at New York's Polo Grounds.

July 11

1927 — White Sox execute eight sacrifice bunts against Detroit to tie a big league record.

1937 — Verle Tiefenthaler — 1962, P G-3

1950 — Every other major league park having hosted an All-Star Game, the classic returned to Comiskey Park. The National League won 4–3 on Red Schoendienst's dramatic 14th-inning homer.

1982 — Harold Baines' second grand slam of the week to lead White Sox to 16–7 clubbing of Toronto. (A)

July 12

1891 — Hank Schreiber — 1914, OF G-1

1897 — "Hod" Fenner — 1921, P G-2

1927 — Jack Harshman — 1954–57, P G-134

1964 — Pete Ward sets club record with his third grand slam homer of the season.

1968 — Manager Eddie Stanky is fired and Al Lopez comes out of retirement to replace him.

1879 — "Jiggs" Donahue — 1904–09, 1B G-657

1919 — Buck Weaver clears the bases with a single to beat Boston, 14–9, at Comiskey Park.

1921 — Harry Dorish — 1951–55, P G-176

1938 — Don Pavletich — 1969, C–1B G-78

1951 — White Sox outscore Red Sox, 3–2, in 19th inning to win, 5–4, at Comiskey Park. Both teams had played 17 innings the day before in the second game of a doubleheader, with Saul Rogovin going all the way only to lose on a run in the top of the 17th. On successive nights the two clubs set AL records for the longest night game.

1954 — In a slugfest featuring six home runs, Nellie Fox's two-RBI bloop single over shortstop in the bottom of the eighth inning breaks a 9–9 tie and gives AL 11–9 win in All-Star Game at Cleveland.

1955 — Kevin Bell — 1976–80, 3B G-293

1964 — The Sox trade first baseman Joe Cunningham to Washington for first baseman Bill Skowron and pitcher Carl Bouldin. Frank Kreutzer, a pitcher, is sent to Washington to complete the deal on July 28.

July 14

1915 — With rain threatening and the Philadelphia A's trailing 4–2 and attempting stall tactics, Sox pitcher Red Faber walks around the bases and is credited with three stolen bases in one inning. Ironically, the game went nine innings and Sox won, 6–4, with Faber's run being the decider.

1928 — Ed Walsh Jr. wins his first major league game, beating the Red Sox in Boston, 11–4. The younger Walsh won only 11 major league games while his Hall of Fame father won 195. All of those combined 206 victories came with the Sox.

1947 — Steve Stone — 1973, 1977–78, P, G-100

1953 — Billy Pierce, first White Sox pitcher to win All-Star starting assignment, blanks NL for three innings on one hit. Nationals, however, go on to win, 5–1, at Cincinnati's Crosley Field.

1976 — Sox trade outfielder Rich Coggins to Phillies for outfielder Wayne Nordhagen.

1979 — Claudell Washington hits three homers while Rusty Torres and Jim Morrison club one apiece as Sox whip Tigers, 12–4, at Comiskey Park.

July 15

1874 — Mike Heydon — 1904, C G-4

1891 — Jim Breton — 1913–15, 3B G-107

1907 — White Sox rout New York Highlanders, 15–0.

1932 — Second baseman Jackie Hayes handles 34 consecutive chances without an error as White Sox and Red Sox play consecutive 11-inning games in Boston on July 14–15. White Sox won both games, 9–8 and 4–2.

July 16

1887 — Joe Jackson — 1915–20, OF G-649

1905 — Lou Garland — 1931, P G-7

1907 — Ed Walsh sets a major league record for chances accepted by a pitcher in an extra-inning game (15). He also had a record 12 assists in the 13-inning contest.

1910 — Bill Norman — 1931–32, P G-37

1912 — Milt Bocek — 1933–34, OF G-30

1936 — Eddie Fisher — 1962–66, 1972–73, P G-286

1937 — Lee Elia — 1966, SS G-80

July 17

1938 — Deron Johnson — 1975, 1B–DH G-148

1942 — Don Kessinger — 1977–79, SS-MGR G-226

1959 — Early Wynn and the Yankees' Ralph Terry match two-hitters, but Jim Landis' ninth-inning hit drives home the game's only runs in 2–0 cliffhanger at Yankee Stadium. Jim McAnany's single earlier in the inning spoiled Terry's no-hit bid.

1975 — Wilbur Wood starts consecutive Sox games due to All-Star break and pitches second straight shutout, beating Detroit, 5–0.

July 18

1917 — Leo Wells — 1942, 1946, 3B-SS G-80

1921 — Black Sox trial opens.

1930 — Outfielder Bob Fothergill is purchased from Detroit.

1936 — In second game of doubleheader against Athletics in Philadelphia, the Sox dump A's, 21–14, as Rip Radcliff has six hits, four singles and two doubles. White Sox also win first game, 7–4, and doubleheader the next day, 11–5 and 8–2.

1939 — J. Louis Comiskey dies—his widow Grace Comiskey and children inherit ownership.

1948 — Pat Seerey slugs four home runs in 11 innings in first of twin bill against A's in Philadelphia. Seerey connected in three straight innings (4–6), but did not hit another four-bagger until the 11th. The fourth homer won the game for the Sox, 12–11. (In his other two appearances, Seerey fouled out and walked.)

July 19

1891 — Jim Scoggins — 1913, P G-1

Robert Smith — 1913, P G-1

1899 — Joe Kiefer — 1920, P G-2

1906 — Jackie Hayes — 1932–40, 2B G-809

1910 — Harry Kinzy — 1934, P G-13

1916 — Phil Cavaretta — 1954–55, 1B–OF G-77

1920 — Babe Ruth re-sets his major league home run record with his 30th and 31st of season against the Sox's Dickie Kerr in New York.

1964 — Pitcher Gary Peters hits a pinch-hit home run in the 13th inning to beat Kansas City, 3–2.

July 20

1897 — Happy Foreman — 1924, P G-5

1936 — Sox buy pitcher Bill Dietrich from Washington.

1940 — White Sox pound Athletics in Philadelphia, 19–7.

1957 — Dick Donovan pitches his second one-hitter of the season, 4–0, over Boston. His previous one-hitter was over Cleveland on May 25, also won by a 4–0 score.

1968 — Sox trade infielder Wayne Causey to Angels for infielder-outfielder Woodie Held.

July 21

1877 — Irving Young — 1910–11, P G-51

1881 — Johnny Evers — 1922, '24, 2B–MGR G-1

1918 — Chet Hajduk — 1941, PH G-1

1935 — Moe Drabowsky — 1972, P G-7

1949 — Bought pitcher Mickey Haefner from Washington.

1959 — Richard Barnes — 1982, P G-6

1982 — White Sox erupt for 6 twelfth inning runs in Detroit for 9–3 victory.

July 22

1910 — George Caithamer — 1934, C G-5

1922 — Jim Rivera — 1952–61, OF G-1010

1944 — Sparky Lyle — 1982, P G-11

1962 — Floyd Robinson gets six hits in one game, all singles. Sox beat Red Sox, 7–3.

July 23

1917 — Ray Scarborough — 1950, P G-27

1920 — Bought outfielder Amos Strunk from Athletics.

1926 — Johnny Groth — 1954–55, OF G-157

1931 — Joe Stanka — 1959, P G-2

1937 — Dean Look — 1961, OF G-3

1940 — Hank Allen — 1972–73, 1B–3B–OF G-37

1961 — Roy Sievers hits two home runs in one game for the fifth time during the season (against Baltimore at Chicago).

1968 — After returning as manager for less than two weeks, Al Lopez undergoes an emergency appendectomy and misses 36 games. Coach Les Moss runs the team in his absence.

July 24

1909 — Ed Madjeski — 1934, C G-85

1912 — Alex Carrasquel — 1949, P G-3

1942 — Cotton Nash — 1967, 1B 3

July 25

1944 — Buddy Bradford — 1966–70, 1972–76, OF G-473

1954 — Jack Harshman sets all-time White Sox mark for strikeouts in single game with 16 vs. Boston.

1965 — John Romano's grand slam beats Tigers to end six-game losing streak. Smoky Burgess sets a major league record with his 108th career pinch-hit.

July 26

1892 — Sam Jones — 1932–35, P G-129

1914 — Ellis Kinder — 1956–57, P G-30

1923 — Hoyt Wilhelm — 1963–68, P G-361

1939 — Pete Ward — 1963–69, 3B–OF–1B, G-899

1948 — Bought pitcher Randy Gumpert from Yankees.

1968 — Traded pitcher Don McMahon to Detroit for pitcher Dennis Ribant.

July 27

1905 — Rudolph Leopold — 1928, P G-2

1923 — Ray Boone — 1958–59, 1B 86

July 28

1930 — Ted Lepcio — 1961, IF G-5

1931 — Gus Keriazakos — 1950, P G-1

> Bob Fothergill hits a homer and triple in one inning—the eighth. Sox score 11 in eighth to beat host Yankees, 14–12.

1935 — Pitcher Ted Lyons clubs two doubles in the second inning at Cleveland.

1952 — Acquired outfielder Jim Rivera and catcher Darrell Johnson from St. Louis Browns, sending outfielder Ray Coleman and catcher J. W. Porter to the Browns.

1959 — White Sox move into first place to stay with a 4–3 victory over the Yankees, behind Billy Pierce's pitching and Al Smith's eighth-inning, two-run homer.

1976 — John "Blue Moon" Odom and Francisco Barrios combine to no-hit Oakland, 2–1.

July 29

1910 — Patsy Dougherty spoils no-hitter of Ed Summers of Detroit. It was the fourth time in his career that Dougherty had the only hit for his team in a game (the third time with Sox).

1928 — Ken Landenberger — 1952, 1B G-2

1943 — Signed infielder Tony Cuccinello as a free agent (released earlier by Braves).

1951 — Ken Kravec — 1975–80, P G-123

1963 — Joel Horlen comes within one out of no-hitter, then loses 2–1 to Senators.

1967 — Traded outfielder Jim King to Cleveland for outfielder Rocky Colavito. Infielder Marv Staehle is assigned to Cleveland to complete deal, October 26.

July 30

1912 — Charles Uhlir — 1934, OF G-14

1925 — White Sox stop 13-game winning streak of Washington's Stanley Coveleskie with 11-1 victory in Washington.

1944 — Pat Kelly — 1971–76, OF G-692

1947 — Jim Spencer — 1976–77, 1B G-278

1952 — Lou Kretlow tosses his second two-hitter in six days, white-washing Yankees, 7–0.

1957 — Steve Trout — 1978–82, P G-115

July 31

1870 — Joe Sugden — 1901, C G-48

1910 — Lee Tannehill socks first Comiskey Park home run vs. Detroit, a grand slam.

1912 — Jess Landrum — 1938, 2B G-4

Archie Wise — 1932, P G-3

1920 — Fred Bradley — 1948–49, P G-9

1943 — Billy Wynne — 1968–70, P G-33

1951 — Bought outfielder Ray Coleman from St. Louis Browns.

1972 — Dick Allen ties an unofficial major league record with two inside-the-park home runs in one game against the Twins in Minnesota. Allen had two runners ahead of him in the first inning and one on in the fifth.

AUGUST 1

1947 — Tony Muser — 1971–75, 1B G-310

1950 — Milt May — 1979, C G-65

1977 — Texas outslugs White Sox, 11–6, in the longest nine-inning night game in American League history, 3:56, one minute short of the longest nine-inning game in AL history.

August 2

1898 — Emmett Bowles — 1922, P G-1

1899 — Tink Riviere — 1925, P G-3

1902 — Joe Klinger — 1930, 1B–C G-4

1906 — Doc White shuts out Boston, 3–0, as the White Sox start an American League record 19-game winning streak that puts them in thick of pennant race.

1924 — Lloyd Merriman — 1955, PH G-1

1968 — Traded infielder Tim Cullen to Washington for infielder Ron Hansen.

1979 — Don Kessinger resigns as manager and retires as player during first season in dual role. Tony LaRussa is promoted from the White Sox' top farm club at Iowa to be the new manager.

August 3

1874 — Ed McFarland — 1902–07, C G-323

1889 — Wally Mayer — 1911–12, 1914–15, C G-69

1902 — Doug Taitt — 1929, OF G-47

1906 — Ed Walsh one-hits Boston, 4–0, his second one-hitter of season.

1911 — Art Evans — 1932, P G-7

1956 — White Sox outslug Orioles, 11–3, in the first inning, tying the AL record for most runs scored by both teams in the first inning.

1959 — Nellie Fox's seventh-inning RBI single proves to be the deciding run in a 5–3 American League victory in the season's second All-Star Game, played at the Los Angeles Coliseum.

August 4

1885 — William "Tex" Jones — 1911, 1B G-9

1902 — Homer Blankenship — 1922–23, P G-8

1906 — White Sox shut out Boston for the third straight time, 1–0, with Roy Patterson hurling the shutout.

1910 — Sox and A's play 16-inning, 0–0 game.

1911 — Lee Tannehill becomes the only major league shortstop to execute two unassisted double plays in the same season. A further oddity is that they both came in the same game, the first game of a doubleheader.

1918 — Don Kolloway — 1940–43, 1946–49, 2B G-683

1920 — Bob Keegan — 1953–58, P G-136

1938 — Rip Radcliff collects eight hits in 10 at-bats in a doubleheader.

1939 — Dennis Higgins — 1966–67, P G-51

1942 — Angel Bravo — 1969, OF G-27

   Cleon Jones — 1976, OF G-12

1956 — White Sox set club record of six home runs at Comiskey Park as Jim Rivera hits two and Less Moss, Larry Doby, Jack Harshman, and Walt Dropo add one each in win over Baltimore.

August 5

1904 — Vic Frasier — 1931–33, '39, P G-95

1927 — Rocky Krsnich — 1949, 1952–53, 3B G-120

1949 — Luke Appling ties major league record by playing 2,153 games at shortstop. It was his last year as the regular White Sox shortstop. Before retiring, Appling played 2,218 at short.

August 6

1872 — Sam Mertes — 1901–2, 2B–OF G-266

1904 — Nick Altrock handles 13 chances with an error, setting a major league record for pitchers.

1905 — Chad Kimsey — 1932–33, P G-35

1912 — Bud Hafey — 1935, PH G-2

1935 — The Sox beat the Yankees, 9–8, in 15 innings. Zeke Bonura steals home for the winning run. (H)

1937 — Camilo Carreon — 1959–64, C G-301

1955 — By not playing, Nellie Fox ended 274 game playing streak . . . but began a 798-game skein the following day.

1959 — White Sox and Orioles battle to 18-inning, 1–1 tie.

August 7

1929 — Don Larsen — 1961, P G-25

1936 — Jerry McNertney — 1964, 1966–68, C G-247

1954 — Steve Kemp — 1982, OF G-160

August 8

1965 — Bill Skowron hits his 200th major league home run vs. Cleveland.

1977 — A White Sox player hits two home runs in one game for the 10th time this season, setting a club record, when Lamar Johnson smacks a pair vs. Seattle. Eric Soderholm, Richie Zisk, and Jim Spencer each duplicate the feat within the next week and the Sox end the season with 15. Ironically, Johnson had the only Sox two-home-run game in 1976.

August 9

1917 — Nemo Leibold sets major league record (since tied) for most errorless chances by a rightfielder.

1939 — Claude Osteen — 1975, P G-37

1942 — Tommie Agee — 1965–67, OF G-328

1946 — Gerry Moses — 1975, C G-2

1977 — White Sox hit six home runs (Eric Soderholm 2; one each for Chet Lemon, Oscar Gamble, Jim Essian, and Royle Stillman), tying the club record at Comisky Park in victory over Mariners.

August 10

1892 — Elmer Jacobs — 1927, P G-25

1911 — Taft Wright — 1940–42, 1946–48, OF G-741

1923 — Pete Gebrian — 1947, P G-27

1925 — Bought pitcher James Edwards from Cleveland.

1927 — Bob Chakales — 1955, P G-7

1933 — Rocky Colavito — 1967, OF G-60

1981 — In opening game of major league's first-ever second half, White Sox beat Boston, 7–1.

August 11

1910 — Ed Walsh strikes out 15 batters for second time in his career—vs. Boston.

1926 — Sox' five-run 13th inning defeats Indians, 7–2, at Cleveland.

1946 — Eddie Leon — 1973–74, SS G-158

1962 — Joe Cunningham doubles and triples in the same inning—the fourth.

August 12

1891 — William Lathrop — 1913–14, P G-25

1892 — Ray Schalk — 1912–28, C–MGR G-1755

1893 — John Michaelson — 1921, P G-2

1899 — John Black — 1924, 2B G-6

1900 — Spence Harris — 1925–26, OF G-136

1907 — Ed Walsh records 11 assists in one game for second time this season. Five pitchers have accomplished this feat, Walsh being the only pitcher to do it twice.

1910 — Traded pitcher Frank Smith and third baseman Bill Purtell to Red Sox for third baseman Harry Lord and second baseman Amby McConnell.

1935 — Ken McBride — 1959, P G-11

August 13

1874 — Fielder Jones — 1901–8, OF–MGR G-1158

1906 — White Sox battle New York to 0–0 tie, only blemish during 19-game winning streak.

1907 — Art Shires — 1928–30, 1B G-170

1943 — Luke Appling gets his 2,000th major league hit.

August 15

1888 — Babe Borton — 1912–13, 1B G-59

1891 — Fred Lamline — 1912, P G-1

1905 — Leslie Cox — 1926, P G-2

1919 — Happy Felsch tied a major league record with four outfield assists in one game. Felsch's strong arm also helped him set major league record for outfielders of 15 doubleplays in one season—1919.

1937 — Joel Horlen — 1961–71, P G-380

1939 — First night game ever played in Comiskey Park by White Sox. Johnny Rigney's hurling beats Browns, 5–2.

August 15

1889 — Harry Smith — 1912, P G-1

1922 — White Sox, with 21 singles and Red Sox, with 14, combine to set AL record.

1924 — Frank Whitman — 1946, '48, SS G-20

1926 — James Goodwin — 1948, P G-8

1936 — John Buzhardt — 1962–67, P G-175

1944 — John Matias — 1970, LB–OF G-58

1958 — Randy Johnson — 1980, OF–1B G-12

1973 — Acquired pitcher Jim Kaat on waivers from Minnesota.

August 16

1884 — Joe Hovlik — 1911, P G-12

58

1897 — Bob Fothergill — 1930–32, OF G-275

1926 — White Sox and Tigers play second consecutive scoreless tie at Comiskey Park. In all, the teams battled scoreless for 15 straight innings.

1927 — Babe Ruth, on the way to his famous 60-home-run season, becomes the first player to hit a home run over the Comiskey Park roof. Tommy Thomas was the Sox pitcher. The outfield grandstand roof was added in the spring of 1927.

1931 — Don Rudolph — 1957–59, P G-16

1974 — In 13-inning game vs. Yankees, Jorge Orta collects five hits for third time that season—one game short of major league mark.

1978 — Rookie Ross Baumgarten beats Texas, 6–2. In doing so, the lefthanded hurler won games at four different levels of organized baseball during the same season.

August 17

1896 — Doug McWeeny — 1921–22, '24, P G-44

1900 — Elmer Pence — 1922, OF G-1

1901 — Charles Embry — 1923, P G-1

1906 — Johnny Watwood — 1929–32, OF–1B G-359

1907 — Ed Durham — 1933, P G-24

1913 — Rudy York — 1947, 1B G-102

1972 — Acquired pitcher Eddie Fisher from Angels for infielder Bruce Miller. Catcher Bruce Kimm was sent to Angels to complete the deal, Sept. 1, 1972.

August 18

1890 — Buck Weaver — 1912–20, SS–3B G-1254

1917 — White Sox regain first place to stay during winningest campaign in club history. Defeat of Philadelphia moved Boston back into second place after Red Sox had taken over first place for one day.

1920 — Bob Kennedy — 1939–42, 1946–48, 1955–57, 3B–OF G-699

1946 — Jim Magnuson — 1970–71, P G-28

1977 — Traded pitcher Larry Anderson to Cubs for pitcher Steve Renko.

August 19

1891 — Al DeVormer — 1918, C G-8

1912 — Lester Rock — 1936, 1B G-2

1915 — Bill Nagel — 1945, 1B G-67

1930 — Shortstop Luke Appling is acquired from Atlanta Crackers in Southern Association.

1950 — Larry Doby Johnson — 1978, C G-3

1970 — In the ninth inning against the Red Sox in Boston, Luis Aparicio becomes only White Sox pinch-hitter to hit safely twice in the same inning.

August 20

1908 — Al Lopez — 1957-65, 1968-69, MGR

1915 — Traded pitcher Ed Klepfer and outfielders Bob Roth and Larry Chappell to Cleveland for outfielder Joe Jackson.

1919 — Earl Harrist — 1947-48, '53, P G-51

1928 — Art Shires hits triple and three singles in his first major league game.

1957 — Bob Keegan no-hits Washington, 6-0, in second game of doubleheader at Comiskey Park.

August 21

1875 — Frank Isbell — 1901-9, 1B-2B G-1074

1903 — James Holmes has four outfield assists in one game to tie major league record.

1920 — Whitey Platt — 1946, OF G-84

Gerry Staley — 1956-61, P G-270

1926 — Ted Lyons no-hits the Red Sox, 6-0, in only 67 minutes at Boston.

1933 — Yankees and White Sox battle to 3-3, 18-inning tie at Chicago.

August 22

1879 — John McAleese — 1901, P G-1

1891 — Happy Felsch — 1915-20, OF G-749

1912 — George Meyer — 1938, 2B G-24

1923 — Sloppy Thurston strikes out the side on nine pitches in the 12th inning vs. Athletics.

1958 — Nellie Fox sets mark for consecutive games without striking out (98).

1965 — John Buzhardt's 2-1 victory caps a doubleheader sweep of A's and a 10-game winning streak.

1980 — White Sox owners vote to sell the team to Edward J. DeBartolo, Sr., for $20 million. The sale was later turned down twice by American League owners.

August 23

1870 — George Davis — 1902, 1904–9, SS G-862

1888 — Paul Meloan — 1910–11, OF G-66

1890 — James Crabb — 1912, P G-2

1906 — White Sox extend win streak to 19—still club record.

1918 — Ken Holcombe — 1950–52, P G-59

1922 — George Kell — 1954–56, 3B–1B G-220

1924 — Sherm Lollar — 1952–63, C G-1358

1934 — John Romano — 1958–59, 1965–55, C G-301

1942 — Danny Murphy — 1969–70, P G-68

1948 — Ron Blomberg — 1978, 1B–DH G-61

1972 — Dick Allen becomes the first White Sox player to hit a home run into the centerfield bleachers at Comiskey Park (off Lindy McDaniel of Yankees).

1981 — Chicago wallops Toronto, 13–2, on 21 hits.

August 24

1887 — Harry Hooper — 1921–25, OF G-662

1897 — Francis Pratt — 1921, PH G-1

1956 — Tony Bernazard — 1981–82, 2B G-243

August 25

1928 — Darrell Johnson — 1952, C G-22

1950 — Stan Perzanowski — 1971, '74, P G-7

1959 — Traded outfielder Harry Simpson and infielder Bob Sagers to Pittsburgh for first baseman Ted Kluszewski.

1981 — Robin Yount's ninth inning leadoff bloop double spoils Dennis Lamp's no-hit bid. Lamp settles for a one-hit, 5–1 triumph over the Brewers in Milwaukee.

August 26

1914 — Eddie Cicotte strikes out 15 Yankees.

1949 — After opening the game by surrendering a run on a walk and two singles, Bob Kuzava strikes out six consecutive Red Sox to tie an American League record.

1961 — Ed Short moves up from traveling secretary and publicity director to succeed Hank Greenberg as general manager.

August 27

1880 — Ed Hahn — 1906–10, OF G-499

1894 — Eddie Mulligan — 1921–22, 3B G-255

1910 — Over 20,000 fans watch two amateur teams play a night game at Comiskey Park, the first night-baseball game ever played in an American League park. The lights were temporary and it wasn't until 1939 that the White Sox played a home game at night.

1911 — Ed Walsh no-hits Boston, 5–0.

1931 — Joe Cunningham — 1962–64, 1B G-256

1932 — Jim King — 1967, OF G-23

1935 — White Sox and Yankees each strand 15 runners.

1946 — Ed Herrmann — 1967, 1969–74, C G-643

1981 — Playing its first home game since June 11 (due to strike), Chicago beats Yankees, 3–1, on Greg Luzinski's three-run, eighth-inning homer. Two batters later, game was stopped by rain.

August 28

1892 — Robert Roth — 1914–15, OF–3B G-104

1896 — Aaron Ward — 1927, 2B G-145

1909 — White Sox draw seven straight walks from Washington pitching in second inning.

1911 — Joe Martin — 1938, PH G-1

August 29

1876 — Elmer Stricklett — 1904, P G-1

1919 — Orval Grove — 1940–49, P G-207

1939 — Dave Nicholson — 1963–65, OF G-277

1953 — Marvis Foley — 1979–80, 1982, C G-140

1965 — White Sox beat Boston, 3–2, on both ends of a doubleheader and rookie Bob

Locker saves both games. Ron Hansen sets major league record for shortstops by handling 28 chances in a doubleheader. His 18 chances in the 14-inning first game tied an AL mark for extra-inning games. Hansen had the least amount of innings.

1975 — Ken Henderson switch hits a pair of home runs—the only White sox player ever to do so.

August 30

1872 — Davey Dunkle — 1903, P G-11

1880 — Charlie Armbruster — 1907, C G-1

1925 — Ted Wilson — 1952, OF G-8

1927 — Gordon Goldsberry — 1949–51, 1B G-131

1959 — White Sox sweep third doubleheader of season from second place Cleveland, and also sweep four-game series at Indians' Municipal Stadium, increasing lead to comfortable 5½ games.

1960 — Ricky Seilheimer — 1980, C G-21

1981 — Acquired pitcher Jerry Koosman from Minnesota for minor league infielders Ivan Mesa, Ron Perry and Randy Johnson.

August 31

1898 — Sarge Connally — 1921, 1923–29, P G-205

1905 — Frank Smith one-hits Washington for second time this season.

1910 — Ira Hutchinson — 1933, P G-1

1919 — Jack Wallaesa — 1947–48, SS–OF, G-114

1926 — Ray Morehart ties a major league record with nine hits in a doubleheader (10 at-bats).

1935 — Vern Kennedy no-hits St. Louis, 5–0. Kennedy is also the batting star with a bases-loaded triple.

1941 — Ted Lyons pitches his last incomplete game in the major leagues against the Browns in St. Louis. He completed his last three starts of 1941, all 20 of his starts in 1942 and, returning from the armed forces, all five of his starts in 1946.

1951 — Saul Rogovin shuts out his former teammates for the second time, 2–0, after being traded earlier in the season by Detroit.

1953 — Bill Nahorodny — 1977–79, C G-179

1954 — Claudell Washington — 1978–80, OF G-249

1955 — Silvio Martinez — 1977, P G-10.

August 31 (continued)

1980 — Ed Farmer picks up a save in each game (nos. 23 and 24) as White Sox rally with eight runs in last two innings of first game and four runs in last two innings of nightcap to sweep Indians, 10–8 and 8–7, at Cleveland.

SEPTEMBER 1

1888 — Roy Wolfe — 1912, '14, OF G-10

1921 — Joe Erautt — 1950–51, C G-32

1930 — Dean Stone — 1962, P G-27

1943 — Fred Rath — 1968–69, P G-8

1948 — White Sox draw 13 walks off Dick Weik of Detroit.

September 2

1880 — Fred Payne — 1909–11, C G-189

1889 — Chief Chouneau — 1910, P G-1

1900 — Joe Heving — 1933–34, P G-73

1918 — Buck Weaver hits safely eight times in 10 at-bats in a doubleheader.

1937 — Boze Berger and Mike Kreevich become the first AL players to open game with back-to-back home runs (off Johnny Marcum of Boston).

1941 — Jerry Crider — 1970, P G-32

1950 — Lamar Johnson — 1974–81, 1B G-687

1956 — Fred Howard — 1979, P G-28

1959 — White Sox score 10 runs after two are out and no one on base against Detroit.

1970 — Vice President and Director of Player Personnel Ed Short is fired and replaced by Roland Hemond.

1973 — White Sox back Stan Bahnsen with club record six double plays in 13–3 win over California.

1981 — Chet Lemon swats 5,000th homer in Sox history.

September 3

1913 — Kerby Farrell — 1945, 1B G-103

1916 — Eddie Stanky — 1966–68, MGR.

1920 — Sandy Consuegra — 1953–56, P G-140

1922 — Morrie Martin — 1954–56, P G-82

1951 — Alan Bannister — 1976–80, SS–OF–2B G-442

1970 — Manager Don Gutteridge is fired and Chuck Tanner is hired to replace him. Bill Adair runs the team until Sept. 15 when Tanner's season with Hawaii in the Pacific Coast League is finished.

September 4

1887 — Red Corriden — 1950, MGR.

1912 — Gordon Maltzberger — 1943–44, 1946–47, P G-135

1913 — Clarence Fieber — 1932, P G-3

1936 — Jim McAnany — 1958–60, OF G-75

1937 — Mike Kreevich hits four doubles in four consecutive times at bat, as Chicago beats Tigers in Detroit, 9–1.

1959 — Early Wynn beats Cleveland, 3–2, in Chicago, as White Sox open up a 6½ game lead over the second place Indians, their largest bulge of season.

1960 — A virus ends Nellie Fox's consecutive game streak at 798.

September 5

1893 — Don Rader — 1913, OF-3B, G-2

1895 — Ted Jourdan — 1916–18, 20; 1B G-75

1900 — Merv Shea — 1934–37, C G-147

1919 — Tom Jordan — 1944, '46, C G-24

1920 — Gene Bearden — 1953, P G-31

1980 — Rookie Lamarr Hoyt two-hits Blue Jays in Toronto, 3–0, for his first major league shutout, raising record to 7–2.

September 6

1888 — Red Faber — 1914–33, P G-670

1903 — Doc White one-hits Cleveland over 10 innings.

1905 — Frank Smith no-hits Detroit, 15–0. This is the widest margin of victory during a no-hitter in modern major league history. He had pitched two one-hitters earlier in the season. Doc White shut out the Tigers in the first of two games, 2–0.

1911 — Vallie Eaves — 1939–40, P G-7

1934 — Tom Flanigan — 1954, P G-2

September 7

1936 — Charles Lindstrom — 1958, C G-1

1970 — Sox use 41 players in twinbill vs. A's.

September 8

1906 — Frank Stewart — 1927, P G-1

1916 — Tom Turner — 1940–44, C G-218

1945 — Ossie Blanco–1970, 1B G-34

1977 — Bought catcher Bill Nahorodny from Phillies.

September 9

1908 — Johnny Marcum — 1939, P–PH G-38

1921 — Earl Sheely scores five runs in White Sox 20–15 win over Detroit at Comiskey Park.

1928 — White Sox break open game with eight runs in ninth inning to beat Cleveland, 10–1.

1931 — Earl Averill, Jr. — 1960, C G-10

September 10

1884 — Jack Lapp — 1916, C G-40

1905 — Irv Jeffries — 1930--31, 3B–SS G-119

1924 — Ted Kluszewski — 1959–60, 1B G-112

1939 — Detroit stops Johnny Rigney's 11-game win streak, 5–1, in first game of doubleheader.

1951 — Randy Wiles — 1977, P G-5

1967 — Joel Horlen no-hits Detroit, 6–0. Cisco Carlos also shuts out Detroit in the second game of the twin bill, 4–0, with help from Hoyt Wilhelm and Bob Locker.

September 11

1911 — Les Tietje — 1933–36, P G-69

1936 — White Sox collect 26 hits vs. Athletics.

September 12

1904 — Doc White begin shutout string of five straight games.

1907 — Ollie Bejma — 1939, 2B G-90

1908 — Battling to the wire for the AL pennant, Chicago and Detroit play fourth straight extra-inning game.

1916 — Ralph Hamner — 1946, P G-25

1959 — Early Wynn defeats Orioles, 6–1, in Baltimore, for 20th victory of season. It was his fifth (and last) 20-win season of career, but only first with Sox.

1964 — Bought catcher Smoky Burgess from Pittsburgh.

September 13

1896 — Roy Wilson — 1928, P G-1

1906 — Thornton Lee — 1937-47, P G-262

1967 — White Sox nip Cleveland, 1–0, in 17 innings.

1974 — Dick Allen announces that he is quitting the team with 16 games remaining, but he still wins the AL home run title.

September 14

1967 — Don Buford's 10th-inning grand slam beats Cleveland, 4–0, as Cisco Carlos goes all the way for the win.

September 15

1875 — George Rohe — 1905-7, INF G-253

1876 — Nick Altrock — 1903-9, P G-186

1887 — Harry Suter — 1909, P G-18

1900 — Bud Clancy — 1924-30, 1B G-449

Harry McCurdy — 1926-28, C G-179

1901 — White Sox set major league record with five triples in eighth inning against Milwaukee. Sox also had sixth triple in game for AL record.

1906 — Charles Biggs — 1932, P G-6

1937 — Charlie Smith — 1962-64, 3B G-71

September 15 (continued)

1978 — White Sox erupt in 10th inning at Seattle to beat Mariners, 8–3, and avoided becoming the first team not to win an extra inning game for an entire season. Sox lost their previous eight attempts.

September 16

1901 — Ken Ash — 1925, P G-2

1905 — Joseph Vance — 1935, P G-10

1928 — Vito Valentinetti — 1954, P G-1

1944 — Chuck Brinkman — 1969–74, C G-144

1953 — Chris Knapp — 1975–77, P G-40

September 17

1898 — Earl Webb — 1933, OF–1B G-58

1913 — Robert Uhle — 1938, P G-1

1917 — Allen Gettel — 1948–49, P G-43

1918 — Bob Dillinger — 1951, 3B G-89

1920 — White Sox hit six triples against the Yankees

1938 — Merv Connors hits three consecutive home runs and a double off A's Jim Reninger in first game of twin bill at Chicago. Sox won both, 8–4 and 7–4.

1940 — Cisco Carlos — 1967–69, P G-62

1956 — Thad Bosley — 1978–80, OF G-172

September 18

1948 — Ken Brett — 1976–77, P G-40

Lee Richard — 1971–72, 1974–75, SS–3B–OF G-173

1982 — In second game of doubleheader, Oakland and White Sox tie AL record (also co-held by Sox) for longest nine inning night game, 3:56.

September 19

1925 — Washington's Bobby Veach spoiled Ted Lyons' no-hit bid in the ninth inning. Lyons settles for a one-hitter as Chicago won 17–0 in the second game of a doubleheader in Washington.

1926 — White Sox sweep a five-game series with Red Sox with second straight 6–3 win at Chicago.

1946 — Ron Lolich — 1971, OF G-2

1951 — Nardi Contreras — 1980, P G-8

1978 — Ron Blomberg's eight-inning grand slam home run brings 7–3 victory in second game of doubleheader for sweep of A's in Oakland.

September 20

1902 — Jimmy Callahan pitches White Sox' first no-hitter (second in AL history), beating Detroit, 3–0. White Sox were involved in the first two American League no-hitters and won both—even though they were the no-hit victims in the first one. (See May 9, 1901.)

1908 — Zeke Bonura — 1934–37, 1B G-529

Frank Smith no-hits A's, 1–0, in Philadelphia. It was the second no-hitter of his career and he is still the only pitcher with two no-hitters for the Sox.

1941 — Dennis Ribant — 1968, P G-17

1943 — Rich Morales — 1967–73, INF G-336

1958 — Jim Siwy — 1982, P G-2

September 21

1917 — Joe Haynes — 1941–48, P G-219

September 22

1920 — Bob Lemon — 1977–78, MGR

Chicago grand jury convenes to investigate charges that White Sox players fixed the 1919 World Series.

1923 — Tom Wright — 1952–53, OF G-137

1939 — Stover McIlwain — 1957–58, P G-2

1959 — White Sox clinch first pennant in 40 years with 4–2 victory over second-place Indians in Cleveland. Reliever Gerry Staley, entering the game in the ninth inning with bases loaded, threw one pitch—inducing Vic Power to ground to Luis Aparicio for game-ending double play. Early Wynn was the starter and winner; Jim Rivera and Al Smith homered.

1961 — Floyd Robinson's ninth-inning grand slam sets club record of seven in one season—but White Sox fall short in game, 8–6, as Baltimore's Jim Gentile ties a major league record in the same game with his fifth grand slam of the season.

1977 — Bought outfielder Bob Molinaro from Detroit.

September 23

1889 — Walter Schaller — 1913, OF G-34

1898 — George Murray — 1933, P G-2

1920 — Marino Pieretti — 1948–49, P G-80

September 23 (continued)

1936 — Luke Appling hits a home run, double and two singles to overtake Cleveland's Earl Averill and become the first (and only) White Sox player to win the AL batting title. Appling repeated as champion in 1943.

1952 — Jim Morrison — 1979–82, 2B–3B G-370

Dennis Lamp — 1981–82, P G-71

September 24

1910 — Dixie Walker — 1936–37, OF G-180

1917 — Charlie Cuellar — 1950, P G-2

1919 — White Sox clinch pennant with 6–5 win over Browns, eliminating Cleveland.

1944 — White Sox sweep all 11 games at Comiskey Park vs. Washington as Thornton Lee and Eddie Lopat chalk up 9–3 and 2–0 doubleheader win.

1948 — Eric Soderholm — 1977–79, 3B, G-329

1950 — Don Kirkwood — 1977, P G-16

1963 — White Sox stop Baltimore, 15–0.

1972 — Dick Allen slugs 37th homer of season—now a club record.

1977 — Jack Brohamer becomes only the second player in Sox history to hit for the cycle as Sox beat Mariners, 8–3. Brohamer also had a second double.

September 25

1905 — Greg Mulleavy — 1930–32, SS G-78

1916 — Norm Schlueter — 1938–39, C G-69

1920 — Lefty Williams beats Cleveland, 5–1, in Cleveland, helped by Joe Jackson's home run. Sox take two out of three in series and pull back within a half game of league-leading Indians.

September 26

1895 — Bernie Neis — 1927, OF G-45

1904 — John Cortazzo — 1923, PH G-1

1905 — Johnny Hodapp — 1932, OF–2B G-68

Ed Walsh pitches complete game victories in both games of a doubleheader (10–5 and 3–1).

1906 — Pat Caraway — 1930–32, P G-109

1912 — Dick Clarke — 1944, 3B G-63

1917 — Thurman Tucker — 1942–44, 1946–47, OF G-480

1943 — White Sox score 13 runs in fourth inning vs. Washington.

1950 — Bugs Moran — 1974, P G-15

September 27

1905 — Chicago scores 15 runs against Red Sox in game called after six innings in Boston.

1907 — Whitlow Wyatt — 1933–36, P G-82

1926 — Jerry Scala — 1948–50, OF G-80

1944 — Virle Rounsaville — 1970, P G-8

1967 — White Sox blow chance to regain first place with their final three games at home, losing a doubleheader to A's, 5–2 and 4–0, at Kansas City.

1981 — Ross Baumgarten and Lamarr Hoyt combine to surrender AL record-tying eight consecutive singles at start of game in Oakland, but Hoyt settles down to shut out Oakland the rest of the way on two hits as White Sox rally for 9–5 win. Sox crashed five homers to take nightcap, 10–3.

September 28

1885 — Wilbur Good — 1918, OF G-35

1889 — Rip Jordan — 1912, P G-4

1892 — Jack Fournier — 1912–17, 1B–OF G-444

1895 — Harold Bubser — 1922, PH G-3

Glen Moulder — 1948, P G-33

1920 — Chicago grand jury indicts eight White Sox players (pitchers Ed Cicotte and Lefty Williams, outfielders Joe Jackson and Happy Felsch, third baseman Buck Weaver, shortstop Swede Risberg, first baseman Chick Gandil, and infielder Fred McMullin) on charges that they conspired to throw the 1919 World Series. With his club still trailing Cleveland by a half-game, owner Charles Comiskey immediately suspended the eight players.

1932 — Third baseman Jimmie Dykes and outfielders Al Simmons and Mule Haas are bought from Philadelphia Athletics for $150,000.

1974 — White Sox strand 18 men in a nine-inning game against the A's in Oakland.

September 29

1901 — Tony Rensa — 1937–39, C G-99

1908 — Ed Walsh starts and wins both ends of a doubleheader against Boston, allowing only one run on seven hits and one walk.

1909 — Oris Hockett — 1945, OF G-106

1914 — John Johnson — 1945, P G-29

1922 — Don Wheeler — 1949, C G-67

1924 — Ed McGhee — 1950, 1954–55, OF G-71

1935 — After winning first game, 3–2, White Sox beat pennant-winning Tigers, 14–2, in six innings in Chicago. They connected for 10 singles in the second inning off of AL won-lost percentage champion, Eldon Auker.

1936 — Hal Trosky, Jr. — 1958, P G-2

1967 — White Sox lose to Washington, 1–0, on an unearned run in the first inning as Phil Ortega outduels Tommy John at Comiskey Park. Loss eliminates Sox from pennant race. Despite being in first place for 89 days during the season, the Sox finish fourth during the wild '67 campaign. They were three games back, losing their last three games at home to Washington.

September 30

1904 — Doc White pitches fifth straight shutout and sixth shutout for month of September (3-hitter vs. New York).

1921 — Catcher Ray Schalk records three assists in the eight inning.

1948 — Rusty Torres — 1978–79, OF G-106

1949 — Acquired shortstop Chico Carrasquel from the Dodger organization for cash and two minor league players.

1956 — At age of 16 years and 10 months, Jim Derrington becomes the youngest major league pitcher to start a game since 1900. With one single in two at-bats, he also becomes the youngest AL player to hit safely. Unfortunately, he lost to Kansas City, 7–6.

OCTOBER 1

1916 — On the White Sox's final day of the regular season, Cleveland beats Sox in first game of doubleheader, ending Chicago's chances of catching Red Sox for pennant.

1919 — Ed Cicotte gives up five fourth-inning runs and Sox manage only six hits off the Redlegs' Dutch Reuther, as Cincinnati takes opening game of World Series at home, 9–1.

1920 — In first game following indictment and suspension of eight players in 1919

World Series, Red Faber loses to Browns, 8–6, while Cleveland splits pair with Tigers. White Sox trail by two games with two remaining.

1926 — Bob Boyd — 1951, 1953–54, 1B-OF G-96

1937 — Al Brice — 1961, P G-3

1950 — Gus Zernial hits four home runs in a doubleheader, three in the second game at Comiskey Park.

1956 — Vance Law — 1982, SS–3B G-114

1959 — While Dodgers are looking for the White Sox speed, Ted Kluszewski turns on the power with two home runs and five RBIs as Sox coast to 11–0 triumph in Game 1 of World Series in Chicago. Early Wynn and Gerry Staley combine for the shutout.

October 2

1891 — Eddie Murphy — 1915–21, OF G-359

1908 — Ed Walsh strikes out 15, but loses, 1–0, as Addie Joss hurls perfect game for Indians at Cleveland in the midst of tight American League pennant race.

1919 — In the fourth inning, Lefty Williams' sudden three-walk wild streak is capped by Larry Kopf's triple, enabling home-standing Cincinnati to win 4–2 on only four hits and take a 2–0 lead in World Series.

1920 — White Sox beat Browns, 10–7, but Cleveland beats Detroit, 10–1, clinching pennant with one game remaining in season.

1921 — Ralph Weigel — 1948, C G-66

1949 — Greg Pryor — 1978–81, INF G-394

1951 — Bob Coluccio — 1975, '77, OF G-81

1959 — With homers accounting for all their runs, Dodgers win Game 2 of World Series in Chicago, 4–3, evening the series. White Sox took 2–1 lead into seventh, but Dodgers tied score on Chuck Essegian's pinch homer, and Charlie Neal's second home run of the game with one aboard proved to be just enough.

1977 — A crowd of 20,953 breaks Comiskey Park attendance mark (1,657,135).

October 3

1874 — Alfred Shaw — 1908, C G-32

1903 — Charlie Dorman — 1923, C G-1

1905 — Johnny Riddle — 1930, C G-25

1917 — Frank Kalin — 1943, PH G-4

1919 — Dickie Kerr stifles Cincinnati on three hits for 3–0 victory at Chicago, pulling White Sox within two games to one in World Series. Chick Gandil's second-inning double for two runs was the key blow.

1936 — Jack Lamabe — 1966–67, P G-37

1948 — Jack Onslow is hired to replace Ted Lyons as manager.

1949 — Jim Breazeale — 1978, 1B G-25

1954 — Joe Gates — 1978–79, 2B G-24

1965 — Eddie Fisher sets an American League record with his 82nd mound appearance in game at Comiskey Park.

October 4

1892 — Delos Brown — 1914, PH G-1

1919 — With both teams' bats silent, Ed Cicotte's two fifth-inning errors lead to the only two runs of the game as Reds win 2–0 in Chicago, taking a 3–1 game lead behind the pitching of Jimmy Ring.

1922 — Don Lenhardt — 1951, OF G-64

1931 — Joe Kirrene — 1950, '54, 3B G-10

1944 — Tony LaRussa — 1979–82, MGR.

1959 — In the seventh inning in L.A., Carl Furillo's pinch-hit, two-run single with the bases loaded gives Dodgers a 3–1 victory. White Sox fall behind, two games to one in World Series, despite out-hitting Dodgers, 12–5, in the third game.

1963 — White Sox release Sherm Lollar, ending his major league career.

1980 — Fifty-seven-year-old Minnie Minoso becomes the second player in major league history to play in five decades, with pinch-hitting appearance at Comiskey Park. Ed Farmer notches his 30th save of the year in a 4–2 win over Angels.

1981 — Jerry Hairston hits eighth inning grand slam, then singles in winning run with his sixth RBI of the game as White Sox outslug Twins, 13–12, in Chicago.

October 5

1887 — Felix Chouinard — 1910–11, OF G-38

1904 — Sammy West — 1942, OF G-49

1908 — Ed Walsh beats Detroit, 6–1, to move White Sox within a half-game of league-leading Tigers. Cleveland splits doubleheader with St. Louis and they are eliminated from pennant race. The victory is Walsh's fortieth of the season.

1919 — White Sox face fifth straight different starter and Hod Eller pitches the Reds' second straight three-hit shutout for a 5–0 victory in Game 5 of World Series at Chicago. Edd Roush's triple caps a four-run sixth inning which broke a scoreless duel between Eller and the Sox's Lefty Williams. Sox fall behind four games to one, but are still alive as World Series switched to best-of-nine format in 1919.

1959 — Falling behind 4–0 in first three innings at L.A., Sox rally to tie the score in the seventh, with Sherm Lollar's three-run homer the key blow. But Gil Hodges' homer in the eighth gives Dodgers 5–4 victory and a 3–1 advantage in games in World Series.

October 6

1908 — Having pitched in 13 of the previous 16 games, Ed Walsh is bypassed as a starter in season finale in Chicago with pennant on the line. Doc White is tabbed instead, but he is knocked out after two innings and Detroit wins, 7–0, to take the pennant. Loss puts White Sox in third place, 1½ behind Detroit and one game behind Cleveland. Had Sox won, they would have won pennant by percentage points over Cleveland (an 89–63 record, compared to 90–64). Game was played behind locked gates as Charles Comiskey feared interference from overflow crowds would hurt the home team's chances.

1917 — Happy Felsch hits White Sox's first World Series home run and it proves to be the deciding run as Ed Cicotte outduels the Giants' Slim Sallee, 2–1, in World Series opener in Chicago.

1959 — Setting World Series attendance records for third straight game, 92,706 in L.A. Coliseum watch Sherm Lollar's double-play grounder score game's only run and send World Series from West Coast back to Chicago with Sox trailing Dodgers, three games to two. Pitching of Bob Shaw and Dick Donovan, plus defensive replacement Jim Rivera's over-the-shoulder catch off Charlie Neal with two on and two out in seventh inning, frustrate a fine pitching performance by a young Sandy Koufax.

Greg Walker — 1982, DH G-11

October 7

1881 — James Durham — 1902, P–OF G-5

1917 — White Sox take a 2–0 lead in games in World Series over the Giants with a 7–2 win in Chicago, highlighted by the pitching of Red Faber and three hits apiece by Joe Jackson and Buck Weaver. A five-run fourth broke the game open for the Sox.

1919 — Dickie Kerr struggles early, but hangs in for his second World Series victory, as White Sox beat Redlegs, 5–4, in Cincinnati, when Chick Gandil singles home Buck Weaver in the tenth inning. White Sox now trail four games to two.

1921 — Al Sima — 1954, P G-5

1922 — Grady Hatton — 1954, 3B G-13

1925 — Ted Blankenship and the Cubs' Grover Alexander duel for 19 innings in opening game of Chicago City Series before game is called at a 2–2 tie.

1926 — Ted Blankenship shuts out Cubs, 3–0, to win city series, four games to three.

1956 — Rudy Law — 1982, OF G-121

October 8

1887 — Ping Bodie — 1911–14, OF G-516

Donie Bush — 1930–31, MGR.

1910 — Wally Moses — 1942–46, OF G-628

1918 — Bob Gillespie — 1947–48, P G-50

1919 — Ed Cicotte returns to form to beat Reds in Cincinnati, 4–1, and suddenly the White Sox pull to within four games to three in the World Series.

1921 — George "Catfish" Metkovich — 1949, OF G-93

1959 — Dodgers spurt to 8–0 in first four innings and hang on to win, 9–3, and take World Series, four games to two. Host White Sox stage fourth inning rally on Ted Kluszewski's three-run homer. But Dodger relief hero Larry Sherry, with a win or save in each Dodger victory, clinches game for L.A., with 5⅔ scoreless innings.

October 9

1906 — Winners of a record 116 games during the regular season, Cubs are heavily favored over the weak-hitting White Sox in World Series. But the Sox prevail in Game 1, 2–1, when Frank Isbell's sixth-inning single drives in Fielder Jones and Nick Altrock outduels Three Finger Brown. The first World Series game between the cross-town rivals is played in snow flurries at the Cubs' home park.

1912 — Mickey Haefner — 1949–50, P G-38

1919 — Lefty Williams retires first batter, but does not retire another as Cincinnati rolls for four runs in first inning to coast to 10–5 victory in Chicago and take World Series over White Sox, five games to three.

Rumors of a fix were abundant during the Series and an investigation started at end of 1920 season led to eight players banned from organized baseball for life. (See September 28, 1920.)

1939 — Mike Hershberger — 1961–64, '71, OF G-513

1941 — Jeoff Long — 1964, 1B–OF G-23

1946 — Jim Qualls — 1972, OF G-11

1948 — Frank Lane hired as general manager, replacing Leslie O'Connor.

1950 — Brian Downing — 1973–77, C G-453

Cubs coast to a 7–1 win at the Sox home park, evening the World Series at one game apiece.

1914 — Italo Chelini — 1935–37, P G-254

1916 — Floyd Baker — 1945–51, 3B G-590

1917 — Traveling to New York and rain delay cools off White Sox as Rube Benton shuts them out, 2–0, pulling Giants within two games to one in World Series. Ed Cicotte surrenders only five hits, but Dave Robertson's triple and Walter Holke's double in the fourth do him in.

1922 — Saul Rogovin — 1951–53, P G-79

1950 — Paul Richards signed as manager, replacing interim skipper Red Corriden.

October 11

1878 — Frank Roth — 1906, C G-16

1901 — Ernie Smith — 1930, SS G-24

1906 — Ed Walsh strikes out 12 and shuts out host Cubs on two-hits as White Sox regain lead in World Series, two games to one. Sox manage only four hits off Jack Pfiester, but one of them is George Rohe's bases-loaded triple, accounting for all the White Sox runs.

1917 — Vince Castino — 1943–45, C G-88

For the second straight day the White Sox are shut out in New York, this time, 5–0, by Ferdie Schupp. The Giant hitting star was Bennie Kauff, who powered two homers, evening the World Series at 2–2.

1926 — Joe Ginsberg — 1960–61, C G-34

1930 — Bill Fischer — 1956–58, P G-53

October 12

1874 — Jimmy Burke — 1901, SS G-42

1883 — Charlie French — 1910, 2B–OF G-45

1890 — Dixie Davis — 1915, P G-2

Joe Jenkins — 1917, 1919, C G-21

1906 — A two-hitter by Three Finger Brown allows the Cubs to tie the World Series, 2–2, with a 1–0 triumph over host Sox, Johnny Evers singled home Frank Chance for the only run off of White Sox' Nick Altrock.

1931 — Lew Fonseca named player-manager, replacing Donie Bush.

October 13

1877 — Hamilton Patterson — 1909, OF G-1

1888 — Jack Onslow — 1949–50, MGR

1891 — Fred McMullin — 1916–20, 3B G-303

1894 — Swede Risberg — 1917–20, SS G-476

1906 — Frank Isbell establishes World Series record with four doubles, overcoming six White Sox errors, as Sox takes 3–2–game lead in World Series with an 8–6 victory over the host Cubs.

1914 — Frankie Hayes — 1946, C G-53

1917 — In a wild game in Chicago, with six White Sox errors, three Giant miscues, and both teams combining for 26 hits, Eddie Collins singles in game-winning run as part of three-run eight-inning outburst to beat Giants, 8–5. White Sox take a 3-games-to-2 World Series lead.

1970 — Traded first baseman Gail Hopkins and John Matias to Royals for outfielder Pat Kelly and pitcher Don O'Riley.

October 14

1906 — Rapping Three Finger Brown for seven runs in the first two innings, host White Sox beat Cubs, 8–3, and win World Series, four games to two. Subbing at shortstop for Lee Tannehill, George Davis had three RBIs for the second straight game. Jiggs Donahue also added three RBIs and Edgar Hahn had four hits. Strangely, it was the only game won by the home team in the White Sox' upset triumph.

October 15

1902 — Evar Swanson — 1932–34, OF G-275

1903 — Mule Haas — 1933–37, OF G-517

1908 — Hugo Klaener — 1934, P G-3

1917 — Three Giant errors lead to four unearned runs by the White Sox as Red Faber goes all the way to win Game 6 at New York and along with it, the World Series title, four games to two.

October 16

1881 — Moxie Manvel — 1908, P G-17

1921 — Matt Batts — 1954, C G-55

1924 — Bob Cain — 1949–50, P G-46

1940 — Dave DeBusschere — 1962–63, P G-36

1949 — Hugh Yancy — 1972, '74, '76, INF G-7

1952 — Traded infielder Willie Miranda and outfielder Hank Edwards to St. Louis Browns for infielder Joe DeMaestri.

October 17

1917 — John Ostrowski — 1949-50, OF–3B G-71

1933 — Bob Powell — 1955, '57, PH G-2

1945 — Bob Christian — 1969-70, OF G-51

October 18

1895 — Babe Pinelli — 1918, 3B G-24

1902 — Charlie Berry — 1932-33, C G-158

1912 — Guy Curtright — 1943-46, OF G-331

1915 — George Gick — 1937-38, P G-2

1927 — Marv Rotblatt — 1948, 1950-51, P G-35

1931 — Andy Carey — 1961, 3B G-56

1938 — Bobby Knoop — 1969-70, 2B G-234

1949 — Ed Farmer — 1979-81, P G-148

1952 — Rudy Hernandez — 1972, SS G-8

1955 — Traded infielder Bobby Adams to Baltimore for outfielder Cal Abrams.

October 19

1943 — Sandy Alomar — 1967-69, 2B G-167

1949 — Traded catcher Joe Tipton to Philadelphia Athletics for second baseman Nellie Fox.

1972 — Traded outfielder Walt Williams to Cleveland for infielder Eddie Leon.

1978 — Shortstop Don Kessinger named player-manager.

October 20

1883 — Cuke Barrows — 1909-12, OF G-32

1895 — John Russell — 1921-22, P G-16

1909 — Bruce Campbell — 1930-32, OF G-18

October 21

1887 — Roy Corhan — 1911, SS G-43

     Thomas Quinlan — 1915, OF G-42

1916 — Eddie Carnett — 1944, OF–1B G-126

1917 — Frank Papish — 1945–48, P G-120

1951 — Ron Pruitt — 1980, OF–C G-33

October 22

1933 — Ron Jackson — 1954–59, 1B G-186

1941 — Wilbur Wood — 1967–78, P G-578

1942 — Cecil Upshaw — 1975, P G-29

1953 — Rich Wortham — 1978–80, P G-83

October 23

1886 — Lena Blackburne — 1910, 1912, 1914–15, 1927–29, INF–MGR G-320

1910 — William J. Sullivan, Jr. — 1931–33, 3B–1B G-239

1920 — Vern Stephens — 1953, '55, 3B G-66

1933 — Jake Striker — 1960, P G-2

October 24

1907 — Grant Bowler — 1931–32, P G-17

1929 — Jim Brosnan — 1963, P G-45

1944 — John Jeter — 1973, OF G-89

1951 — Traded infielder Floyd Baker to Washington for infielder Willie Miranda.

October 25

1946 — Don Eddy — 1970–71, P G-29

1955 — Traded shortstop Chico Carrasquel and outfielder Jim Busby to Cleveland for outfielder Larry Doby.

October 26

1866 — Kid Gleason — 1919–23, MGR

1880 — Lee Tannehill — 1903–12, 3B–SS G-1089

1931 — Charles A. Comiskey, owner and founder of the Chicago White Sox, dies at the age of 72.

1947 — Bill Gogolewski — 1975, P G-19

1957 — Harry Chappas — 1978–80, SS G-72

October 27

1876 — Patsy Dougherty — 1906–11, OF G-703

1900 — Red Proctor — 1923, P G-2

1936 — Lee Stange — 1970, P G-16

1952 — Pete Vuckovich — 1975–76, P G-37

October 28

1879 — Frank Smith — 1904–10, P G-247

1883 — Frank Lange — 1910–13, P G-129

1894 — John Bischoff — 1925, C G-7

1896 — Roxy Snipes — 1923, PH G-1

1904 — Elias Funk — 1932–33, OF G-132

1914 — Johnny Rigney — 1937–42, 1946–47, P G-198

1972 — Traded pitcher Vicente Romo to San Diego for outfielder John Jeter.

October 30

1897 — Elwood Wirtz — 1924, C G-6

1930 — Don Nicholas — 1952, '54, OF G-10

1956 — Al Lopez is hired as manager, succeeding Marty Marion.

October 31

1901 — Ray Flaskamper — 1927, SS G-26

1939 — Ed Stroud — 1966–67, '71, OF G-85

1941 — Ed Spiezio — 1972, 3B G-74

1943 — Fred Klages — 1966–67, P G-15

1945 — Bill Voss — 1965–68, OF G-87

NOVEMBER 1

1931 — Russ Kemmerer — 1960–62, P G-103

1950 — Luke Appling retires as player and is named manager of White Sox' Memphis farm club.

November 2

1888 — Dutch Zwilling — 1910, OF G-27

1946 — Tom Paciorek — 1982, 1B G-104

November 3

1895 — Frank Willson — 1918, '27, OF G-11

1959 — Traded first baseman Ron Jackson to Red Sox for pitcher Frank Baumann.

November 4

1909 — Skeeter Webb — 1940–44, 2B–SS, G-342

1920 — Val Heim — 1942, OF, G-13

1927 — Carl Sawatski — 1954, C G-43

1933 — Tito Francona — 1958, OF G-41

1965 — Al Lopez retires as manager of Sox; Eddie Stanky is signed as successor on Dec. 14.

November 5

1890 — Flame Delhi — 1912, P G-1

1893 — Clarence Yaryan — 1921–22, C G-81

1895 — Spencer Heath — 1920, P G-4

1905 — Carl Fischer — 1935, P G-24

1914 — Mark Mauldin — 1934, 3B G-10

November 6

1876 — Dave Altizer — 1909, OF–1B G-116

Danny Green — 1902–5, OF G-523

1911 — Frank Gabler — 1938, P G-18

1928 — Bill Wilson — 1950, 1953–54, OF G-32

1943 — White Sox buy first baseman Hal Trosky from Cleveland. Trosky missed the

1947 — Skip Pitlock — 1974–75, P G-41

November 7

1938 — Jim Kaat — 1973–75, P G-92

1958 — Reggie Patterson — 1981, P G-6

November 8

1884 — Mutz Ens — 1912, 1B G-3

1907 — Tony Cuccinello — 1943–45, 3B G-190

1908 — John Stoneham — 1933, OF G-10

November 9

1908 — Roy Schalk — 1944–45, 2B G-279

1920 — Bill Mueller — 1942, '45, OF G-39

November 10

1896 — Jimmie Dykes — 1933–46, 3B–MGR, G-580

1903 — George Blackerby — 1928, OF G-30

1934 — Norm Cash — 1958–59, 1B G-71

1948 — Catcher Aaron Robinson traded to Detroit for pitcher Billy Pierce and cash.

November 11

1885 — Jack Ness — 1916, 1B G-75

1912 — Hal Trosky, Sr. — 1944, '46, 1B G-223

1926 — Eddie Collins is released as player and manager. Catcher Ray Schalk named player-manager.

November 12

1906 — Red Evans — 1936, P G-18

1926 — Don Johnson — 1954, P G-46

November 13

1886 — Ralph Kreitz — 1911, C G-7

1913 — Jack Hallett — 1940–41, P G-24

1925 — Jim Delsing — 1948, 56, OF G-75

November 14

1943 — Danny Lazar — 1968–69, P G-17

1951 — Traded pitcher Randy Gumpert and outfielder Don Lenhardt to Boston for pitcher Chuck Stobbs and infielder Mel Hoderlein.

November 15

1880 — Hi Jasper — 1914–15, P G-19

1884 — Red Kelly — 1910, OF G-14

1888 — Pat Ragan — 1919, P G-1

1901 — John Dobb — 1924, P G-2

1904 — George Cox — 1928, P G-26

1937 — Bob Farley — 1962, 1B G-35

1948 — Outfielder Taft Wright sold to Philadelphia A's.

November 16

1883 — Rollie Zeider — 1910–13, INF G-351

1888 — Carl Manda — 1914, 2B G-9

1891 — Ralph Bell — 1912, P G-3

1943 — Greg Bollo — 1965–66, P G-18

1976 — Signed Bob Lemon as manager, replacing Paul Richards, who returned to scouting.

November 17

1913 — Lee Stine — 1934–35, P G-5

1923 — Mike Garcia — 1951, PH G-6

1933 — Dan Osinski — 1969, P G-51

1936 — Gary Bell — 1969, P G-23

1952 — Dave Frost — 1977, P G-4

November 18

1890 — Raymond Shook — 1916, PH G-1

1924 — Rocky Nelson — 1951, PH G-6

1926 — Roy Sievers — 1960–61, 1B G-268

1953 — Gil Rondon — 1979, P G-4

November 19

1892 — Everett Scott — 1926, SS G-40

1898 — Harry Courtney — 1922, P G-18

1922 — George Yankowski — 1949, C G-12

1943 — Aurelio Monteagudo — 1967, P G-1

November 20

1869 — Clark Griffith — 1901–2, P–MGR G-70

1891 — Leon Cadore — 1923, P G-1

1917 — Jess Dobernic — 1939, P G-4

1945 — Jay Johnstone — 1971–72, OF G-237

November 21

1893 — Ziggy Hasbrook — 1916–17, 1B G-11

1899 — Augie Swentor — 1922, C G-1

1908 — Paul Richards — 1951–54, '76, MGR

1924 — Warren Hacker — 1961, P G-42

1941 — Tom McCraw — 1963–70, 1B–OF G-994

1952 — Bill Almon — 1981–82, SS G-214

November 22

1889 — Amos Strunk — 1920–24, OF G-319

1946 — Cy Acosta — 1972–74, P G-101

     Rich McKinney — 1970–71, 2B–3B–OF G-157

1948 — Traded pitcher Joe Haynes to Cleveland for catcher Joe Tipton.

1950 — Greg Luzinski — 1981–82, DH G-263

November 23

1887 — Bubber Jonnard — 1920, C G-1

1906 — Wilbur Wehde — 1930–31, P G-12

1920 — Jake Jones — 1941–42, 1946–47, 1B G-79

November 23 (continued)

1942 — Jerry Nyman — 1968–69, P G-29

1955 — Todd Cruz — 1980, SS G-90

November 24

1964 — Sold pitcher Fritz Ackley to St. Louis Cardinals.

November 25

1875 — Fred Parent — 1908–11, SS–OF G-339

1917 — Len Perme — 1942, '46, P G-8

1951 — Bucky Dent — 1973–76, SS G-509

November 26

1866 — Hugh Duffy — 1910–11, MGR.

1898 — John Kerr — 1929–31, 2B G-325

1914 — Ed Weiland — 1949–52, P G-10

1916 — Bob Elliott — 1953, 3B G-67

1920 — Bud Sheely — 1951–53, C G-101

1980 — Outfielder Ron LeFlore signs as a free agent with a two-million dollar multi-year contract. He played out his option with Montreal.

November 27

1919 — Danny Reynolds — 1945, SS–2B G-29

1938 — While hunting, pitcher Monty Stratton injures his leg with an accidental discharge from his own pistol, ending a promising major league career when amputation is required.

1961 — Traded outfielder Minnie Minoso to Cardinals for first baseman Joe Cunningham.

1981 — Traded outfielder Chet Lemon to Detroit for outfielder Steve Kemp.

November 28

1951 — Traded infielder Joe DeMaestri, first baseman Gordon Goldsberry, catcher Gus Niarhos, pitcher Dick Littlefield, and outfielder Jim Rivera to St. Louis Browns for catcher Sherm Lollar, pitcher Al Widmar, and infielder Tom Upton; then sent Upton to Washington for infielder Sam Dente.

1961 — Traded first baseman Roy Sievers to Phillies for pitcher John Buzhardt and third baseman Charlie Smith.

November 29

1885 — Scotty Alcock — 1914, 3B G-54

1911 — Harry Boyles — 1938–39, P G-11

1914 — Joe Orengo — 1945, 3B G-17

1922 — Minnie Minoso — 1951–57, 1960–61, '64, '76, '80; OF G-1379

1939 — Jim Derrington — 1956–57, P G-21

1967 — Traded pitchers Bruce Howard and Roger Nelson and infielder Don Buford to Baltimore for shortstop Luis Aparicio, outfielder Russ Snyder and first baseman-outfielder John Matias.

1972 — Traded pitcher Tom Bradley to San Francisco for pitcher Steve Stone and outfielder Ken Henderson.

November 30

1896 — Larry Duff — 1922, P G-3

1935 — Steve Hamilton — 1970, P G-3

1955 — Traded pitcher Virgil Trucks to Detroit for outfielder-third baseman Bubba Phillips.

1961 — Traded pitchers Billy Pierce and Don Larsen to Giants for pitchers Eddie Fisher and Dom Zanni and first baseman Bob Farley. Received pitcher Verle Tiefenthaler to complete deal, August 17, 1962.

1970 — Traded outfielder Ken Berry, second baseman Syd O'Brien, and pitcher Billy Wynne to California for pitcher Tom Bradley, catcher Tom Egan, and outfielder Jay Johnstone.

DECEMBER 1

1901 — Mike Cvengros — 1923–25, P G-89

1917 — Marty Marion — 1954–56, MGR

1925 — Cal McLish — 1961, P G-31

1964 — Traded pitcher Frank Baumann to Cubs for catcher Jimmie Schaffer.

Traded pitcher Ray Herbert and first baseman Jeoff Long to Phillies for outfielder Danny Cater and shortstop Lee Elia.

1965 — Traded outfielder Dave Nicholson and catcher Bill Heath to Houston for pitchers Jack Lamabe and Ray Cordeiro.

1970 — Traded shortstop Luis Aparicio to Red Sox for second baseman Mike Andrews and shortstop Luis Alvarado.

December 1 (continued)

1975 — Sox great Nellie Fox dies of cancer.

December 2

1899 — Ray Morehart — 1924, '26, 2B–SS G-104

1937 — Traded pitcher Vern Kennedy, third baseman Tony Piet, and outfielder Dixie Walker to Detroit for third baseman Marv Owen, outfielder Gee Walker and catcher Mike Tresh.

1971 — Traded infielder Rich McKinney to Yankees for pitcher Stan Bahnsen.

Traded pitcher Tommy John and infielder Steve Huntz to Dodgers for first baseman Dick Allen.

December 3

1872 — Pat Dolan — 1903, 1B–OF G-27

1901 — Bennie Tate — 1930–32, C G-165

1925 — Harry Simpson — 1959, OF G-38

1945 — Steve Huntz — 1971, INF G-35

1952 — Larry Anderson — 1977, P G-6

1957 — Traded pitchers Jack Harshman and Russ Heman, outfielder Larry Doby, and first baseman Jim Marshall to Baltimore for pitcher Ray Moore, infielder Billy Goodman, and outfielder Tito Francona.

December 4

1885 — Shano Collins — 1910–20, OF–1B G-1335

1920 — Bill Metzig — 1944, 2B G-5

1924 — Dick Strahs — 1954, P G-9

1931 — Traded infielder John Kerr and outfielder Carl Reynolds to Washington for pitchers Bump Hadley and Sam Jones and second baseman Jackie Hayes.

1948 — Traded pitcher Frank Papish to Cleveland for pitchers Ernie Groth and Bob Kuzava.

1957 — Traded outfielder Minnie Minoso and infielder Fred Hatfield to Cleveland for pitcher Early Wynn and outfielder Al Smith.

December 5

1901 — Carey Selph — 1932, 3B–2B G-116

1968 — Traded pitcher Jack Fisher to Cincinnati for catcher Don Pavletich and pitcher Don Secrist.

1974 — Traded infielder Eddie Leon to Yankees for pitcher Cecil Upshaw.

1977 — Traded pitchers Chris Knapp and Dave Frost and catcher Brian Downing to Angels for outfielders Bobby Bonds and Thad Bosley and pitcher Richard Dotson.

December 6

1899 — Jocko Conlan — 1934–35, OF G-128

1913 — After progressing westward through the United States, the White Sox and the Giants play the first overseas game of their "around the world" tour at Keio University in Tokyo. Sox won, 9–4.

1920 — Gus Niarhos — 1950–51, C G-107

1946 — Signed pitcher Red Ruffing, previously released by the Yankees.

1951 — Traded first baseman Rocky Nelson to Dodgers for third baseman Hec Rodriguez.

1954 — Traded pitchers Don Johnson and Don Ferrarese, catcher Matt Batts, and infielder Fred Marsh to Baltimore for pitcher Bob Chakales, catcher Clint Courtney, and infielder Jim Brideweiser.

Traded first baseman Ferris Fain and Jack Phillips and pitcher Leo Crittante to Detroit for first baseman Walt Dropo, outfielder Bob Nieman, and pitcher Ted Gray.

1959 — Traded catcher John Romano, first baseman Norm Cash, and third baseman Bubba Phillips to Cleveland for pitchers Don Ferrarese and Jake Striker, catcher Dick Brown, and outfielder Minnie Minoso.

December 7

1906 — Tony Piet — 1935–37, 2B-3B G-286

1927 — Dick Donovan — 1955–60, P G-212

1950 — Rich Coggins — 1976, OF G-32

December 8

1892 — Ellis Johnson — 1912, '15, P G-6

1914 — Second baseman Eddie Collins is bought from Philadelphia Athletics for $50,000.

1936 — In a three-team deal, White Sox send pitcher Jack Salveson to Washington, pitcher Thornton Lee goes from Cleveland to White Sox, and pitcher Earl Whitehill goes from Washington to Cleveland.

1939 — Traded outfielder Ray Radcliff to St. Louis Browns for outfielder Moose Solters.

December 8 (continued)

Traded outfielder Gee Walker to Washington for outfielder Taft Wright and pitcher Pete Appleton.

1951 — Steve Dillard — 1982, 2B G-16

1954 — Bought infielder Cass Michaels from Philadelphia Athletics.

1959 — Traded outfielder Johnny Callison to Phillies for third baseman Gene Freese.

December 9

1921 — Charles Kress — 1949–50, 1B G-100

1928 — Joe DeMaestri — 1951, INF G-56

1941 — Traded outfielder Mike Kreevich and pitcher Jack Hallett to Athletics for outfielder Wally Moses.

December 10

1889 — Jimmy Johnston — 1911, OF G-1

1931 — Bob Roselli — 1961–62, C G-57

1935 — Sold outfielder Al Simmons to Detroit for $75,000.

1939 — Bob Priddy — 1968–69, P G-46

1944 — Steve Renko — 1977, P G-8

1952 — Traded pitcher Chuck Stobbs to Washington for Mike Fornieles, also a pitcher.

1963 — Traded second baseman Nellie Fox to Houston for pitcher Jim Golden and outfielder Danny Murphy.

1975 — Traded pitcher Jim Kaat and shortstop Mike Buskey to Phillies for pitchers Dick Ruthven and Roy Thomas and outfielder-infielder Alan Bannister.

Group headed by Bill Veeck buys White Sox.

1976 — Traded pitchers Rich Gossage and Terry Forster to Pittsburgh for outfielder Richie Zisk and pitcher Silvio Martinez.

December 11

1903 — Raymond Phelps — 1935–36, P G-42

1924 — Hal Brown — 1951–52, P G-55

Second baseman Eddie Collins is named player-manager, replacing Johnny Evers.

1934 — Lee Maye — 1970–71, OF G-38

1950 — Traded pitchers Ray Scarborough and Bill Wight to Boston for pitchers Joe Dobson and Dick Littlefield and outfielder Al Zarilla.

1953 — Traded infielders Connie Ryan and Rocky Krsnich and pitcher Saul Rogovin to Cincinnati for outfielder Willard Marshall.

1973 — Traded pitchers Steve Stone and Ken Frailing and catcher Steve Swisher to Cubs for third baseman Ron Santo (pitcher Jim Kremmel was sent to Cubs to complete the deal, 12-18-73).

1975 — Traded third baseman Bill Melton and pitcher Steve Dunning to California for first baseman Jim Spencer and outfielder Morris Nettles.

1981 — Traded catcher Jim Essian, shortstop Todd Cruz, and outfielder Rod Allen to Seattle for first baseman-outfielder Tom Paciorek.

December 12

1891 — Thomas D. Daly — 1913–15, OF G-91

1933 — Traded catcher Charlie Berry to Athletics for pitcher George Earnshaw and catcher John Pasek.

1944 — Traded outfielder Ed Carnett to Cleveland for outfielder Oris Hockett.

1945 — Ralph Garr — 1976–79, OF G-490

1975 — Traded outfielder Ken Henderson and pitchers Dick Ruthven and Danny Osborn to Atlanta for outfielder Ralph Garr and infielder Larvell Blanks. Then Blanks was dealt to Cleveland for second baseman Jack Brohamer.

Traded pitcher Rich Hinton and catcher Jeff Sovern to Cincinnati for pitcher Clay Carroll.

1980 — Acquired second baseman Tony Bernazard from Montreal for pitcher Rich Wortham.

December 13

1916 — Hank Majeski — 1950–51, 3B G-134

1923 — Larry Doby — 1956–57, '59, '78, OF–MGR, G-280

1936 — J. C. Martin — 1959–67, C G-649

1947 — Dave Hamilton — 1975–77, P G-130

1969 — Traded pitcher Gary Peters and catcher Don Pavletich to Red Sox for infielder Syd O'Brien and pitcher Billy Farmer. Farmer retired and was replaced in the deal by Gerry Janeski, 3-9-70.

December 14

1873 — John Anderson — 1908, OF G-123

1894 — James Edwards — 1925–26, P G-4

1897 — Maurice Archdeacon — 1923–25, OF G-127

1899 — Robert Lawrence — 1924, P G-1

1904 — James S. Moore — 1930–32, P G-43

1905 — Robert Weiland — 1928–31, P G-45

1913 — Edgar Smith — 1939–43, 1946–47, P G-188

1921 — Bobby Adams — 1955, 3B G-28

1923 — Paul LaPalme — 1956–57, P G-65

1949 — Traded pitcher Ed Klieman to Philadelphia Athletics for third baseman Hank Majeski.

1950 — Traded outfielder Mike McCormick to Washington for outfielder Bud Stewart.

1966 — Traded catcher John Romano and pitcher Lee White to Cardinals for pitcher Don Dennis and outfielder Walt Williams.

December 15

1910 — George Stumpf — 1936, OF G-10

1920 — Eddie Robinson — 1950–52, 1B G-425

1929 — Ray Herbert — 1961–64, P G-109

1931 — Sammy Esposito — 1952, 1955–63, 3B–SS G-542

1932 — Traded outfielders Bob Fothergill, Bob Seeds, Johnny Hodapp and Greg Mulleavy to Red Sox for pitcher Ed Durham and infielder Harold Rhyne.

1944 — Stan Bahnsen — 1972–75, P G-136

1945 — Harry Grabiner retires as general manager after 22 years and is replaced by Leslie O'Connor, former secretary to Baseball Commissioner Landis.

1950 — Mike Proly — 1978–80, P G-114

1960 — Traded third baseman Gene Freese to Cincinnati for pitchers Juan Pizarro and Cal McLish.

1961 — Charles A. Comiskey II sells his minority (46%) ownership of team. For first time in history of White Sox, no one from the Comiskey family is a principal owner.

1966 — Traded outfielder Floyd Robinson to Cincinnati for pitcher Jim O'Toole.

1967 — Traded outfielder Tommie Agee and infielder Al Weis to Mets for pitchers Jack Fisher and Billy Wynne, outfielder Tommy Davis, and catcher Buddy Booker.

1969 — Traded outfielder Angel Bravo to Cincinnati for pitcher Gerry Arrigo.

December 16

1876 — Samuel Strang — 1902, 3B G-137

1898 — Frank Shellenback — 1918–19, P G-37

December 17

1876 — Roy Patterson — 1901–7, P G-184

1903 — Karl Swanson — 1928–29, 2B G-24

1936 — Jerry Adair — 1966–67, IF G-133

1975 — Signed Paul Richards as manager, replacing Chuck Tanner, who was allowed to accept the manager's job at Oakland.

December 18

1893 — Dominic Mulrenan — 1921, P G-12

1930 — Bill Skowron — 1964–67, 1B G-347

1940 — Traded pitcher Jack Knott to Athletics for infielder Dario Lodigiani.

1944 — Syd O'Brien — 1970, 3B–2B, G-121

December 19

1879 — Mike Welday — 1907, '09, OF G-53

1943 — Walt Williams — 1967–72, OF G-603

1945 — Art Kusnyer — 1970, C G-4

December 20

1886 — Joe Berger — 1913–14, 2B–SS G-124

1894 — Butch Henline — 1930–31, C G-14

1949 — Oscar Gamble — 1977, OF–DH G-137

December 21

1897 — Harold Haid — 1933, P G-6

1925 — Bob Rush — 1960, P G-9

December 21 (continued)

1938 — Traded infielder Lou "Boze" Berger to Red Sox for infielder Eric McNair.

1948 — Bought outfielder Steve Souchock from the Yankees.

December 22

1896 — Harvey McClellan — 1919–24, SS–3B G-344

December 23

1879 — Frank Owen — 1903–9, P G-186

1899 — Alphonse "Tommy" Thomas — 1926–32, P G-246

1943 — Jerry Koosman — 1981–82, P G-50

December 24

1950 — Purchased the contract of first baseman Bob Boyd from Colorado Springs farm club.

December 25

1887 — Morrie Rath — 1912–13, 2B G-247

1899 — Tom Gulley — 1926, OF G-16

1903 — Red Barnes — 1930, OF G-85

1908 — Ben Chapman — 1941, OF G-57

1927 — Nellie Fox — 1950–63, 2B G-2115

1938 — Jack Hamilton — 1969, P G-8

December 26

1936 — Wayne Causey — 1966–68, 2B G-261

1947 — Carlton Fisk — 1981–82, C G-231

1950 — Jorge Orta — 1972–79, 2B–OF–3B, G-990

December 27

1922 — Connie Johnson — 1953, 1955–56, P G-39

1949 — Ernesto Escarrega — 1982, P G-38

December 28

1900 — Ted Lyons — 1923–42, 1946–48, P–MGR G-705

1947 — Aurelio Rodriguez — 1982, 3B G-118

Comiskey Park — the oldest ballpark in the major leagues. The first game played in the historic park was on July 1, 1910, when St. Louis beat the Sox, 2-0.

An illustrious group of Hall of Famers who spent significant portions of their careers on the South Side of Chicago: Red Faber,

URBAN CLARENCE FABER
CHICAGO A.L. 1914-1933
DURABLE RIGHTHANDER WHO WON 253,
LOST 211, E.R.A. 3.13 GAMES IN TWO DECADES
WITH WHITE SOX. VICTOR IN 3 GAMES
OF 1917 WORLD'S SERIES AGAINST GIANTS.
WON 20 OR MORE GAMES IN SEASON
FOUR TIMES, THREE IN SUCCESSION.

RAYMOND WILLIAM SCHALK
CHICAGO A.L. 1912 TO 1928
NEW YORK N.L. 1929
HOLDER OF MAJOR LEAGUE RECORD FOR
MOST YEARS LEADING CATCHER IN FIELDING
EIGHT YEARS; MOST PUTOUTS, NINE YEARS
MOST ASSISTS IN ONE MAJOR LEAGUE (1810)
MOST CHANCES ACCEPTED (8965). CAUGHT
FOUR NO-HIT GAMES INCLUDING PERFECT
GAME IN 1922.

ALOYSIUS HARRY SIMMONS
PLAYED WITH 7 MAJOR LEAGUE CLUBS 1924-
1944. STAR WITH PHILA.(A.L.). BATTED
.308 TO .392 FROM 1924 TO 1934. LEADING
BATTER .381 IN 1930, .390 IN 1931. MOST
HITS BY A.L. RIGHT-HANDED BATTER WITH
2831. LED LEAGUE RUNS BATTED IN, RUNS
SCORED, HITS AND TOTAL BASES SEVERAL
SEASONS. HIT 3 HOME RUNS, JULY 15, 1932.
LIFETIME BATTING AVERAGE .334.

EDWARD TROWBRIDGE COLLINS
PHILADELPHIA - CHICAGO
PHILADELPHIA, A.L. -1906-1930
FAMED AS BATSMAN, BASE RUNNER
AND SECOND BASEMAN AND ALSO AS
FIELD CAPTAIN. BATTED .333 DURING
MAJOR LEAGUE CAREER, SECOND ONLY
TO TY COBB IN MODERN BASE STEALING
MADE 3313 HITS IN 2826 GAMES.

Ray Schalk, Al Simmons, Eddie Collins, Ed Walsh, Clark Griffith, Charles Comiskey, and Ted Lyons.

EDWARD ARTHUR WALSH
"BIG ED"

OUTSTANDING RIGHTHANDED PITCHER OF CHICAGO A.L. FROM 1904 THROUGH 1916. WON 40 GAMES IN 1908 AND WON TWO GAMES IN THE 1906 WORLD SERIES. TWICE PITCHED AND WON TWO GAMES IN ONE DAY, ALLOWING ONLY ONE RUN IN DOUBLEHEADER AGAINST BOSTON ON SEPT. 29, 1908. FINISHED BIG LEAGUE PITCHING CAREER WITH BOSTON N.L. IN 1917.

CLARK C. GRIFFITH

ASSOCIATED WITH MAJOR LEAGUE BASEBALL FOR MORE THAN 50 YEARS AS A PITCHER, MANAGER AND EXECUTIVE. SERVED AS A MEMBER OF THE CHICAGO AND CINCINNATI TEAMS IN THE N.L. AND THE CHICAGO, NEW YORK AND WASHINGTON CLUBS IN THE A.L. COMPILED MORE THAN 200 VICTORIES AS A PITCHER, MANAGER OF THE CINCINNATI N.L. AND CHICAGO, NEW YORK AND WASHINGTON A.L. TEAMS FOR 20 YEARS.

CHARLES A. COMISKEY
"THE OLD ROMAN"

STARTED 50 YEARS OF BASEBALL AS ST. LOUIS BROWNS FIRST-BASEMAN IN 1882 AND WAS FIRST MAN AT THIS POSITION TO PLAY AWAY FROM THE BAG FOR BATTERS. AS BROWNS' MANAGER-CAPTAIN-PLAYER WON 4 STRAIGHT AMERICAN ASSOCIATION PENNANTS STARTING 1885, WORLD CHAMPIONS FIRST 2 YEARS. OWNER AND PRESIDENT CHICAGO WHITE SOX 1900 TO 1931.

THEODORE AMAR LYONS
CHICAGO A.L. 1923 TO 1946

ENTIRE ACTIVE PITCHING CAREER OF 21 SEASONS WITH CHICAGO A.L. WON 260 GAMES, LOST 230. TIED FOR LEAGUE'S MOST VICTORIES 1925 AND 1927, BEST EARNED RUN AVERAGE, 2.10 IN 1942 WHEN HE STARTED AND FINISHED ALL 20 GAMES. PITCHED NO-HIT GAME, AUG. 21, 1926 AGAINST BOSTON PITCHED 21-INNING GAME MAY 24, 1929.

Fielder Jones was a star outfielder and manager of the 1906 World Champion White Sox, who defeated the Cubs in the fall classic.

(above) Jim Kaat, one of a handful of major leaguers who played in four different decades, joined the Sox at the end of his career when most thought he had outlived his usefulness as a pitcher. In his two seasons with the club the lefthander won 21 and 20 games, respectively.

(left) A solid hitter for parts of nine seasons in a White Sox uniform, Carlos May saw action as both a first baseman and an outfielder. Tragedy struck May early in his career when he lost his right thumb in a gun accident while serving in the Marine Reserves.

(left) In eight seasons with the Sox, "Jungle Jim" Rivera proved to be an exciting performer both as a productive hitter and a fine defensive outfielder.

(right) Billy Pierce was the ace of the White Sox pitching staff for most of his 13 seasons with the club. He was a two-time 20-game winner with the Sox and finished his 18-year career in the major leagues with 211 wins.

(above) William "Kid" Gleason managed the 1919 American League champion White Sox in his first year as a big league skipper.

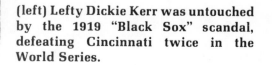

(left) Lefty Dickie Kerr was untouched by the 1919 "Black Sox" scandal, defeating Cincinnati twice in the World Series.

Hall of Fame shortstop Luke Appling played all of his 20 major league seasons in a White Sox uniform. "Old Aches and Pains" ended his career with a .310 lifetime batting average and two batting titles to his credit. He won his first batting crown with a career-high .388 in 1936.

(left) A 22-year major league veteran, Jimmy Dykes played for the Sox from 1933 to 1939 and managed the club from 1934 to 1946.

(right) Hall of Fame outfielder Al Simmons had back-to-back years of .331 and .334 in 1933 and 1934 for the Sox.

(above) Monty Stratton's promising career, in which he won 15 games in both 1937 and 1938, ended tragically in November of '38 when the pitcher injured a leg (which required amputation) in a hunting accident. Pictured on the right watching Stratton attempt a comeback is Hall of Fame hurler Dizzy Dean.

(left) One of the most powerful sluggers in White Sox history, first baseman Zeke Bonura led the club in home runs and runs batted in 1934-1937 — his only years with the team. His .345 batting mark in 1937 was also a club high.

A four-time All-Star shortstop with the Sox in his six seasons in Chicago, Chico Carrasquel provided some exciting shortstop play in the early 1950s.

Sox righthander Sandy Consuegra led the American League in
winning percentage (.842) with a 16-3 record in 1954.

Turk Lown and Gerry Staley
(right) gave the Sox an outstanding bullpen combination in their
pennant-winning year of 1959.
Lown was 9-2 with a 2.89 earned
run average and a league-leading
15 saves. Staley compiled an 8-5
mark, a fine 2.24 ERA and 14
saves.

Truly one of the great shortstops in baseball history, Luis
Aparicio was known for his spectacular defensive ability
and his remarkable knack for stealing bases. In each of his
first seven seasons in the majors — all with the Sox —
Aparicio led the AL in stolen bases, with a high of 56 in the
pennant-winning year of 1959.

One of the most popular Sox players ever, Nellie Fox was a perennial All-Star second baseman in his 14 seasons in Chicago. The high point of his career came in 1959, when "Little Nel" was voted the league's Most Valuable Player Award for the pennant-winning Sox.

(right) The superb centerfield play of Jim Landis was a major reason for the Sox' success in their pennant-winning season of 1959.

(below) Along with Gerry Staley, Turk Lown gave the Sox outstanding relief pitching during their pennant winning season of 1959. Lown was 9-2, with a 2.89 ERA, and led the league with 15 saves.

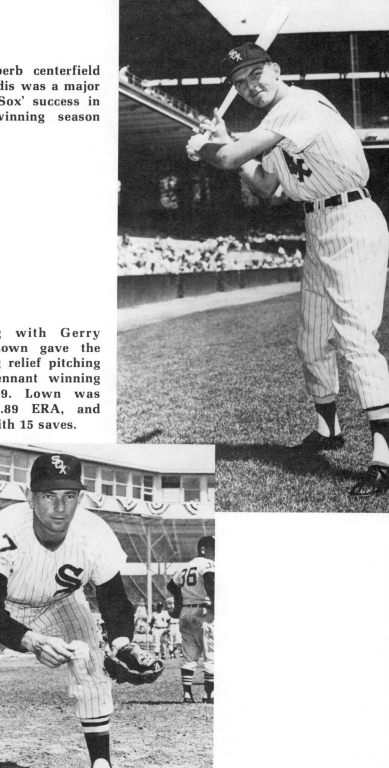

(left) One of the National League premier sluggers in the 1950s, Ted Kluszewski came to the Sox during the 1959 pennant stretch and was a key figure in Chicago's success. In the World Series that year against the Dodgers, "Big Klu" clouted three homers, drove in 10 runs and batted .391.

(below) All-Star catcher Sherm Lollar was the White Sox' major power source in the late 1950s when the club was primarily known for its pitching, speed, and defense. In 1958 and 1959 he clouted 20 and 22 homers, respectively, and drove in 84 runs each season.

Hall of Famer Manager Al Lopez piloted the Sox to the '59 pennant. "The Senor" also managed Cleveland to the AL title in 1954, giving him the distinction of being the only skipper, other than the Yankees' Casey Stengel, to win an American League flag in the decade of the 1950s.

The stereotype of a great relief pitcher, Hoyt Wilhelm had six outstanding seasons in a Sox uniform from 1963-68. In those years he recorded earned run averages of 2.64, 1.99, 1.81, 1.66, 1.31, and 1.73, with a total of 98 saves.

(left) Tommie Agee, who spent three seasons with the Sox, was named the American League Rookie of the Year in 1966 by virtue of his 22 homers, 86 RBIs, and outstanding defensive play in centerfield.

(right) Joel Horlen was one of the real pitching mainstays for the White Sox in the 1960s. He enjoyed his best season in 1967 with a 19-7 record and a league-leading 2.06 earned run average. His remarkable season was capped off on September 10, when he twirled a no-hitter against Detroit at Comiskey Park.

(left) One of the greatest pinch-hitters of all time, Smoky Burgess played 18 years in the major leagues. He finished his outstanding career in a Sox uniform in 1967.

A native of Chicago, promotional genius Bill Veeck owned the White Sox from 1959 to 1961 and from 1976 to 1980.

(right) Throughout much of the 1960s, Gary Peters was the ace of an excellent White Sox pitching staff. He won the AL Rookie of the Year Award in 1963 with a 19-8 record and league-leading 2.33 ERA. The next season he became a 20-game winner for the only time in his career with a 20-8 mark and a fine 2.50 earned run average.

(below) Floyd Robinson was one of the American League's most skillful hitters in the early 1960s, batting .310 in 1961, .312 in 1962, and .301 in 1964 during his seven years with the White Sox.

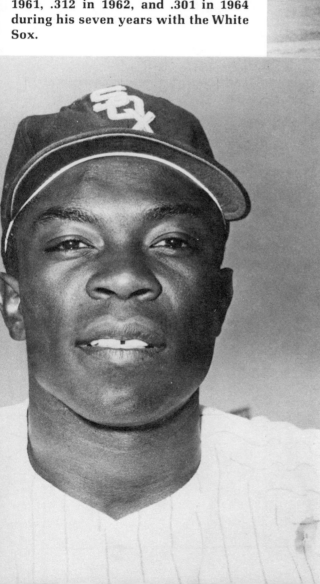

(left) One of the outstanding defensive centerfielders of his day, Johnny Mostil (who signed this picture for co-author Art Berke before his death in 1970) compiled a .301 lifetime batting average in his 10 major league seasons, all with the Sox.

(below) One of only 14 pitchers in major league history through 1981 to win as many as 300 games, Early Wynn was the leader of the Sox pitching staff with 22 victories in the pennant-winning year of 1959. He was elected to the Baseball Hall of Fame in 1971.

Slugger Dick Allen came to the Sox in 1972 and established himself as one of the greatest power hitters in Sox annals. That very same year he won the league's MVP award as a result of his 37 homers, 113 RBIs (both tops in the AL), and .308 batting mark. His homer total in '72 still stands as a White Sox single-season record.

(left) Lefthanded knuckleballer Wilbur Wood performed as both a starter and a reliever in his 12 seasons with the Sox. He was a four-time 20-game winner, who led the league in victories (24) and innings pitched, in both 1972 and 1973.

(right) In 1971 Chuck Tanner took over the managership of the White Sox, who compiled a 56-106 record the year before for a last-place finish in the American League West. By 1972 the club had improved to an 87-67 mark and a second-place finish behind eventual World Champion Oakland. That same year, Tanner was voted the top manager in baseball. He piloted the club through 1975.

(above) An outstanding hitter for the Sox during the 1970s, Jorge Orta enjoyed his best seasons in Chicago in 1974 and 1975, when he batted .316 and .304, respectively.

(left) Bill Melton became the first White Sox player to lead the American League in homers with 33 in 1971. He had other outstanding years as well, with 23 four-baggers in 1969, 33 in 1970, 20 in 1973, and 21 in 1974.

(left) Richie Zisk provided an abundance of power for the Sox in 1977 with 30 homers, a club-leading 101 RBIs, along with a .290 batting average.

(below) Designated hitter Oscar Gamble clouted a club-high 31 home runs in 1977.

Tony LaRussa became the White Sox field manager in 1979.

(left) One of baseball's finest pitchers, Britt Burns became an All-Star at the age of 22 in 1981 — a year after being named the "American League Rookie Pitcher of the Year."

(right) After 11 seasons with the Philadelphia Phillies, Chicago native Greg Luzinski became the Sox designated hitter in 1981. Re-establishing the fact he was one of the game's most feared sluggers, Luzinski powered 21 homers in the strike-shortened season. As a result of his fine performance, he was named the league's top DH.

Perhaps the most popular player in the history of the White Sox franchise, Minnie Minoso was certainly one of the most exciting to watch, both offensively and defensively. He played for the Sox in five different periods — 1951-57, 1960-61, 1964, 1976, and 1980. With a lifetime batting average close to .300 and almost 200 homers to his credit in his career with four different teams, Minoso hit over .300 seven times in a White Sox uniform.

Minoso became one of a handful of major leaguers to play in four different decades when he left the Sox coaching lines to hit in 1976. And, with a pinch-hitting appearance, the 57-year-old Minoso became the second player in history to play in five different decades.

An All-Star catcher with the Boston Red Sox for more than a decade, Carlton Fisk joined the White Sox in 1981. His presence gave the youthful Sox roster a touch of respectability.

COMISKEY'S CHAMPION WHITE SOX – 1917

The 1917 World Champion Chicago White Sox, pictured left to right: Theodore Jourdan, 1B; Fred McMullin, 3B; Claude Williams, P; Joe Jenkins, C; Joe Jackson, LF; James Scott, P; Reb Russell, P; Red Faber, P; Chick Gandil, 1B; Byrd Lynn, C; Dave Danforth, P; Happy Felsch, CF; Ray Schalk, C; Pants Rowland, MGR.; Kid Gleason, Coach; Eddie Collins, 2B; Harry Liebold, RF; Ed Cicotte, P; Swede Risberg, SS; Buck Weaver, 3B; Joe Benz, P; Robert Byrne, Utilityman; Mellie Wolfgang, P; John Collins, OF; Eddie Murphy, OF. Insets, left to right: Harry Grabiner, Secretary; Charles A. Comiskey, President; J. Louis Comiskey, Treasurer.

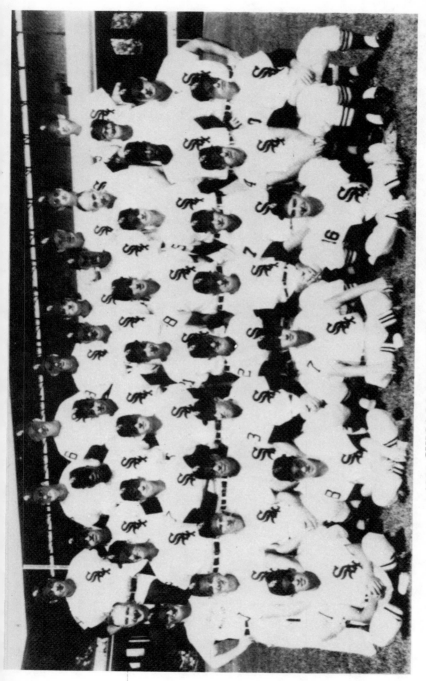

1959 CHICAGO WHITE SOX — AL CHAMPIONS

Front Row – Left to right – Luis Aparicio, Batboy, Batboy, BP Catcher Joe Heinsen, Second Row – (seated)– Sherman Lollar, Billy Goodman, Coaches Don Gutteridge and Tony Cuccinello, Manager Al Lopez, Coaches John Cooney and Ray Berres, Sam Esposito, John Romano. Third Row– Dick Donovan, Turk Lown, Bob Shaw, Gerry Staley, Barry Latman, Ken McBride, Al Smith, Ted Kluszewski. Fourth row – Jim Rivera, Earl Battey, Rudolfo Arias, Norm Cash, Jim Landis, Trainer Eddie Froelich, Visiting Clubhouse Man Art Colledge. Top row – Early Wynn, Earl Torgeson, Joe Stanka, Ray Moore, Jim McAnany, Nelson Fox, Billy Pierce and John "Bubba" Phillips.

December 29

1884 — Lou Fiene — 1906–9, P G-26

1911 — Bill Knickerbocker — 1941, 2B G-89

1934 — Ramon Conde — 1962, 3B G-14

December 30

1905 — John Pomorski — 1934, P G-3

1944 — Bought infielder Floyd Baker from St. Louis Browns.

December 31

1884 — Bobby Byrne — 1917, 3B G-1

1919 — Tommy Byrne — 1953, P-PH G-18

   Loyd Christopher — 1947, OF G-7

1924 — Ted Gray — 1955, P G-2

1931 — Traded pitcher Bob Weiland to Red Sox for pitcher Milt Gaston.

1940 — Traded catcher Ken Silvestri to Yankees for infielder William Knickerbocker.

Players with Incomplete Birth Date Available

Joe Barrens — played 1912, OF G-2
James "Red" Bowser — born 1886, played 1910, OF G-1
Ed Hughes — played 1902, C G-1
Sam McMackin — played 1902, P G-1
Andrew "Peaches" Nelson — played 1908, P G-3
Frank Shugart — 1867, played 1901, SS G-107
Edward Wright — played 1916, SS G-8

WHITE SOX REGULARS
1901–81

1901
1B Isbell
2B Mertes
3B Hartman
SS Shugart
OF Hoy
OF McFarland
OF Jones
C   Sullivan
    Sugden

1902
1B Isbell
2B Daly
3B Strang
SS Davis
OF Mertes
OF Green
OF Jones
C   Sullivan
    McFarland

1903
1B Isbell
2B Daly
    Magoon
3B Callahan
SS Tannehill
OF Holmes
    Hallman
OF Green
OF Jones
C   McFarland
    Slattery

1904
1B Isbell
    J. Donahue
2B Dundon
3B Tannehill
SS Davis
OF Holmes
    Callahan
OF Green
OF Jones
C   Sullivan

1905
1B J. Donahue
2B Dundon
3B Tannehill
SS Davis
OF Holmes
    Callahan
OF Green
OF Jones
C   Sullivan
    McFarland

1906
1B J. Donahue
2B Isbell
3B Tannehill
    Rohe
SS Davis
OF Hahn
OF Dougherty
    O'Neill
OF Jones
C   Sullivan

1907
1B J. Donahue
2B Isbell
3B Rohe
    Quillin
SS Davis
OF Hahn
OF Dougherty
OF Jones
C   Sullivan

1908
1B J. Donahue
    Isbell
2B Davis
    Atz
3B Tannehill
SS Parent
OF Hahn
OF Dougherty
OF Jones
C   Sullivan

1909
1B Isbell
    Altizer
2B Atz
3B Tannehill
    Purtell
SS Tannehill
    Parent
OF Hahn
    Parent
OF Dougherty
OF White
    Altizer
C   Sullivan
    Owens

1910
1B Mullen
      Gandil
2B French
      Zeider
3B Purtell
      Lord
SS Blackburne
      Zeider
OF Parent
      S. Collins
OF Dougherty
OF Browne
      Meloan
      Zwilling
C   Sullivan
      Payne

1911
1B S. Collins
      Zeider
2B McConnell
      Tannehill
3B Lord
SS Corhan
      Tannehill
OF McIntyre
OF Bodie
OF Callahan
C   Sullivan
      Payne

1912
1B Zeider
      Fournier
2B Rath
3B Lord
SS Weaver
OF S. Collins
OF Bodie
OF Callahan
C   Block
      Kuhn

1913
1B Fournier
      Chase
2B Rath
      Berger
3B Lord
SS Weaver
OF S. Collins
OF Bodie
OF Chappell
      Mattick
C   Schalk

1914
1B Fournier
      Chase
2B Blackburne
3B Alcock
      Breton
SS Weaver
OF S. Collins
OF Bodie
      Roth
OF Demmitt
C   Schalk

1915
1B Fournier
2B E. Collins
3B Blackburne
SS Weaver
OF S. Collins
OF Felsch
OF Murphy
C   Schalk

1916
1B Fournier
2B E. Collins
3B Weaver
SS Terry
OF S. Collins
OF Felsch
OF Jackson
C   Schalk

1917
1B Gandil
2B E. Collins
3B Weaver
SS Risberg
OF Jackson
OF Felsch
OF Leibold
C   Schalk

1918
1B Gandil
2B E. Collins
3B McMullin
SS Weaver
OF S. Collins
OF Felsch
OF Leibold
C   Schalk

1919
1B Gandil
2B E. Collins
3B Weaver
SS Risberg
OF Jackson
OF Felsch
OF Leibold
C   Schalk

1920
1B S. Collins
2B E. Collins
3B Weaver
SS Risberg
OF Jackson
OF Felsch
OF Leibold
C   Schalk

1921
1B Sheely
2B E. Collins
3B Mulligan
SS Johnson
OF Falk
OF Strunk
OF Hooper
C   Schalk

1922
1B Sheely
2B E. Collins
3B Mulligan
SS Johnson
OF Falk
OF Mostil
OF Hooper
C   Schalk

1923
1B Sheely
2B E. Collins
3B Kamm
SS McClellan
OF Falk
OF Mostil
OF Hooper
C   Schalk

1924
1B Sheely
2B E. Collins
3B Kamm
SS Barrett
OF Falk
OF Mostil
OF Hooper
C   Crouse

1925
1B Sheely
2B E. Collins
3B Kamm
SS Davis
OF Falk
OF Mostil
OF Hooper
C   Schalk

1926
1B Sheely
2B E. Collins
3B Kamm
SS Hunnefield
OF Falk
OF Mostil
OF Barrett
C   Schalk

1927
1B Clancy
2B Ward
3B Kamm
SS Hunnefield
OF Falk
OF Metzler
OF Barrett
C   McCurdy
    Crouse

1928
1B Clancy
2B Hunnefield
3B Kamm
SS Cissell
OF Falk
OF Mostil
OF Metzler
C   Crouse
    Berg

1929
1B Shires
2B Kerr
3B Kamm
SS Cissell
OF Metzler
OF Hoffman
OF Reynolds
C   Berg

1930
1B Clancy
    Watwood
2B Cissell
3B Kamm
SS Hunnefield
    Mulleavy
    Smith
OF Jolley
OF Barnes
    Fothergill
OF Reynolds
C   Tate
    Crouse

1931
1B Blue
2B Kerr
3B Jeffries
    Sullivan
SS Cissell
    Appling
OF Watwood
    Simons
OF Fothergill
    Fonseca
OF Reynolds
C   Tate
    Grube

1932
1B Blue
2B Appling
    Hayes
3B Selph
    Sullivan
    Kress
SS Appling
    Kress
OF Funk
OF Fothergill
    Kress
OF Seeds
C   Grube
    Berry

1933
1B Kress
2B Hayes
3B Dykes
SS Appling
OF Simmons
OF Haas
OF Swanson
C   Grube
    Berry

98

1934
1B Bonura
2B Hayes
   Boken
3B Dykes
   Hopkins
SS Appling
OF Simmons
OF Haas
   Conlan
OF Swanson
C Shea
   Madjeski

1935
1B Bonura
2B Hayes
   Piet
3B Dykes
   Hopkins
SS Appling
OF Simmons
OF Haas
   Washington
OF Radcliff
C Sewell

1936
1B Bonura
2B Hayes
   Piet
3B Dykes
SS Appling
OF Kreevich
OF Haas
   Rosenthal
OF Radcliff
C Sewell

1937
1B Bonura
2B Hayes
3B Piet
   Berger
SS Appling
OF Kreevich
OF F. Walker
OF Radcliff
C Sewell

1938
1B Kuhel
2B Hayes
   Meyer
   Berger
3B Owen
SS Appling
   Berger
OF Kreevich
OF G. Walker
OF Radcliff
   Steinbacher
C Sewell
   Rensa

1939
1B Kuhel
2B Hayes
   Bejma
3B Owen
   McNair
SS Appling
OF Kreevich
OF G. Walker
OF Radcliff
   Rosenthal
C Tresh

1940
1B Kuhel
2B Webb
   McNair
3B Kennedy
SS Appling
OF Kreevich
OF Solters
OF Wright
C Tresh

1941
1B Kuhel
2B Knickerbocker
   Kolloway
3B Kennedy
   Lodigiani
SS Appling
OF Kreevich
OF Hoag
   Solters
OF Wright
C Tresh

1942
1B Kuhel
2B Kolloway
3B Kennedy
   Lodigiani
SS Appling
OF Moses
OF Hoag
OF Wright
   West
C Tresh
   Turner

1943
1B Kuhel
2B Kolloway
   Webb
3B Grant
   Hodgin
   Cuccinello
SS Appling
OF Moses
OF Tucker
OF Curtright
C Tresh
   Turner

1944
1B Trosky
2B Schalk
3B Hodgin
   Clarke
SS Webb
OF Moses
OF Tucker
OF Curtright
   Carnett
C Tresh
   Turner

1945
1B Farrell
   Nagel
2B Schalk
3B Cuccinello
SS Michaels
   Appling
OF Moses
OF Hockett
OF Dickshot
C Tresh

99

1946
1B   Trosky
       Kuhel
2B   Michaels
       Kolloway
3B   Wells
       Lodigiani
       Kolloway
SS   Appling
OF   Kennedy
       Platt
OF   Tucker
OF   Wright
C   Tresh
       Hayes

1947
1B   York
       Jones
2B   Kolloway
       Michaels
3B   Baker
       Michaels
SS   Appling
OF   Kennedy
OF   Philley
OF   Tucker
       Wright
C   Tresh
       Dickey

1948
1B   Lupien
2B   Kolloway
       Michaels
3B   Baker
       Appling
SS   Michaels
       Appling
OF   Hodgin
       Seerey
OF   Philley
OF   Wright
C   Weigel
       Robinson

1949
1B   Kress
       Goldsberry
2B   Michaels
3B   Baker
SS   Appling
OF   Metkovich
       Souchock
OF   Philley
OF   Adams
       Zernial
       Ostrowski
C   Wheeler
       Tipton

1950
1B   Robinson
2B   Fox
3B   Majeski
SS   Carrasquel
OF   Rickert
       McCormick
OF   Philley
OF   Zernial
C   Masi

1951
1B   Robinson
2B   Fox
3B   Dillinger
       Minoso
SS   Carrasquel
OF   Zarilla
OF   Busby
OF   Stewart
       Minoso
C   Masi
       Niarhos

1952
1B   Robinson
2B   Fox
3B   Rodriguez
SS   Carrasquel
       Miranda
OF   Coleman
       Stewart
OF   Mele
OF   Minoso
C   Lollar

1953
1B   Fain
2B   Fox
3B   Elliott
       Krsnich
SS   Carrasquel
OF   Rivera
OF   Mele
OF   Minoso
C   Lollar

1954
1B   Fain
       Cavaretta
2B   Fox
3B   Michaels
       Marsh
SS   Carrasquel
OF   Rivera
OF   Groth
OF   Minoso
C   Lollar
       Batts

1955
1B	Dropo
2B	Fox
3B	Kell
SS	Carrasquel
OF	Rivera
OF	Nieman
	Busby
OF	Minoso
C	Lollar

1956
1B	Dropo
2B	Fox
3B	Esposito
	Hatfield
SS	Aparicio
OF	Rivera
OF	Doby
OF	Minoso
C	Lollar

1957
1B	Dropo
	Torgeson
2B	Fox
3B	Esposito
	Phillips
SS	Aparicio
OF	Rivera
	Landis
OF	Doby
OF	Minoso
C	Lollar
	Battey

1958
1B	Torgeson
	Boone
2B	Fox
3B	Goodman
SS	Aparicio
OF	Landis
OF	Smith
OF	Rivera
	Mueller
C	Lollar

1959
1B	Torgeson
	Cash
	Kluszewski
2B	Fox
3B	Goodman
	Phillips
SS	Aparicio
OF	Landis
OF	Smith
OF	Rivera
	McAnany
C	Lollar

1960
1B	Sievers
2B	Fox
3B	Freese
SS	Aparicio
OF	Landis
OF	Smith
OF	Minoso
C	Lollar

1961
1B	Sievers
2B	Fox
3B	Carey
	A. Smith
SS	Aparicio
OF	Landis
OF	Robinson
	A. Smith
OF	Minoso
C	Lollar
	Carreon

1962
1B	Cunningham
2B	Fox
3B	A. Smith
	C. Smith
SS	Aparicio
OF	Landis
OF	Robinson
OF	Hershberger
C	Lollar
	Carreon

1963
1B	McCraw
	Cunningham
2B	Fox
3B	Ward
SS	Hansen
OF	Landis
OF	Robinson
OF	Hershberger
	Nicholson
C	Carreon
	Martin

1964
1B	McCraw
	Skowron
2B	Weis
3B	Ward
SS	Hansen
OF	Landis
	Nicholson
OF	Robinson
OF	Hershberger
C	Martin

1965
1B	Skowron
2B	Buford
3B	Ward
SS	Hansen
OF	Cater
OF	Robinson
OF	Berry
C	Martin
	Romano

1966
1B	McCraw
2B	Weis
	Adair
3B	Buford
SS	Elia
	Adair
OF	Agee
OF	Robinson
OF	Berry
C	Martin
	Romano

1967
1B McCraw
2B Causey
    Weis
3B Buford
SS Hansen
OF Agee
OF Ward
    Williams
OF Berry
C   Josephson
    Martin

1968
1B McCraw
2B Alomar
    Cullen
3B Ward
    Kenworthy
SS Aparicio
OF Davis
OF Bradford
    Voss
OF Berry
C   Josephson

1969
1B McCraw
    Hopkins
2B Knoop
    Morales
3B Melton
SS Aparicio
OF Bradford
    May
OF Williams
OF Berry
C   Pavletich
    Herrmann

1970
1B McCraw
    Hopkins
2B Knoop
3B Melton
3B O'Brien
SS Aparicio
OF May
OF Melton
    Williams
OF Berry
C   Herrmann
    Josephson

1971
1B May
2B Andrews
3B Melton
SS Richard
    Alvarado
OF Reichardt
OF Williams
    Stroud
OF Johnstone
    Kelly
C   Herrmann
    Egan

1972
1B Allen
    Muser
2B Andrews
3B Melton
SS Alvarado
OF Reichardt
    May
OF Williams
OF Johnstone
    Kelly
C   Herrmann
    Egan

1973
1B Allen
    Muser
2B Orta
3B Melton
SS Leon
OF May
OF Henderson
    Jeter
OF Kelly
    Hairston
C   Herrmann

1974
1B Allen
    Muser
2B Orta
3B Melton
    Santo
SS Dent
OF May
OF Henderson
OF Kelly
    Sharp
C   Herrmann

1975
1B D. Johnson
2B Orta
3B Melton
SS Dent
OF May
    Hairston
OF Henderson
    Nyman
OF Kelly
    Sharp
C   Downing

1976
1B Spencer
    L. Johnson
2B Brohamer
3B Bell
    Stein
SS Dent
OF Bannister
    Orta
OF Lemon
OF Garr
    Kelly (DH)
C   Downing

1977
1B Spencer
    L. Johnson
2B Orta
3B Soderholm
SS Bannister
OF Garr
OF Lemon
OF Zisk
    Gamble (DH)
C   Downing
    Essian

1978
1B L. Johnson
    Blomberg (DH)
2B Orta
3B Soderholm
SS Bannister
    Kessinger
OF Garr
OF Lemon
OF Bonds
    Washington
C   Essian

1979		1980		1981		1982	
1B	L. Johnson	1B	Squires	1B	Squires	1B	Paciorek
2B	Orta		L. Johnson		L. Johnson		Squires
3B	Morrison	2B	Morrison	2B	Bernazard	2B	Bernazard
SS	Pryor	3B	Pryor	3B	Morrison	3B	Rodriguez
OF	Nordhagen	SS	Cruz	SS	Almon		Morrison
OF	Lemon		Pryor	OF	Baines	SS	Almon
OF	Washington	OF	Baines	OF	Lemon		V. Law
C	Colbern		Nordhagen	OF	Leflore	OF	Baines
	Foley	OF	Lemon		Luzinski (DH)	OF	LeFlore
	Nahorodny	OF	Washington	C	Fisk		R. Law
		C	Kimm			OF	Kemp
							Luzinski (DH)
						C	Fisk

YEAR-BY-YEAR RECORDS

Key Members of Pitching Staffs
(20-game winners indicated in parentheses)

1901
C. Griffith (24)
R. Patterson (20)
N. Callahan
J. Katoll
E. Harvey

1902
N. Callahan
R. Patterson
W. Piatt
C. Griffith
N. Garvin

1903
D. White
R. Patterson
P. Flaherty
F. Owen

1904
F. Owen (21)
N. Altrock (20)
D. White
F. Smith
R. Patterson
E. Walsh

1905
F. Owen (21)
N. Altrock (22)
F. Smith
D. White
E. Walsh

1906
N. Altrock (21)
F. Owen
E. Walsh
D. White
R. Patterson
F. Smith

1907
D. White (27)
E. Walsh (25)
F. Smith (23)
N. Altrock

1908
E. Walsh (40)
F. Smith
D. White
F. Owen
N. Altrock

1909
F. Smith (24)
J. Scott
E. Walsh
D. White
B. Burns

1910
E. Walsh
D. White
J. Scott
F. Olmstead
I. Young
F. Lange
F. Smith

1911
E. Walsh (26)
D. White
J. Scott
F. Lange
F. Olmstead
J. Baker
I. Young

1912
E. Walsh (27)
J. Benz
D. White
E. Lange
E. Cicotte
R. Peters

Key Members of Pitching Staffs (continued)

1913
R. Russell (21)
J. Scott (20)
E. Cicotte
J. Benz
D. White
E. Walsh

1914
J. Benz
E. Cicotte
J. Scott
R. Faber
R. Russell
M. Wolfgang

1915
R. Faber (24)
J. Scott (24)
J. Benz
R. Russell
E. Cicotte

1916
R. Russell
L. Williams
R. Faber
E. Cicotte
J. Scott
J. Benz
M. Wolfgang
D. Danforth

1917
E. Cicotte (28)
R. Faber
L. Williams
R. Russell
D. Danforth
J. Scott

1918
E. Cicotte
F. Shellenback
J. Benz
D. Danforth
R. Russell
L. Williams

1919
E. Cicotte (29)
L. Williams (23)
D. Kerr
R. Faber
G. Lowdermilk

1920
R. Faber (23)
L. Williams (22)
E. Cicotte (21)
D. Kerr (21)
R. Wilkinson

1921
R. Faber (25)
D. Kerr
R. Wilkinson
S. Hodge
D. McWeeny
D. Mulrenan

1922
R. Faber (21)
C. Robertson
D. Leverett
S. Hodge
T. Blankenship
H. Courtney

1923
C. Robertson
R. Faber
M. Cvengros
T. Blankenship
D. Leverett
S. Thurston

1924
S. Thurston (20)
T. Lyons
R. Faber
S. Connally
T. Blankenship
M. Cvengros
C. Robertson

1925
T. Lyons (21)
R. Faber
T. Blankenship
S. Thurston
C. Robertson
M. Cvengros
S. Connally

1926
T. Lyons
T. Thomas
T. Blankenship
R. Faber
J. Edwards
S. Thurston
S. Connally

1927
T. Lyons (22)
T. Thomas
T. Blankenship
S. Connally
R. Faber

1928
T. Thomas
T. Lyons
G. Adkins
R. Faber
T. Blankenship
E. Walsh, Jr.

1929
T. Thomas
T. Lyons
R. Faber
H. McKain
G. Adkins
E. Walsh, Jr.

1930
T. Lyons (22)
P. Caraway
T. Thomas
R. Faber
D. Henry
E. Walsh, Jr.
G. Braxton
H. McKain

1931
V. Frasier
T. Thomas
P. Caraway
R. Faber
H. McKain
T. Lyons

1932
T. Lyons
S. Jones
M. Gaston
V. Frasier
P. Gregory
R. Faber

1933
T. Lyons
S. Jones
M. Gaston
E. Durham
J. Heving
J. Miller
P. Gregory
R. Faber

1934
G. Earnshaw
T. Lyons
M. Gaston
S. Jones
L. Tietje
P. Gallivan
J. Heving
W. Wyatt

1935
J. Whitehead
V. Kennedy
T. Lyons
L. Tietje
S. Jones
R. Phelps
C. Fischer
W. Wyatt

1936
V. Kennedy (21)
J. Whitehead
S. Cain
T. Lyons
M. Stratton
C. Brown
R. Phelps

1937
V. Kennedy
T. Lee
T. Lyons
J. Whitehead
M. Stratton
B. Dietrich
C. Brown

1938
T. Lee
T. Lyons
M. Stratton
J. Whitehead
J. Rigney
J. Knott

1939
T. Lee
J. Rigney
E. Smith
T. Lyons
J. Knott
B. Dietrich
C. Brown

1940
J. Rigney
T. Lee
E. Smith
T. Lyons
J. Knott
B. Dietrich
C. Brown

1941
T. Lee (22)
E. Smith
J. Rigney
T. Lyons
B. Dietrich
B. Ross
J. Hallett

1942
J. Humphries
E. Smith
T. Lyons
B. Ross
J. Haynes
J. Wade
O. Grove

1943
O. Grove
J. Humphries
E. Smith
B. Dietrich
B. Ross
T. Lee
J. Haynes
G. Maltzberger
J. Wade

1944
B. Dietrich
O. Grove
E. Lopat
J. Humphries
J. Haynes
T. Lee
G. Maltzberger

1945
T. Lee
O. Grove
E. Lopat
J. Humphries
B. Dietrich
E. Caldwell
J. Haynes

Key Members of Pitching Staffs (continued)

1946
E. Lopat
O. Grove
J. Haynes
E. Smith
F. Papish
E. Caldwell
J. Rigney
R. Hamner

1947
E. Lopat
F. Papish
J. Haynes
O. Grove
B. Gillespie
E. Harrist
T. Lee
P. Gebrian
G. Maltzberger
E. Caldwell

1948
B. Wight
J. Haynes
A. Gettel
M. Pieretti
H. Judson
F. Papish
O. Grove
G. Moulder

1949
B. Wight
R. Gumpert
B. Pierce
B. Kuzava
M. Pieretti
H. Judson
M. Surkont
M. Haefner

1950
B. Pierce
B. Wight
B. Cain
R. Gumpert
R. Scarborough
H. Judson
K. Holcombe
L. Aloma

1951
B. Pierce
S. Rogovin
K. Holcombe
J. Dobson
R. Gumpert
L. Kretlow
H. Judson
H. Dorish

1952
B. Pierce
S. Rogovin
J. Dobson
M. Grisson
C. Stobbs
H. Dorish
L. Aloma
B. Kennedy

1953
B. Pierce
V. Trucks
M. Fornieles
H. Dorish
S. Rogovin
S. Consuegra
J. Dobson
B. Keegan

1954
V. Trucks
B. Keegan
B. Pierce
J. Harshman
S. Consuegra
D. Johnson
H. Dorish
M. Martin

1955
B. Pierce
D. Donovan
J. Harshman
V. Trucks
S. Consuegra
C. Johnson
H. Byrd
M. Fornieles
D. Howell

1956
B. Pierce (20)
D. Donovan
J. Harshman
J. Wilson
B. Keegan
G. Staley
D. Howell

1957
B. Pierce (20)
D. Donovan
J. Wilson
J. Harshman
B. Keegan
B. Fischer
G. Staley
D. Howell
P. LaPalme

1958
D. Donovan
B. Pierce
E. Wynn
J. Wilson
R. Moore
G. Staley
T. Lown

1959
E. Wynn (22)
B. Shaw
B. Pierce
D. Donovan
B. Latman
G. Staley
T. Lown

1960
E. Wynn
B. Pierce
B. Shaw
F. Baumann
R. Kemmerer
G. Staley
H. Score
D. Donovan
T. Lown

1961
J. Pizarro
F. Baumann
B. Pierce
C. McLish
R. Herbert
E. Wynn
T. Lown
D. Larsen
W. Hacker

1962
R. Herbert (20)
J. Pizarro
E. Fisher
E. Wynn
J. Buzhardt
F. Baumann
J. Horlen
D. Zanni
T. Lown

1963
G. Peters
R. Herbert
J. Pizarro
H. Wilhelm
J. Buzhardt
J. Horlen
E. Fisher
J. Brosnan

1964
G. Peters (20)
J. Pizarro
J. Horlen
J. Buzhardt
H. Wilhelm
E. Fisher
R. Herbert
D. Mossi

1965
J. Horlen
J. Buzhardt
T. John
G. Peters
E. Fisher
B. Howard
H. Wilhelm

1966
T. John
J. Horlen
G. Peters
J. Buzhardt
B. Howard
J. Lamabe
B. Locker
J. Pizarro
H. Wilhelm
E. Fisher

1967
G. Peters
J. Horlen
T. John
B. Locker
B. Howard
W. Wood
H. Wilhelm
J. Buzhardt

1968
J. Horlen
J. Fisher
T. John
G. Peters
W. Wood
C. Carlos
B. Priddy
H. Wilhelm
B. Locker

1969
J. Horlen
T. John
G. Peters
B. Wynne
W. Wood
D. Osinski

1970
T. John
G. Janeski
J. Horlen
W. Wood
J. Crider
B. Johnson
D. Murphy
B. Miller

1971
W. Wood (22)
T. Bradley
T. John
B. Johnson
J. Horlen
S. Kealey
V. Romo

1972
W. Wood (24)
S. Bahnsen (21)
T. Bradley
T. Forster
D. Lemonds
R. Gossage

1973
W. Wood (24)
S. Bahnsen
S. Stone
T. Forster
E. Fisher
C. Acosta

1974
J. Kaat (21)
W. Wood (20)
S. Bahnsen
T. Forster
B. Johnson
S. Pitlock
R. Gossage

1975
J. Kaat (20)
W. Wood
C. Osteen
R. Gossage
J. Jefferson
D. Hamilton
S. Bahnsen
T. Forster

Key Members of Pitching Staffs (continued)

1976
R. Gossage
B. Johnson
K. Brett
F. Barrios
T. Forster
P. Vuckovich
D. Hamilton
C. Carroll

1977
F. Barrios
S. Stone
K. Kravec
C. Knapp
W. Wood
L. LaGrow
B. Johnson
K. Brett
D. Hamilton

1978
S. Stone
K. Kravec
F. Barrios
W. Wood
J. Willoughby
L. LaGrow

1979
K. Kravec
F. Barrios
L. LaGrow
M. Proly
E. Farmer
R. Wortham
R. Baumgarten
S. Trout

1980
R. Baumgarten
B. Burns
S. Trout
D. Dotson
E. Farmer
R. Wortham
K. Kravec

1981
R. Baumgarten
S. Trout
B. Burns
D. Dotson
E. Farmer
L. Hoyt
D. Lamp
K. Hickey

1982
L. Hoyt
D. Dotson
D. Lamp
J. Koosman
B. Burns
S. Trout
S. Barojas
K. Hickey

White Sox Year-by-Year

* number of games ahead or games behind at end of season

Year	Pos.	W-L	Pct.	GA-GB*	Manager	Attendance
1901	1	83-53	.610	4	Clark Griffith	354,350
1902	4	74-60	.552	8	Clark Griffith	337,898
1903	7	60-77	.438	30½	James J. Callahan	286,183
1904	3	89-65	.578	6	Callahan-Felder Jones	557,123
1905	2	92-60	.605	3	Fielder Jones	687,419
1906	1	93-58	.616	3	Fielder Jones	585,202
1907	3	87-64	.576	5½	Fielder Jones	667,307
1908	3	88-64	.579	1½	Fielder Jones	636,096
1909	4	78-74	.513	20	William J. Sullivan	478,400
1910	6	68-85	.444	35½	Hugh Duffy	552,084
1911	4	77-74	.510	24	Hugh Duffy	583,208
1912	4	78-76	.506	28	James J. Callahan	602,241
1913	5	78-74	.513	17½	James J. Callahan	644,501
1914	6	70-84	.455	30	James J. Callahan	469,290
1915	3	93-61	.604	9½	Clarence Rowland	539,461
1916	2	89-64	.578	2	Clarence Rowland	679,923
1917	1	100-54	.649	9	Clarence Rowland	684,521
1918	6	57-67	.460	17	Clarence Rowland	195,081
1919	1	88-52	.629	3½	William Gleason	627,186
1920	2	96-58	.623	2	William Gleason	833,492
1921	7	62-92	.403	36½	William Gleason	543,650
1922	5	77-77	.500	17	William Gleason	602,860
1923	7	69-85	.448	30	William Gleason	573,778
1924	8	66-87	.431	25½	John Evers	606,658
1925	5	79-75	.513	18½	Edward T. Collins	832,231
1926	5	81-72	.529	9½	Edward T. Collins	710,339
1927	5	70-83	.458	39½	Ray W. Schalk	614,423

Year	Pos.	Record	Pct.	GB	Manager	Attendance
1928	5	72-82	.468	29	Schalk-Russ Blackburne	494,152
1929	7	59-93	.388	46	Russell Blackburne	426,795
1930	7	62-92	.403	40	Owen J. Bush	406,123
1931	8	56-97	.366	51½	Owen J. Bush	403,550
1932	7	49-102	.325	56½	Lewis A. Fonseca	233,198
1933	6	67-83	.447	31	Lewis A. Fonseca	397,789
1934	8	53-99	.349	47	Fonseca-James Dykes	236,559
1935	5	74-78	.487	19½	James Dykes	470,281
1936	3	81-70	.536	20	James Dykes	440,810
1937	3	86-68	.588	16	James Dykes	589,245
1938	6	65-83	.439	32	James Dykes	338,278
1939	4	85-69	.552	22½	James Dykes	594,104
1940	4	82-72	.532	8	James Dykes	660,336
1941	3	77-77	.500	24	James Dykes	677,077
1942	6	66-82	.466	34	James Dykes	425,734
1943	4	82-72	.532	16	James Dykes	508,962
1944	7	71-83	.461	18	James Dykes	563,539
1945	6	71-78	.477	15	James Dykes	657,981
1946	5	74-80	.481	30	Dykes-Lyons	983,403
1947	6	70-84	.455	27	Ted Lyons	876,948
1948	8	51-101	.336	44½	Ted Lyons	777,844
1949	6	63-91	.409	34	Jack Onslow	937,151
1950	6	60-94	.390	38	Onslow-Corriden	781,330
1951	4	81-73	.526	17	Paul Richards	1,328,234
1952	3	81-73	.526	14	Paul Richards	1,231,675
1953	3	89-65	.578	11½	Paul Richards	1,141,353
1954	3	94-60	.610	17	Richards-Marion	1,231,629
1955	3	91-63	.591	9	Marty Marion	1,175,684
1956	3	85-69	.552	12	Marty Marion	1,000,090
1957	2	90-64	.584	8	Al Lopez	1,135,668
1958	2	82-72	.532	10	Al Lopez	797,451
1959	1	94-60	.610	5	Al Lopez	1,423,144
1960	3	87-67	.565	10	Al Lopez	1,644,460
1961	4	86-76	.531	23	Al Lopez	1,146,019
1962	5	85-77	.525	11	Al Lopez	1,131,562
1963	2	94-68	.580	10½	Al Lopez	1,158,848
1964	2	98-64	.605	1	Al Lopez	1,250,053
1965	2	95-67	.586	7	Al Lopez	1,130,519
1966	4	83-79	.512	15	Eddie Stanky	990,016
1967	4	89-73	.549	3	Eddie Stanky	985,634
1968	8 (Tie)	67-95	.414	36	Stanky-Lopez	803,775
1969	5	68-94	.420	29	Lopez-Gutteridge	589,546
1970	6	56-106	.346	42	Gutteridge-Adair-Tanner	495,355
1971	3	79-83	.488	22½	Chuck Tanner	833,891
1972	2	87-67	.565	5½	Chuck Tanner	1,186,018
1973	5	77-85	.475	17	Chuck Tanner	1,316,527
1974	4	80-80	.500	9	Chuck Tanner	1,163,596
1975	5	75-86	.466	22½	Chuck Tanner	770,800
1976	6	64-97	.398	25½	Paul Richards	914,945
1977	3	90-72	.556	12	Bob Lemon	1,657,135
1978	5	71-90	.441	20½	Lemon-Larry Doby	1,491,100
1979	5	73-87	.456	14	Don Kessinger-LaRussa	1,280,702
1980	5	70-90	.438	26	Tony LaRussa	1,200,365
1981	3	54-52	.509	8½	Tony LaRussa	946,651
1982	3	87-75	.537	6	Tony LaRussa	1,567,787

Pitching Leaders

Year	Wins	Earned Run Average	Innings Pitched
1901	C. Griffith, 24-7	N. Callahan, 2.42	R. Patterson, 312
1902	R. Patterson, 19-14	N. Garvin, 2.21	N. Callahan, 282
1903	D. White, 16-15	D. White, 2.13	D. White, 300
	R. Patterson, 16-15		
1904	F. Owen, 21-15	D. White, 1.71	F. Owen, 315
1905	N. Altrock, 22-12	D. White, 1.76	F. Owen, 334
1906	N. Altrock, 21-12	D. White, 1.52	F. Owen, 293
1907	D. White, 27-13	E. Walsh, 1.60	E. Walsh, 422
1908	E. Walsh, 40-15	E. Walsh, 1.42	E. Walsh, 464
1909	F. Smith, 24-17	E. Walsh, 1.41	F. Smith, 365
1910	E. Walsh, 16-20	E. Walsh, 1.27	E. Walsh, 370
1911	E. Walsh, 26-18	E. Walsh, 2.22	E. Walsh, 369
1912	E. Walsh, 27-17	E. Walsh, 2.15	E. Walsh, 393
1913	R. Russell 21-17	E. Cicotte, 1.58	R. Russell, 316
1914	J. Scott, 16-18	E. Cicotte, 2.04	J. Benz, 283
1915	R. Faber, 24-14	J. Scott, 2.03	R. Faber, 300
	J. Scott, 24-11		
1916	R. Russell, 17-11	E. Cicotte, 1.78	R. Russell, 264
	R. Faber, 17-9		
1917	E. Cicotte, 28-12	E. Cicotte, 1.53	E. Cicotte, 347
1918	E. Cicotte, 12-19	J. Benz, 2.51	E. Cicotte, 266
1919	E. Cicotte, 29-7	E. Cicotte, 1.82	E. Cicotte, 307
1920	R. Faber, 23-13	R. Faber, 2.99	R. Faber, 319
1921	R. Faber, 25-15	R. Faber, 2.48	R. Faber, 331
1922	R. Faber, 21-17	R. Faber, 2.80	R. Faber, 353
1923	R. Faber, 14-11	H. Thurston, 3.05	C. Robertson, 255
1924	H. Thurston, 20-14	H. Thurston, 3.80	H. Thurston, 291
1925	T. Lyons, 21-11	T. Blankenship, 3.16	T. Lyons, 263
1926	T. Lyons, 18-16	T. Lyons, 3.01	T. Lyons, 284
1927	T. Lyons, 22-14	T. Lyons, 2.84	T. Lyons, 308
			T. Thomas, 308
1928	T. Thomas, 17-16	T. Thomas, 3.08	T. Thomas, 283
1929	T. Thomas, 14-18	T. Thomas, 3.19	T. Thomas, 260
	T. Lyons, 14-20		
1930	T. Lyons, 22-15	T. Lyons, 3.78	T. Lyons, 298
1931	V. Frasier, 13-15	R. Faber, 3.82	V. Frasier, 254
1932	T. Lyons, 10-15	T. Lyons, 3.28	T. Lyons, 231
	S. Jones, 10-15		
1933	T. Lyons, 10-21	S. Jones, 3.36	T. Lyons, 228
	S. Jones, 10-12		
	E. Durham, 10-6		
1934	G. Earnshaw, 14-11	G. Earnshaw, 4.52	G. Earnshaw, 227
1935	T. Lyons, 15-8	T. Lyons, 3.02	J. Whitehead, 222
1936	V. Kennedy, 21-9	V. Kennedy, 4.63	V. Kennedy, 274
1937	M. Stratton, 15-5	M. Stratton, 2.40	V. Kennedy, 221
1938	M. Stratton, 15-9	T. Lee, 3.49	T. Lee, 245
1939	T. Lee, 15-11	T. Lyons, 2.76	T. Lee, 235
	J. Rigney, 15-8		
1940	E. Smith, 14.9	J. Rigney, 3.11	J. Rigney, 281
	J. Rigney, 14-18		
1941	T. Lee, 22-11	T. Lee, 2.37	T. Lee, 300
1942	T. Lyons, 14-6	T. Lyons, 2.10	J. Humphries, 228

1943	O. Grove, 15-9	O. Grove, 2.75	O. Grove, 216
1944	B. Dietrich, 16-17	J. Haynes, 2.57	B. Dietrich, 246
1945	T. Lee, 15-12	T. Lee, 2.44	T. Lee, 228
1946	E. Lopat, 13-13	E. Lopat, 2.73	E. Lopat, 231
	E. Caldwell, 13-4		
1947	E. Lopat, 16-13	J. Haynes, 2.42	E. Lopat, 253
1948	B. Wight, 9-20	B. Wight, 4.80	B. Wight, 223
	J. Haynes, 9-10		
1949	B. Wight, 15-13	B. Wight, 3.31	B. Wight, 245
1950	B. Pierce, 12-16	B. Wight, 3.58	B. Pierce, 219
1951	B. Pierce, 15-14	S. Rogovin, 2.48	B. Pierce, 240
1952	B. Pierce, 15-12	J. Dobson, 2.51	B. Pierce, 255
1953	B. Pierce, 18-12	B. Pierce, 2.72	B. Pierce, 271
1954	V. Trucks, 19-12	S. Consuegra, 2.69	V. Trucks, 265
1955	D. Donovan, 15-9	B. Pierce, 1.97	B. Pierce, 206
1956	B. Pierce, 20-9	J. Harshman, 3.10	B. Pierce, 276
1957	B. Pierce, 20-12	D. Donovan, 2.77	B. Pierce, 257
1958	B. Pierce, 17-11	B. Pierce, 2.68	D. Donovan, 248
1959	E. Wynn, 22-10	B. Shaw, 2.69	E. Wynn, 256
1960	B. Pierce, 14-7	F. Baumann, 2.67	E. Wynn, 237
1961	J. Pizarro, 14-7	J. Pizarro, 3.05	J. Pizarro, 195
1962	R. Herbert, 20-9	E. Fisher, 3.10	R. Herbert, 237
1963	G. Peters, 19-8	G. Peters, 2.33	G. Peters, 243
1964	G. Peters, 20-8	J. Horlen, 1.88	G. Peters, 274
1965	E. Fisher, 15-7	E. Fisher, 2.40	J. Horten, 219
1966	T. John, 14-11	G. Peters, 1.98	T. John, 223
1967	J. Horlen, 19-7	J. Horlen, 2.06	G. Peters, 260
1968	W. Wood, 13-12	W. Wood, 1.87	J. Horlen, 224
1969	J. Horlen, 13-16	T. John, 3.25	J. Horlen, 236
1970	T. John, 12-17	T. John, 3.28	T. John, 269
1971	W. Wood, 22-13	W. Wood, 1.91	W. Wood, 334
1972	W. Wood, 24-17	W. Wood, 2.51	W. Wood, 377
1973	W. Wood, 24-20	T. Forster, 3.23	W. Wood, 359
1974	J. Kaat, 21-13	J. Kaat, 2.92	W. Wood, 320
1975	J. Kaat, 20-14	J. Kaat, 3.11	J. Kaat, 304
1976	K. Brett, 10-12	K. Brett, 3.32	R. Gossage, 224
1977	S. Stone, 15-12	K. Kravec, 4.10	F. Barrios, 231
1978	S. Stone, 12-12	F. Barrios, 4.05	S. Stone, 210
1979	K. Kravec, 15-13	R. Baumgarten, 3.54	K. Kravec, 250
1980	B. Burns, 15-13	B. Burns, 2.84	B. Burns, 238
1981	B. Burns, 10-6	D. Lamp, 2.41	B. Burns, 156
1982	L. Hoyt 19-15	K. Hickey, 3.00	L. Hoyt, 240

Batting Leaders

Year	Batting Average (Min. 400 ABs)	Home Runs	Runs Batted In
1901	F. Jones, .340	S. Mertes, 5	S. Mertes, 98
1902	F. Jones, .321	F. Isbell, 4	G. Davis, 93
1903	D. Green, .309	D. Green, 6	D. Green, 62
1904	D. Green, .265	F. Jones, 3	G. Davis, 69
1905	J. Donahue, 287	3 players, 2	J. Donahue, 76
1906	F. Isbell, .279	F. Jones, 2	G. Davis, 80
1907	P. Dougherty, .270	Rohe, Dougherty, 2	J. Donahue, 68
1908	P. Dougherty, .278	4 players, 1	F. Jones, 50

111

Year	Batting Average		
1909	P. Dougherty, .285	3 players, 1	P. Dougherty, 55
1910	P. Dougherty, .248	C. Gandil, 2	P. Dougherty, 43
1911	M. McIntyre, .323	P. Bodie, 4	P. Bodie, 97
1912	P. Bodie, .294	Lord, Bodie, 5	S. Collins, 81
1913	B. Weaver, .272	P. Bodie, 8	B. Weaver, 52
1914	S. Collins, .274	J. Fournier, 6	S. Collins, 65
1915	E. Collins, .332	J. Fournier, 5	S. Collins, 85
1916	J. Jackson, .341	H. Felsch, 7	J. Jackson, 78
1917	H. Felsch, .308	H. Felsch, 6	H. Felsch, 102
1918	B. Weaver, .300	E. Collins, 2	S. Collins, 56
1919	J. Jackson, .351	Felsch, Jackson, 7	J. Jackson, 96
1920	J. Jackson, .382	H. Felsch, 14	J. Jackson, 121
1921	E. Collins, .337	E. Sheely, 11	E. Sheely, 95
1922	E. Collins, .324	B. Falk, 12	Sheely, Hooper, 80
1923	E. Collins, .360	H. Hooper, 10	E. Sheely, 88
1924	B. Falk, .352	H. Hooper, 10	E. Sheely, 103
1925	E. Collins, .346	E. Sheely, 9	E. Sheely, 111
1926	B. Falk, .345	B. Falk, 8	B. Falk, 108
1927	B. Falk, .327	B. Falk, 9	Barrett, Falk, 83
1928	W. Kamm, .308	Barrett, Metzler, 3	W. Kamm, 84
1929	C. Reynolds, .317	C. Reynolds, 11	C. Reynolds, 67
1930	C. Reynolds, .359	C. Reynolds, 22	S. Jolley, 114
1931	L. Blue, .304	C. Reynolds, 6	C. Reynolds, 77
1932	B. Seeds, .290	R. Kress, 9	L. Appling, 63
1933	A. Simmons, .331	A. Simmons, 14	A. Simmons, 119
1934	A. Simmons, .344	Z. Bonura, 27	Z. Bonura, 110
1935	L. Appling, .307	Z. Bonura, 21	Z. Bonura, 92
1936	L. Appling, .388	Z. Bonura, 12	Z. Bonura, 138
1937	Z. Bonura, .345	Z. Bonura, 19	Z. Bonura, 100
1938	R. Radcliff, .330	G. Walker, 16	G. Walker, 87
1939	E. McNair, .324	J. Kuhel, 15	G. Walker, 111
1940	L. Appling, .348	J. Kuhel, 27	J. Kuhel, 94
1941	T. Wright, .322	J. Kuhel, 12	T. Wright, 97
1942	D. Kolloway, .273	W. Moses, 7	D. Kolloway, 60
1943	L. Appling, .328	J. Kuhel, 5	L. Appling, 55
1944	R. Hodgin, .295	H. Trosky, 10	H. Trosky, 70
1945	T. Cuccinello, .308	Dickshot, Cutright, 4	Roy Schalk, 65
1946	L. Appling, .309	T. Wright, 7	L. Appling, 55
1947	T. Wright, .324	R. York, 15	R. York, 64
1948	L. Appling, .314	P. Seerey, 18	P. Seerey, 64
1949	C. Michaels, .308	S. Souchock, 7	C. Michaels, 83
1950	E. Robinson, .311	G. Zernial, 29	G. Zernial, 93
1951	O. Minoso, .324	E. Robinson, 29	E. Robinson, 117
1952	Fox, Robinson, .296	E. Robinson, 22	E. Robinson, 104
1953	O. Minoso, .313	O. Minoso, 15	O. Minoso, 104
1954	O. Minoso, .320	O. Minoso, 19	O. Minoso, 116
1955	G. Kell, .312	W. Dropo, 19	G. Kell, 81
1956	O. Minoso, .316	L. Doby, 24	L. Doby, 102
1957	N. Fox, .317	Rivera, Doby, 14	O. Minoso, 103
1958	N. Fox, .300	S. Lollar, 20	S. Lollar, 84
1959	N. Fox, .306	S. Lollar, 22	S. Lollar, 84
1960	A. Smith, .315	R. Sievers, 28	O. Minoso, 105
1961	F. Robinson, .310	A. Smith, 28	A. Smith, 93

1962	F. Robinson, .312	A. Smith, 16	F. Robinson, 109
1963	P. Ward, .295	Ward, Nicholson, 22	P. Ward, 84
1964	F. Robinson, .301	P. Ward, 23	P. Ward, 94
1965	D. Buford, .283	Romano, Skowron, 18	B. Skowron, 78
1966	T. Agee, .273	T. Agee, 22	T. Agee, 86
1967	Buford, Berry, .241	P. Ward, 18	P. Ward, 62
1968	T. Davis, .268	P. Ward, 15	Ward, Davis, 50
1969	W. Williams, .304	B. Melton, 23	B. Melton, 87
1970	L. Aparicio, .313	B. Melton, 33	B. Melton, 96
1971	C. May, .294	B. Melton, 33	B. Melton, 86.
1972	Allen, May, .308	R. Allen, 37	R. Allen, 113
1973	P. Kelly, .280	Melton, May, 20	C. May, 96
1974	J. Orta, .316	R. Allen, 32	K. Henderson, 95
1975	J. Orta, .304	D. Johnson, 18	J. Orta, 83
1976	R. Garr, .300	Orta, Spencer, 14	J. Orta, 72
1977	R. Garr, .300	O. Gamble, 31	R. Zisk, 101
1978	L. Johnson, .273	E. Soderholm, 20	L. Johnson, 72
1979	C. Lemon, .318	C. Lemon, 17	C. Lemon, 86
1980	C. Lemon, .292	J. Morrison, W. Nordhagen, 15	L. Johnson, 81
1981	W. Nordhagen, .308	G. Luzinski, 21	G. Luzinski, 62
1982	R. Law, .318	H. Baines, 25	H. Baines, 105

ALL-TIME RECORDS

Club Season Records

Most runs .... 920 in 1936
Most runs, game .... Chicago 29, Kansas City 6, 4/23/55
Most hits .... 1597 in 1936
Most bases on balls .... 702 in 1949
Highest batting average .... 294 in 1920
Lowest batting average .... 211 in 1910
Most .300 hitters .... 8 in 1924
Most singles .... 1199 in 1936
Most doubles .... 314 in 1926
Most triples .... 102 in 1915
Most homers .... 192 in 1977
Most grand slam homers .... 7 in 1961
Most home runs by pinch-hitters .... 6 in 1953 & 1961
Highest slugging average .... 444 in 1977
Most runs-batted-in .... 862 in 1936
Most stolen bases .... 280 in 1901
Most passed balls .... 45 in 1965
Most errors .... 345 in 1901
Most consecutive errorless games .... 9 in 1955 & 1964
Fewest errors .... 107 in 1957
Highest fielding average .... 982 in 1957 & 1962
Most double plays .... 187 in 1970 & 1974
Most walks issued .... 628 in 1934
Fewest walks, issued .... 255 in 1906
Most strikeouts, pitching .... 976 in 1971
Most saves .... 53 in 1965
Most shutouts .... 32 in 1906
Highest ERA .... 5.41 in 1934
Lowest ERA .... 1.99 in 1905

Individual Records

Batting

Most years, league .... 20, Lucius B. Appling
Most games .... 163, Donald A. Buford, 1966
Most at-bats .... 649, J. Nelson Fox, 1956
Most at-bats, league .... 8857, Lucius B. Appling
Most runs .... 135, John A. Mostil, 1925
Most runs, league .... 1319, Lucius B. Appling
Most hits .... 222, Edward T. Collins, 1920
Most hits, league .... 2749, Lucius B. Appling
Most singles .... 169, Edward T. Collins, 1920
Most singles, league .... 2162, Lucius B. Appling
Most doubles .... 45, Floyd A. Robinson, 1962
Most doubles, league .... 440, Lucius B. Appling
Most triples .... 21, Joseph J. Jackson, 1916
Most triples, league .... 104, John F. Collins; 104, J. Nelson Fox
Most homers, righthanded batter .... 37, Richard A. Allen, 1972
Most homers, lefthanded batter .... 31, Oscar Gamble, 1977
Most homers, season, at home, righthanded batter ..... 27, Richard A. Allen, 1972
Most homers, season, on road .... 18, Richie Zisk, 1977
Most homers, season, at home, lefthanded batter ...... 15, Lawrence E. Doby, 1956
Most homers, rookie season .... 27, Henry J. Bonura, 1934
Most homers one month .... 13, Richard A. Allen, July, 1972
Most homers, league, righthanded batter .... 154, William E. Melton
Most homers, league, lefthanded batter .... 97, Peter T. Ward
Most homers with bases filled, season .... 3, Peter T. Ward, 1964
Most homers with bases filled, league .... 4, J. Sherman Lollar; 4, Bill Melton;
            Walter Dropo; 4, Oscar E. Felsch; 4, Alphonse E. Smith; 4, Peter T. Ward
Most total bases .... 336, Joseph J. Jackson, 1920
Most total bases, league .... 3528, Lucius B. Appling
Most sacrifice hits .... 40, George S. Davis, 1905
Most sacrifice flies .... 12, Orestes A. Minoso, 1961
Most stolen bases .... 56, Wallace Moses, 1943; 56, Luis Aparicio, 1959
Most stolen bases, league .... 366, Edward T. Collins
Most caught stealing .... 29, Edward T. Collins, 1923
Most bases on balls .... 127, Luzerne A. Blue, 1931
Most bases on balls, league .... 1302, Lucius B. Appling
Most strikeouts .... 175, David L. Nicholson, 1963
Fewest strikeouts .... 11, J. Nelson Fox, 1958
Most hit by pitch .... 23, Orestes A. Minoso, 1956
Most runs batted in .... 138, Henry J. Bonura, 1936
Most runs batted in, league .... 1116, Lucius B. Appling
Highest batting average .... 388, Lucius B. Appling, 1936
Highest slugging percentage .... 603, Richard A. Allen, 1972
Most consecutive games batted safely during season ... 27, Lucius B. Appling, 1936
Most grounded into double plays .... 27, J. Sherman Lollar, 1959
Fewest grounded into double plays .... 3, Ulysses J. Lupien, 1948
            3 Donald A. Buford, 1966; 3 Donald A. Buford, 1967

Pitching

Most years, league .... 21, Theodore A. Lyons
Most games, lefthander .... 88, Wilbur F. Wood, 1968
Most games, righthander .... 82, Eddie G. Fisher, 1965
Most games, league .... 669, Urban C. Faber
Most games started .... 49, Edward A. Walsh, 1908; 49, Wilbur F. Wood, 1972
Most complete games .... 42, Edward A. Walsh, 1908
Most games finished, lefthander .... 62, Wilbur F. Wood, 1970
Most games finished, righthander .... 60, Eddie G. Fisher, 1965
Most innings .... 464, Edward A. Walsh, 1908
Most innings, league .... 4087, Urban C. Faber
Most games won, season .... 40, Edward A. Walsh, 1908
Most games won, league .... 260, Theodore A. Lyons
Most years winning 20 or more games .... 4, Edward A. Walsh; 4, Urban C. Faber
4, Wilbur Wood
Most games lost .... 25, Patrick J. Flaherty, 1903
Most games lost, league .... 230, Theodore A. Lyons
Highest percentage games won, season—
.842, Sandalio Consuegra (won 16, lost 3 in 1954)
.806, Edward V. Cicotte (won 29, lost 7 in 1919)
Most consecutive games won over 2 seasons .... 14, D. Lamarr Hoyt, 1981–82
Most consecutive games won, season .... 11, John D. Rigney, 1939
11, Gary C. Peters, 1963
Most consecutive games lost, season .... 14, Howard K. Judson, 1949
Most saves, season .... 30, Edward J. Farmer, 1980
Most bases on balls .... 147, L. Vernon Kennedy, 1936
Most bases on balls, league .... 1213, Urban C. Faber
Most strikeouts .... 269, Edward A. Walsh, 1908
Most strikeouts, league .... 1796, W. William Pierce
Most strikeouts, nine-inning game .... 16, Jack Harshman, July 25, 1954
Most shutouts .... 12, Edward A. Walsh, 1908
Most shutouts, league .... 57, Edward A. Walsh
Most 1-0 shutouts won .... 5, Ewell A. Russell, 1913
Most 1-0 shutouts, league .... 13, Edward A. Walsh
Most shutouts lost .... 8, Patrick J. Flaherty, 1903; 8, Edward A. Walsh, 1907
Most 1-0 shutouts, lost .... 4, W. William Pierce, 1955
Most at-bats .... 1690, Edward A. Walsh, 1908
Most runs .... 182, Richard Kerr, 1921
Most earned-runs .... 162, Richard Kerr, 1921
Most hits .... 381, Wilbur F. Wood, 1973
Most hit batsmen .... 16, James Scott, 1909
Most wild pitches .... 17, Thomas E. John, 1970
Most home runs .... 33, W. William Pierce, 1958
Lowest earned-run average, season .... 1.53, Edward V. Cicotte, 346 innings, 1917

Career Hitting "Top Tens"

Games

Appling	2,422
Fox	2,115
Schalk	1,755
E. Collins	1,670
Aparicio	1,511
Minoso	1,373
Lollar	1,358
J. Collins	1,335
Weaver	1,254
Kamm	1,170

At-Bats

Appling	8,857
Fox	8,486
E. Collins	6,064
Aparicio	5,856
Schalk	5,304
Minoso	5,011
Weaver	4,810
J. Collins	4,791
F. A. Jones	4,248
Lollar	4,229

Runs

Appling	1,319
Fox	1,187
E. Collins	1,063
Minoso	893
Aparicio	791
F. A. Jones	692
Weaver	625
Mostil	618
Schalk	579
J. Collins	572

Hits

Appling	2,749
Fox	2,470
E. Collins	2,005
Aparicio	1,575
Minoso	1,523
Schalk	1,345
Weaver	1,310
J. Collins	1,254
Falk	1,219
F. A. Jones	1,156

Doubles

Appling	440
Fox	335
E. Collins	265
Minoso	260
Falk	245
Kamm	243
J. Collins	230
Aparicio	223
Mostil	209
Sheely	207

Triples

J. Collins	104
Fox	104
Appling	102
E. Collins	102
Mostil	82
Jackson	79
Minoso	79
Weaver	69
Kamm	67
Kreevich	65

Home Runs

Melton	154
Minoso	135
Lollar	124
Ward	97
Allen	85
May	85
A. Smith	85
Landis	83
Bonura	79
Orta	79

Total Bases

Appling	3,528
Fox	3,118
E. Collins	2,567
Minoso	2,346
Aparicio	2,036
J. Collins	1,743
Falk	1,714
Weaver	1,710
Lollar	1,698
Schalk	1,676

Runs Batted In

Appling	1,116
Minoso	808
E. Collins	803
Fox	740
Lollar	631
Falk	627
Schalk	596
Kamm	587
Sheely	582
J. Collins	541

Extra Base Hits

Appling	587
Fox	474
Minoso	473
E. Collins	398
J. Collins	351
Falk	345
Kamm	335
Aparicio	320
Lollar	319
Mostil	314

Batting Avg.

Jackson	.340
E. Collins	.331
Bonura	.317
Fal'k	.315
Wright	.312
Appling	.310
Radcliff	.310
Sheely	.305
Minoso	.304
Hooper	.302

Slugging Pct.

Bonura	.518
Jackson	.499
Minoso	.468
Lemon	.451
A. Smith	.444
Falk	.442
Hooper	.436
Melton	.432
Felsch	.427
Mostil	.427

Stolen Bases

Collins, E.	366	Appling	179
Aparicio	318	Mostil	176
Isbell	250	Schalk	176
Jones, F.	206	Weaver	172
Collins, S.	192	Minoso	171

Career Pitching "Top Tens"

ERA		Wins		Innings Pitched	
Walsh	1.81	Lyons	260	Lyons	4,161
Cicotte	2.24	Faber	254	Faber	4,088
White	2.30	Walsh	194	Walsh	2,946
Scott	2.32	Pierce	186	Pierce	2,932
Russell	2.34	Wood	163	Wood	2,524
F. Smith	2.35	White	159	White	2,522
Altrock	2.40	Cicotte	158	Horlen	1,919
Benz	2.42	Horlen	113	Lee	1,889
Owen	2.53	Scott	111	Scott	1,872
Patterson	2.75	Smith	108	Peters	1,560

Strikeouts		Won-Lost Pct.		Games	
Pierce	1,796	Williams	.648	Faber	669
Walsh	1,732	Pizarro	.615	Lyons	594
Faber	1,471	Cicotte	.608	Wood	578
Wood	1,332	Walsh	.601	Pierce	456
Peters	1,098	Donovan	.593	Walsh	426
White	1,095	White	.564	Wilhelm	361
Lyons	1,073	Smith	.560	White	361
Horlen	1,007	Altrock	.556	Cicotte	353
Cicotte	961	Russell	.552	Horlen	329
Scott	945	Pierce	.550	Scott	317

Shutouts		Saves	
Walsh	57	Wilhelm	98
White	42	Forster	74
Pierce	35	Wood	57
Faber	30	Farmer	54
Cicotte	28	Brown	53
Lyons	27	Fisher	48
Scott	26	Locker	47
Smith	25	Lown	43
Wood	24	LaGrow	41
Russell	23	Staley	40

COMISKEY PARK

Despite today's strong interest in older ballparks, Comiskey Park is—relatively—ignored. And yet, the home of the White Sox is the oldest major league ballpark—older than Wrigley Field, Fenway Park, Tiger Stadium, and all the rest.

When Comiskey Park was built, it was a stadium ahead of its time. Charles Comiskey, denied his first choice for a stadium site, went one block west for a plot of land, reportedly the largest in the majors at the time. Like many of the new ballparks of that day, Comiskey Park had a spacious outfield. Unlike these parks, however, it was built with outfield grandstands in both left field and right. When increased interest in baseball necessitated greater seating capacity, all Comiskey had to do was expand the existing stands by extending the double-decking. Other teams built outfield grandstands which reduced the size of the playing fields, resulting in those now famous bandboxes.

When Comiskey Park opened on July 1, 1910, its dimensions were 362 feet down the foul lines and 420 feet to center. Not only was it spacious, it was symmetrical. In this, it

117

was more than fifty years ahead of its time. Although converted football ovals in Cleveland and Baltimore are symmetrical, and newer stadiums in Milwaukee, San Francisco, and Minnesota came close, symmetrical stadiums were not regularly built until the completion of Dodger Stadium in 1962. Every stadium constructed for major league baseball since then has been symmetrical.

The new stands altered the field's dimensions, slightly, to 352 feet down the foul lines and 440 feet to center. Though those distances have been decreased at times by moving home plate or erecting temporary fences, Comiskey Park has always remained a spacious, symmetrical ballpark. Here is a clue to the stadium's relative anonymity. For such features are not compatible with the idiosyncrasies which highlight other old ballparks. There are no slanting fences or sloping outfields, no "Green Monster" or absence of lights. (In fact, Comiskey Park was designed to accommodate lights.)

Even Comiskey Park's novelties have been more futuristic than quaint. Bill Veeck drove opponents to distraction with the addition of the first "exploding" scoreboard in 1960. He also developed the first picnic area in a major league stadium (beneath the left field grandstand). Although the outfield has always been natural grass, an attempt was made (since abandoned) to improve the playing surface by Astroturfing the infield.

With strong architectural links to the past and continual improvements; with an official seating capacity of 46,550, but able to accommodate over 55,000—Comiskey Park is definitely the very early pioneer of today's modern stadiums.

NICKNAMES

Admiral—Claude Berry

Babe—Foster Blackburn, William Borton, Eddie Klieman, Ralph Pinelli, Jay Towne
Bald Eagle—Frank Isbell
Bam—Brian McCall
Bananas—Johnny Mostil
The Beau—Frank Baumann
Bee Bee—Lee Richard
Biff—Walker Schaller
Big Bill—Bill James
Big Ed—Ed Klepfer, Ed Walsh
The Big Bear—Mike Garcia
Big Finn—Lou Fiene
Biggs—Wilbur Wehde
Blackie—Sam Dente, Jim Derrington, Lee Mangum
Blimp—Frankie Hayes
Blitzen—Joe Benz
Blondy—John Ryan
Blue Moon—John Odom
Boob—Eric McNair
Boots—Al Hollingsworth
Boy Wonder—Roy Patterson
Boze—Louis Berger
Braggo—Robert Roth
The Brat—Eddie Stanky
Bruno—James Block
Bruz—Ralph Hamner
Bubba—John Phillips
Bubber—Clarence Jonnard

Bubber—Clarence Jonnard
Bubby—Fred Talbot
Buck—Clyde Crouse, Thomas O'Brien, George Redfern, Lee Ross, George Weaver
Bucketfoot Al—Al Simmons
Buckshot—Glenn Wright, John Skopec
Bucky—Russell Dent
Bud—John Clancy, Daniel Hafey, Hollis Sheely, Harry Sketchley, Edward Stewart
Buddy — Richard Booker, Charles Bradford, Carl Peterson, Eddie Solomon
Bugs—Carl Moran, Joseph Morris
Bull—Ed Durham, Greg Luzinski
Bullet—Frank Miller
Bullfrog Bill—Bill Dietrich
Bump—Irving Hadley
Bunch—Bob Gillespie
Bunions—Rollie Zeider
Bunny—Anthony Brief
Burrhead—Joe Dobson, Ferris Fain
Buster—Cal McLish, Vern Stephens
Butch—Walter Henline, Don Kolloway, Mel Simmons
Butcher Boy—Grady Adkins
Buzz—Doug McWeeny

Cab—Don Kolloway
Cactus—Cliff Cravath
Casey—Charles Jones
Catfish—George Metkovich
Ceylon—Ed Wright
Chad—Clyde Kimsey
Chick—Martin Autry, Bob Chakales, Tony Cuccinello, Charles Gandil, Wally
    Mattick, Frank Naleway, Marino Pieretti
Chico—Alfonso Carrasquel
Chief—Charles Bender, Emmett Bowles, William Chouneau, Vallie Eaves
Chink—Leo Taylor
Citation—Lloyd Merriman
Cotton—Charles Nash
Cozy—Patrick Dolan
The Crab—Johnny Evers
Cracker—Ray Schalk
The Creeper—Ed Stroud
Cuke—Roland Barrows
Cy—Cecelio Acosta, Edwin Twombly, Irv Young

Daddy Wags—Leon Wagner
Dauntless Dave—Dave Danforth
Deacon—Grover Jones, Everett Scott
Death Valley Jim—Jim Scott
Dixie—Frank Davis, Millard Howell, Gorham Leverett, Fred Walker
The Dixie Thrush—Sammy Strang
Doc—Guy White
Ducky—James Holmes
Dummy—William Hoy, George Leitner
Dutch—Charlier Dorman, Bill Fehring, Fred Hartman, Frank Henry, Clarence
    Hoffman, Russ Kemmerer, Hugo Klaener, Fred Lamline, Edward Zwilling

The Earl of Snohomish—Earl Torgeson

Farmer—Ray Moore
Fat Jack—Jack Fisher
Fats—Bob Fothergill, Frank Kalin
Filipino—Dave Altizer
Fingers—Thomas Quinlan
Fire—Virgil Trucks
Flame—Lee Delhi
Flash—Maurice Archdeacon, Ray Flaskamper
Footsie—Johnny Marcum
Frenchy—Stanley Bordagaray, Claude Raymond, Bernard Uhalt
Fuzzy—Al Smith

Gander—Monty Stratton
Gator—Ralph Garr
Gavvy—Cliff Cravath
Goose—Rich Gossage
The Great Gabbo—Frank Gabler
Gulliver—Paul Lehner
Gus—Early Wynn

Hairbreadth Harry—Jack Hamilton
Happy—Oscar Felsch, August Foreman
Hardrock—Clyde Shoun
Harlem Joe—Joe Kiefer
Hawk—Clay Carroll, Bill Mueller, Ken Silvestri
Hi—Harry Jasper
Hod—Horace Farmer
Honest Eddie—Eddie Murphy
Honest John—John Anderson
Honey—John Romano
Hooker—Frank Whitman
Hoot—Hal Trosky, Jr.
Hot Rod—Jim McDonald
Hub—James Hart
Huevo—Vicente Romo

Irish—Roy Corhan, Earl Harrist
Iron Man—Wiley Piatt

Jay Bird—Jay Johnstone
Jigger—Bill Black
Jiggs—John Donahue
Jockey—Bibb Falk
Jocko—John Conlan
Joe E.—Thurman Tucker
Jungle Jim—Manuel Rivera
Junior—Alvin Moore, Vern Stephens

Kangaroo—Davy Jones
Kettle—Elwood Wirtz
Kid—William Gleason, Frank Willson
Kitty—Jim Kaat
Knuckles—Ed Cicotte

Lanky—Raymond Jordan
Lefty—Bob Barnes, Eddie Carnett, Paul Castner, Italo Chelini, John Dobb, Clarence
    Fieber, Wilbur Good, John Goodell, Hal Hudson, Charlie Jackson, Bill Kennedy,
    Paul LaPalme, Thornton Lee, Pryor McBee, Jim Scoggins, Lee Thompson, Bob
    Uhle, Bob Weiland, Bill Wight, Claude Williams, Roy Wilson
Lena—Russell Blackburne
Liz—Elias Funk

Mandrake the Magician—Don Mueller
Mem—Merritt Lovett
Midget—Don Ferrarese
Molly—Paul Meloan
Money Bags—Tom Qualters
Moose—Grant Bowler, Walt Dropo, George Earnshaw, Bill Skowron, Julius Solters
Moses—Joe Shipley
Moxie—Mark Manvel
Muddy—Herold Ruel
Muggsy—Eddie Stanky
Mule—George Haas, Frank Lary
Mutt—Johnny Riddle
Mutz—Anton Ens

Nemo—Harry Leibold
The Nervous Greek—Lou Skizas
Nig—Johnny Grabowski, Frank Smith
Nixey—James Callahan
Noisy—Dick Clarke
No Neck—Walt Williams

Oats—Joe DeMaestri
The Octopus—Marty Marion
Old Aches and Pains—Luke Appling
Old Folks—Ellis Kinder
The Old Fox—Clark Griffith
Ozark Ike—Guz Zernial

Pants—Clarence Rowland
Pappy—Jack Bruner
Peaches—Andy Nelson
Pep—Harry Clark
Piano Legs—Charles Hickman
Pid—Everett Purdy
Pimba—Luis Alvarado
Ping—Frank Bodie
Pinky—Emmett O'Neill
Poco—Doug Taitt
Polly—Howard McLarry, Roy Wolfe
Pop—Clarence Foster, Paul Gregory
Pop Boy—Clarence Smith
Prince Hal—Hal Chase
Professor—Jim Brosnan
Pudge—Carlton Fisk
Pug—Tony Rensa

Rainbow—Steve Trout

Reb—Ewell Russell
Red—Emile Barnes, James Bowser, John Corriden, Dwight Dorman, Russell Evans, Urban Faber, Albert Kelly, Ralph Kress, Walt Kuhn, Ken Landenberger, Jim McClothlin, Robert Ostergard, Noah Proctor, Charles Ruffing, Robert Wilson, Al Worthington
Rip — Raymond Jordan, Raymond Radcliff
Rocky — Glenn Nelson, Bobby Rhawn
The Rope — Bob Boyd
The Round Man—Ron Northey
Roxy—Wyatt Snipes
Rusty—Russ Kemmerer, Russell Kuntz, Rosendo Torres

Sad Sam—Sam Jones
Sandow—Sam Mertes
Sandy—Santos Alomar, Art Herring, Joe Vance
Sarge—George Connally, Bob Kuzava, Hoyt Wilhelm
Scrap Iron—Clint Courtney
Shano—John Collins
Sheriff—Dave Hams
Shine—John Cortazzo
Shoeless Joe—Joe Jackson
Shovel—Clarence Hodge
Shufflin' Phil—Phil Douglas
Si—Homer Blankenship
Silent John—John Whitehead
Silk—Charlie Kavanagh
Skeeter—James Webb
Skeets—George Dickey
Skinny—Hal Brown
Skip—Lee Pitlock
Slats—Russell Blackburne, Marty Marion
Sleepy Bill—Bill Burns
Slim—Charles Embry, Harry Kinzy, Grover Lowdermilk
Smiley—John Bischoff
Smoke—Joe Kiefer
Smoky—Forrest Burgess
Smokey—Stover McIlwain, Charlie Maxwell, Joe Martin
Smudge—Smead Jolley
Spanky — Mike Squires
Sparky — Albert Lyle
The Sphinx—Don Mossi
Spider—Roger Nelson
Squirrel—Danny Reynolds, Roy Sievers
Steady Eddie—Ed Lopat
Stretch—Harry Boyles
Stubby—Joe Erautt, Frank Mack
Sugar—Bob Cain, Marritt Cain
Sugar Boy—Tom Dougherty
Suitcase—Bob Seeds, Harry Simpson
Sunset Jimmy—Jimmy Burke
Swats—Carl Sawatski
Swede—Johnny Johnson, Charles Risberg

Taffy—Taft Wright

Teach—Earl Caldwell
Tex—William Jones, Ewell Russell, Rich Wortham
Tido—Thomas P. Daly
Tink—Arthur Riviere
Tito—John Francona
Toots—Les Tietje
Topsy—George Magoon
The Trojan—Johnny Evers
Truckhorse—Frank Pratt
Turk—Omar Lown
Twitch—Marv Rickert

The Vulture—Phil Regan

What a Man—Art Shires
Whispering Bill—Bill Barrett
Whistlin' Jake—Jake Wade
Whitey—Mizell Platt, Earl Sheely
Wig—Ralph Weigel
Wild Bill—Bill Connelly, Bill Hunnefield
Witto—Luis Aloma
Wito—Ramon Conde

Yam—Clarence Yaryan
Yip—Frank Owen

Zaza—Erwin Harvey
Zeke—Henry Bonura, Al Zarilla
Ziggy—Robert Hasbrook

WHITE SOX WHO LED LEAGUE IN MAJOR CATEGORIES

Hitting

Batting Average
1936 — Luke Appling (.388)
1943 — Luke Appling (.328)

Hits
1952 — Nellie Fox (192)
1954 — Nellie Fox (201—tie)
1957 — Nellie Fox (196)
1958 — Nellie Fox (187)
1960 — Minnie Minoso (184)

Singles
1902 — Fielder Jones (148)
1936 — Rip Radcliff (161)
1952 — Nellie Fox (157)
1954 — Nellie Fox (167)
1955 — Nellie Fox (157)
1956 — Nellie Fox (158)
1957 — Nellie Fox (160)
1959 — Nellie Fox (149)
1965 — Don Buford (129)

Doubles
1942 — Don Kolloway (40)
1945 — Wally Moses (35)
1957 — Minnie Minoso (36—tie)
1962 — Floyd Robinson (45)
1979 — Chet Lemon (44—tied)

Triples
1916 — Joe Jackson (21)
1920 — Joe Jackson (20)
1937 — Dixie Walker (16)
        Mike Kreevich (16)
1943 — Wally Moses (12—tie)
1951 — Minnie Minoso (14—also with Cleveland)
1953 — Jim Rivera (16)
1954 — Minnie Minoso (18)
1956 — Minnie Minoso (11—tie)
1960 — Nellie Fox (10)

Runs Scored
1925 — Johnny Mostil (125)

Hitting (continued)

Home Runs
1915 — Bob Roth (7—3 with White Sox;
4 with Cleveland)
1971 — Bill Melton (33)
1972 — Dick Allen (37)
1974 — Dick Allen (32)

Runs Batted In
1972 — Dick Allen (113)

Total Bases
1916 — Joe Jackson (293)
1954 — Minnie Minoso (304)

Slugging Percentage
1915 — Jake Fournier (.491)
1972 — Dick Allen (.603)
1974 — Dick Allen (.563)

Bases on Balls
1901 — Dummy Hoy (86)
1915 — Eddie Collins (119)
1925 — Willie Kamm (90)
Johnny Mostil (90)
1972 — Dick Allen (99—tie)

Stolen Bases
1901 — Frank Isbell (48)
1908 — Pat Dougherty (47)
1919 — Eddie Collins (33)
1923 — Eddie Collins (49)
1924 — Eddie Collins (42)
1925 — Johnny Mostil (43)
1926 — Johnny Mostil (35)
1951 — Minnie Minoso (31—also with
Cleveland)
1952 — Minnie Minoso (22)
1953 — Minnie Minoso (25)
1955 — Jim Rivera (25)
1956 — Luis Aparicio (21)
1957 — Luis Aparicio (28)
1958 — Luis Aparicio (29)
1959 — Luis Aparicio (56)
1960 — Luis Aparicio (51)
1961 — Luis Aparicio (53)
1962 — Luis Aparicio (31)

Pitching

Winning Percentage
1901 — Clark Griffith (.774, 24–7)
1908 — Ed Walsh (.727, 40–15)
1916 — Ed Cicotte (.682, 15–7)
1917 — "Reb" Russell (.750, 15–5)
1919 — Ed Cicotte (.806, 29–7)
1954 — Sandy Consuegra (.842, 16–3)
1957 — Dick Donovan (.727, 16–6, tie)
1959 — Bob Shaw (.750, 18–6)
1962 — Ray Herbert (.690, 20–9)
1967 — Joel Horlen (.731, 19–7)

Wins
1908 — Ed Walsh (40)
1917 — Ed Cicotte (28)
1919 — Ed Cicotte (29)
1925 — Ted Lyons (21—tie)
1927 — Ted Lyons (22—tie)
1957 — Billy Pierce (20—tie)
1959 — Early Wynn (22)
1964 — Gary Peters (20—tie)
1972 — Wilbur Wood (24—tie)
1973 — Wilbur Wood (24)

Earned Run Average
1906 — Doc White (1.52)
1907 — Ed Walsh (1.60)
1910 — Ed Walsh (1.27)
1917 — Ed Cicotte (1.53)
1921 — Red Faber (2.47)
1922 — Red Faber (2.80)
1941 — Thornton Lee (2.37)
1942 — Ted Lyons (2.10)
1951 — Saul Rogovin (2.78—also with
Detroit)
1955 — Billy Pierce (1.97)
1960 — Frank Baumann (2.68)
1963 — Gary Peters (2.33)
1966 — Gary Peters (1.98)
1967 — Joel Horlen (2.06)

Strikeouts
1908 — Ed Walsh (269)
1909 — Frank Smith (177)
1911 — Ed Walsh (255)
1953 — Billy Pierce (186)
1958 — Early Wynn (179)

Shutouts

1901 — Clark Griffith (5—tie)
1906 — Ed Walsh (10)
1908 — Ed Walsh (12)
1909 — Ed Walsh (8)
1925 — Ted Lyons (5)
1940 — Ted Lyons (4—tie)
1954 — Virgil Trucks (5—tie)
1957 — Jim Wilson (5)
1960 — Early Wynn (4—tie)
1963 — Ray Herbert (7)
1966 — Tommy John (5—tie)
1967 — Tommy John (6)
　　　　Joel Horlen (6)

Saves

1908 — Ed Walsh (7)
1910 — Ed Walsh (6)
1911 — Ed Walsh (7)
1912 — Ed Walsh (10)
1914 — Red Faber (4—tie)
1917 — Dave Danforth (7)
1920 — Dickie Kerr (5—tie)
1937 — Clint Brown (18)
1943 — Gordon Maltzberger (14)
1944 — Gordon Maltzberger (12—tie)
1952 — Harry Dorish (11)
1959 — Turk Lown (15)
1974 — Terry Forster (24)
1975 — Rich Gossage (26)

Games

1907 — Ed Walsh (56)
1908 — Ed Walsh (66)
1909 — Frank Smith (51)
1910 — Ed Walsh (45—tie)
1911 — Ed Walsh (56)
1912 — Ed Walsh (62)
1913 — "Reb" Russell (51)
1915 — Red Faber (50—tie)
1917 — Dave Danforth (50)
1939 — Clint Brown (61)
1942 — Joe Haynes (40)

1952 — Bill Kennedy (47)
1959 — Gerry Staley (67)
1965 — Eddie Fisher (82)
1966 — Eddie Fisher (67—23 with Chicago,
　　　　　　　　　　　　44 with Baltimore)
1967 — Bob Locker (77)
1968 — Wilbur Wood (88)
1969 — Wilbur Wood (76)
1970 — Wilbur Wood (77)

Complete Games

1907 — Ed Walsh (37)
1908 — Ed Walsh (42)
1909 — Frank Smith (37)
1919 — Ed Cicotte (29)
1921 — Red Faber (32)
1922 — Red Faber (31)
1924 — Hollis Thurston (28)
1927 — Ted Lyons (30)
1929 — Tommy Thomas (24)
1930 — Ted Lyons (29)
1941 — Thornton Lee (30)
1956 — Billy Pierce (21—tie)
1957 — Billy Pierce (16)
　　　　Dick Donovan (16)
1958 — Billy Pierce (19—tie)

Innings Pitched

1901 — Ed Walsh (422)
1908 — Ed Walsh (464)
1909 — Frank Smith (365)
1911 — Ed Walsh (369)
1912 — Ed Walsh (393)
1917 — Ed Cicotte (347)
1919 — Ed Cicotte (307—tie)
1922 — Red Faber (353)
1927 — Tommy Thomas (308)
　　　　Ted Lyons (308)
1930 — Ted Lyons (298)
1959 — Early Wynn (256)
1972 — Wilbur Wood (377)
1973 — Wilbur Wood (359)

CLUB TOTALS THROUGH THE YEARS

Hitting

Year	R	HR	BA	League Rank (BA)
1901	819	32	.276	5
1902	675	14	.268	6
1903	516	14	.247	6
1904	600	14	.242	5
1905	613	11	.237	5

Hitting (continued)

Year	R	HR	BA	League Rank (BA)
1906	570	6	.228	8
1907	584	6	.237	7
1908	535	3	.224	8
1909	494	4	.221	8
1910	456	7	.211	8
1911	717	19	.269	6
1912	640	17	.255	7
1913	486	23	.236	8
1914	487	19	.239	7
1915	717	25	.258	3
1916	601	17	.251	2
1917	657	19	.253	3
1918	457	9	.256	4T
1919	668	25	.287	1
1920	794	37	.294	3
1921	683	35	.283	5
1922	691	45	.278	5
1923	692	42	.279	5
1924	793	41	.288	6
1925	811	38	.284	6
1926	730	32	.289	3T
1927	662	36	.278	6
1928	656	24	.270	7
1929	627	37	.268	7
1930	729	63	.276	6
1931	704	27	.260	8
1932	667	36	.267	7
1933	683	43	.272	4
1934	704	71	.263	8
1935	738	74	.275	7
1936	920	60	.292	5
1937	780	67	.280	5T
1938	709	67	.277	5
1939	755	64	.275	6
1940	735	73	.278	3
1941	638	47	.255	8
1942	538	25	.246	7T
1943	573	33	.247	5
1944	543	23	.247	8
1945	596	22	.262	1
1946	562	37	.257	4
1947	553	53	.256	5
1948	559	55	.251	7
1949	648	43	.257	6
1950	625	93	.260	6T
1951	714	86	.270	1
1952	610	80	.252	5
1953	716	74	.258	6
1954	711	94	.267	2
1955	725	116	.268	1
1956	776	128	.267	4
1957	707	106	.260	3

Year	R	HR	BA	League Rank (BA)
1958	634	101	.257	4
1959	669	97	.250	6
1960	741	112	.270	1
1961	765	138	.265	3
1962	707	92	.257	5
1963	683	114	.250	5T
1964	642	106	.247	6T
1965	647	125	.246	4
1966	574	87	.231	10
1967	531	89	.225	8T
1968	463	71	.228	6
1969	625	112	.247	6
1970	633	123	.253	4
1971	617	138	.250	7T
1972	566	108	.238	7
1973	652	111	.256	7T
1974	684	135	.268	3
1975	655	94	.255	7
1976	586	73	.255	7
1977	844	192	.278	4
1978	634	106	.264	7
1979	730	127	.275	7
1980	587	91	.259	12
1981	476	76	.272	2
1982	786	136	.273	5

Pitching

Year	CG	SHO	ERA	League Rank (ERA)
1901	110	11	2.98	1
1902	116	11	3.41	5
1903	114	9	3.02	6
1904	134	26	2.30	3
1905	131	17	1.99	1
1906	117	32	2.13	2
1907	112	17	2.22	1
1908	107	21	2.22	3
1909	112	26	2.04	2
1910	103	23	2.01	2
1911	86	14	3.01	2T
1912	84	14	3.06	3
1913	86	16	2.33	1
1914	74	17	2.48	2
1915	92	17	2.43	3
1916	73	18	2.36	1
1917	79	21	2.16	1
1918	76	10	2.69	4
1919	87	14	3.04	4
1920	112	8	3.59	3
1921	86	7	4.94	8
1922	86	13	3.93	4
1923	74	5	4.03	5
1924	76	1	4.75	8
1925	71	12	4.34	4
1926	85	11	3.74	3

Pitching (continued)

Year	CG	SHO	ERA	League Rank (ERA)
1927	85	10	3.91	2
1928	88	6	3.98	4
1929	78	5	4.41	6
1930	67	2	4.71	5
1931	54	6	5.05	8
1932	50	2	4.82	6
1933	53	8	4.45	6
1934	72	4	5.41	8
1935	80	8	4.38	5
1936	80	5	5.06	6
1937	70	15	4.17	2
1938	83	5	4.36	2
1939	62	5	4.31	4
1940	83	10	3.74	2
1941	106	14	3.52	1
1942	86	8	3.58	4
1943	70	12	3.20	5
1944	64	5	3.58	6
1945	84	13	3.69	7
1946	62	9	3.10	1
1947	47	11	3.64	5
1948	35	2	4.89	7
1949	57	10	4.30	6
1950	62	7	4.41	4
1951	74	11	3.50	2
1952	53	13	3.25	2
1953	57	16	3.41	2
1954	60	21	3.05	2
1955	55	17	3.37	2
1956	65	11	3.73	3
1957	59	16	3.35	2
1958	55	15	3.61	4
1959	44	13	3.29	1
1960	42	11	3.60	3
1961	39	3	4.06	4
1962	50	13	3.73	4
1963	49	19	2.97	1
1964	44	20	2.72	1
1965	21	14	2.99	2
1966	38	22	2.68	1
1967	36	24	2.45	1
1968	20	11	2.75	4
1969	29	10	4.21	11
1970	20	6	4.54	12
1971	46	19	3.13	4
1972	36	14	3.12	8
1973	48	15	3.87	7
1974	55	11	3.94	11
1975	34	7	3.94	8
1976	54	10	4.25	12
1977	34	3	4.25	10
1978	38	9	4.22	12

Year	CG	SHO	ERA	League Rank (ERA)
1979	28	9	4.10	6
1980	32	12	3.92	6
1981	20	8	3.47	4
1982	30	10	3.87	3

Fielding

Year	E	DP	F.A.	League Rank (F.A.)
1901	345	100	.941	5
1902	257	125	.955	1
1903	297	85	.949	7
1904	238	95	.964	1
1905	217	95	.968	1
1906	243	80	.963	2
1907	233	101	.966	1
1908	232	82	.966	1
1909	246	101	.964	1
1910	314	100	.954	6T
1911	252	98	.961	2
1912	291	102	.956	3
1913	255	104	.960	4T
1914	299	90	.955	6
1915	222	95	.965	2
1916	203	134	.968	2T
1917	204	117	.967	2
1918	169	98	.967	3
1919	176	116	.969	2
1920	198	142	.968	4
1921	200	155	.969	2
1922	155	132	.975	1
1923	184	138	.971	2
1924	229	136	.963	8
1925	200	162	.968	4
1926	165	122	.973	1
1927	178	131	.971	1
1928	186	149	.970	3T
1929	188	153	.970	4
1930	235	136	.962	7T
1931	245	131	.961	8
1932	264	170	.958	8
1933	186	143	.970	6
1934	207	126	.966	8
1935	146	133	.976	2
1936	168	174	.973	2T
1937	174	173	.971	6
1938	196	155	.967	7
1939	167	140	.972	2
1940	185	125	.969	5
1941	180	145	.971	5
1942	173	144	.970	5
1943	166	167	.973	5T
1944	183	154	.970	7T
1945	180	139	.970	7T
1946	175	170	.972	6
1947	155	180	.975	7T

Fielding (continued)

Year	E	DP	F.A.	League Rank (F.A.)
1948	160	176	.974	5T
1949	141	180	.977	4T
1950	140	181	.977	5
1951	151	176	.975	4T
1952	123	158	.980	1
1953	125	144	.980	1
1954	108	149	.982	1
1955	111	147	.981	2
1956	122	160	.979	1
1957	107	169	.982	1
1958	114	160	.981	2
1959	130	141	.979	1
1960	109	175	.982	1
1961	128	138	.980	2T
1962	110	153	.982	1
1963	131	163	.979	5
1964	122	164	.981	4T
1965	127	156	.980	4T
1966	159	149	.976	9
1967	138	149	.979	4
1968	151	152	.977	6T
1969	122	163	.981	2
1970	165	187	.975	11
1971	160	128	.975	12
1972	135	136	.977	9T
1973	144	165	.977	7T
1974	147	188	.977	7T
1975	140	155	.978	2T
1976	130	155	.979	4
1977	159	125	.974	12
1978	139	130	.977	8
1979	173	142	.972	13
1980	171	162	.973	14
1981	87	113	.979	8T
1982	151	173	.976	13

WHITE SOX VS. OTHER AMERICAN LEAGUE CLUBS
(Through 1982)

	W	L
Sox vs. Baltimore	217	239
Boston	785	814
California	193	176
Cleveland	811	794
Detroit	774	829
Kansas City	97	117
Milwaukee	90	87
Minnesota	159	200
New York	672	895
Oakland	282	216
Seattle	37	38
Texas	201	142
Toronto	39	30

	G	W	L	T
Sox vs. American League (1901–82):	12,675	6320	6255	100

MANAGERS AND THEIR RECORDS
1901–82

Clark Griffith, 1901–2
83-53
74-60
157-114 (.581)

James Callahan, 1903–4, 1912–14
60-77
22-18
78-76
78-74
70-84
308-329 (.484)

Fielder Jones, 1904–8
67-47
92-60
93-58
87-64
88-64
427-293 (.593)

Billy Sullivan, 1909
78-74 (.513)

Hugh Duffy, 1910–11
68-85
77-74
145-159 (.477)

Clarence "Pants" Rowland, 1915–18
93-81
89-65
100-54
57-67
339-247 (.578)

William "Kid" Gleason, 1919–23
88-52
96-58
62-92
77-77
69-85
392-364 (.519)

Johnny Evers, 1924
66-87 (.431)

Eddie Collins, 1925–26
79-75
81-72
160-147 (.521)

Ray Schalk, 1927–28
70-83
32-42
102-125 (.449)

Lena Blackburne, 1928-29
40-40
59-93
99-133 (.427)

Donie Bush, 1930–31
62-92
56-97
118-189 (.384)

Lew Fonseca, 1932–34
49-102
67-83
4-13
120-198 (.377)

Jimmie Dykes, 1934–46
49-86
74-78
81-70
86-68
65-83
85-69
82-72
77-77
66-82
82-72
71-83
71-78
10-20
899-938 (.489)

Ted Lyons, 1946–48
64-60
70-84
51-101
185-245 (.430)

131

Jack Onslow, 1949–50
63-91
8-22
71-113 (.386)

Red Corriden, 1950
52-72 (.419)

Paul Richards, 1951–54, 1976
81-73
81-73
89-65
91-54
64-97
406-362 (.529)

Marty Marion, 1954–56
3-6
91-63
85-69
179-138 (.565)

Al Lopez, 1957–65, 1968-69
90-64
82-72
94-60
87-67
86-76
85-77
94-68
98-64
95-67
21-26
8-9
840-650 (.564)

Eddie Stanky, 1966–68
83-79
89-73
34-45
206-197 (.511)

Les Moss, 1968
12-24 (.333)

Don Gutteridge, 1969–70
60-85
49-87
109-172 (.388)

Bill Adair, 1970
4-6 (.400)

Chuck Tanner, 1970–75
3-13
79-83
87-67
77-85
80-80
75-86
401-414 (.492)

Bob Lemon, 1977–78
90-72
34-40
124-112 (.525)

Larry Doby, 1978
37-50 (.425)

Don Kessinger, 1979
46-60 (.434)

Tony LaRussa, 1979-
27-27 ('79)
70-90 ('80)
54-52 ('81)
87-75 ('82)
238-244 (.494)

ALL-STAR RECORDS

White Sox Selected to All-Star Game
*Denotes starter

1933
Jimmie Dykes, 3B
*Al Simmons, OF

1934
Jimmie Dykes, 3B
*Al Simmons, OF

1935
*Al Simmons, OF

1936
*Luke Appling, SS
*Rip Radcliff, OF

1937
Luke Sewell, C
Monte Stratton, P (injured, could not play)

1938
*Mike Kreevich, OF

1939
Luke Appling, SS
Ted Lyons, P

1940
*Luke Appling, SS

1941
Luke Appling, SS
Thornton Lee, P
Eddie Smith, P

1942
Eddie Smith, P

1943
Luke Appling, SS

1944
Orval Grove, P
*Thurman Tucker, OF

1946
Luke Appling, SS

1947
Luke Appling, SS
Rudy York, 1B

1948
Joe Haynes, p

1949
*Cass Michaels, 2B

1950
Ray Scarborough, P

1951
Jim Busby, OF

*Chico Carrasquel, SS
*Nellie Fox, 2B
Randy Gumpert, P
Minnie Minoso, OF
Eddie Robinson, 1B

1952
Nellie Fox, 2B
Minnie Minoso, OF
*Eddie Robinson, 1B

1953
*Chico Carrasquel, SS
Nellie Fox, 2B
Ferris Fain, 1B
Minnie Minoso, OF
Billy Pierce, P

1954
*Chico Carrasquel, SS
Nellie Fox, 2B
Bob Keegan, P
Sherm Lollar, C
*Minnie Minoso, OF
Virgil Trucks, P
George Kell, 3B (replaced due to injury)
Ferris Fain, 1B (replaced due to injury)

1955
Chico Carrasquel, SS
*Nellie Fox, 2B
Dick Donovan, P
Sherm Lollar, C
Billy Pierce, P

1956
*Nellie Fox, 2B
Sherm Lollar, C
Billy Pierce, P
Jim Wilson, P

1957
*Nellie Fox, 2B
Minnie Minoso, OF
Billy Pierce, P

1958
*Luis Aparicio, SS
*Nellie Fox, 2B
Sherm Lollar, C
Billy Pierce, P
Early Wynn, P

1959
*Luis Aparicio, SS
*Nellie Fox, 2B
Sherm Lollar, C
Billy Pierce, P
Early Wynn, P

1960
Luis Aparicio, SS
Nellie Fox, 2B
Sherm Lollar, C
*Minnie Minoso, OF
Al Smith, OF
Gerry Staley, P
Early Wynn, P

1961
Nellie Fox, 2B
Billy Pierce, P

1962
*Luis Aparicio, SS
Jim Landis, OF

1963
*Nellie Fox, 2B
Juan Pizarro, P

1964
Gary Peters, P
Juan Pizarro, P

1965
Eddie Fisher, P
Bill Skowron, 1B

1966
Tommie Agee, OF

1967
Tommie Agee, OF
Joe Horlen, P
Gary Peters, P

1968
Tommy John, P
Duane Josephson, C

1969
Carlos May, OF

1970
*Luis Aparicio, SS

1971
Bill Melton, 3B

1972
*Dick Allen, 1B
Carlos May, OF
Wilbur Wood, P

1973
*Dick Allen, 1B
Pat Kelly, OF (replaced Allen because of injury)

1974
*Dick Allen, 1B
Wilbur Wood, P

1975
Bucky Dent, SS
Rich Gossage, P
Jim Kaat, P
Jorge Orta, 2B

1976
Rich Gossage, P

1977
*Richie Zisk, OF

1978
Chet Lemon, OF

1979
Chet Lemon, OF

1980
Ed Farmer, P

1981
*Carlton Fisk, C
Britt Burns, P

1982
*Carlton Fisk, C

*Top vote getter of any All Star member

The Sporting News Major League All-Stars
(1925–60)

1926 — Johnny Mostil, OF
1927 — Ted Lyons, P
1933 — Al Simmons, OF
1934 — Al Simmons, OF
1936 — Luke Appling, SS
1940 — Luke Appling, SS
1941 — Thornton Lee, P
1943 — Luke Appling, SS

1955 — Nellie Fox, 2B
　　　　Billy Pierce, P
1957 — Billy Pierce, P
1958 — Nellie Fox, 2B
　　　　Sherm Lollar, C
　　　　Early Wynn, P
1960 — Minnie Minoso, OF

The Sporting News American League All-Stars
(1961–81)

1963 — Gary Peters, P
1964 — Gary Peters, P
1968 — Luis Aparicio, SS
1970 — Luis Aparicio, SS

1972 — Dick Allen, 1B
　　　　Wilbur Wood, LHP
1974 — Dick Allen, 1B
1975 — Jim Kaat, LHP

The Sporting News Gold Glove Awards (All-Star Fielding)
(Given as a major league award in 1957 and American League only from 1958–81)

1957 — Sherm Lollar, C
　　　　Nellie Fox, 2B
　　　　Minnie Minoso, LF
1958 — Sherm Lollar, C
　　　　Luis Aparicio, SS
1959 — Sherm Lollar, C
　　　　Nellie Fox, 2B
　　　　Luis Aparicio, SS
1960 — Nellie Fox, 2B
　　　　Luis Aparicio, SS
　　　　Minnie Minoso, LF
　　　　Jim Landis, CF
1961 — Luis Aparicio, SS

　　　　Jim Landis, OF
1962 — Luis Aparicio, SS
　　　　Jim Landis, OF
1963 — Jim Landis, OF
1964 — Jim Landis, OF
1966 — Tommie Agee, OF
1968 — Luis Aparicio, SS
1970 — Luis Aparicio, SS
　　　　Ken Berry, OF
1973 — Jim Kaat, P
1974 — Jim Kaat, P
1975 — Jim Kaat, P
1977 — Jim Spencer, 1B
1981 — Mike Squires, 1B

MAJOR AWARD WINNERS

Baseball Writers Association of America (BBWAA) American League Most Valuable Player Award

1959 — Nellie Fox
1972 — Dick Allen

BBWAA Cy Young Award

1959 — Early Wynn

BBWAA Rookie of the Year Award

1956 — Luis Aparicio
1963 — Gary Peters
1966 — Tommie Agee

The Sporting News Major League Player of the Year

1959 — Early Wynn

The Sporting News American League Player of the Year

1959 — Nellie Fox
1972 — Dick Allen

The Sporting News American League Pitcher of the Year

1956 — Billy Pierce
1957 — Billy Pierce
1959 — Early Wynn
1972 — Wilbur Wood

The Sporting News American League Rookie of the Year

1951 — Minnie Minoso
1956 — Luis Aparicio

The Sporting News American League Rookie Player of the Year

1963 — Pete Ward
1966 — Tommie Agee
1969 — Carlos May

The Sporting News American League Rookie Pitcher of the Year

1963 — Gary Peters
1980 — Britt Burns

The Sporting News American League Fireman of the Year Award

1965 — Eddie Fisher
1968 — Wilbur Wood
1974 — Terry Forster
1975 — Rich Gossage

The Sporting News Major League Manager of the Year Award

1972 — Chuck Tanner

The Sporting News Major League Executive of the Year Award

1972 — Roland Hemond
1977 — Bill Veeck

WORLD SERIES

1906

Roster of 1906 World Champion White Sox (93-58)

Manager: Fielder Jones

	POS.	G.
Altrock, Nicholas (Nick)	P	38
Davis, George Stacey	SS129*	133
Donahue, John Augustus (Jiggs)	1B	154
Dougherty, Patrick Henry	OF	75
Dundon, Augustus J.	2B18*	33
Fiene, Louis Henry	P	6
Hahn, Edgar Wm.	OF	130
Hart, James Henry	C15*	17
Hemphill, Frank Vernon	OF	13
Isbell, Wm. Frank	2B132*	143
Jones, Fielder Allison MGR.	OF	144
McFarland, Edward Wm.	C	12
O'Neill, Wm. John	OF93*	94
Owen, Frank Malcolm	P	42
Patterson, Roy Lewis	P	22
Quillin, Lee	SS	3
Rohe, George Anthony	3B57*	74
Roth, Frank Charles	C15*	16
Smith, Frank Elmer	P	20
Sullivan, Wm. Joseph (Billy)	C	118
Tannehill, Lee Ford (SS20)	3B92*	112
Towne, Jay King	C	13
Vinson, Ernest Augustus	OF	10
Walsh, Edward Augustin	P41*	42
White, Guy Harris (Doc)	P	28

1906 World Series Review

In one of the biggest upsets in World Series play, the White Sox—called the "Hitless Wonders" because of a team batting average of .228—defeated the powerful crosstown Cubs, four games to two, in the only all-Chicago fall classic. The Cubs, who established a major league record of 116 victories during the regular season, finished 20 games ahead of the second-place New York Giants of John McGraw. The Sox, whose team batting mark was dead last in the league, finished just three games ahead of the New York Highlanders by virtue of a 19-game winning streak in August.

Utility infielder George Rohe was the hitting hero for the White Sox, batting .333 for the Series in place of regular third baseman George Davis. His triples in both Games 1 and 3 enabled the Sox to win by scores of 2-1 and 3-0. Ed Walsh, who hurled a two-hit shutout with 12 strikeouts in Game 3, and was the winner in Game 5, emerged as the pitching star.

*Number of games at this position.

137

GAME 1

Tuesday, October 9—At West Side Park

White Sox (AL)	AB	R	H	O	A	E
Hahn, rf	3	0	0	1	0	0
Jones, cf	4	1	1	3	0	0
Isbell, 2b	4	0	1	0	1	1
Rohe, 3b	4	1	1	1	2	0
Donahue, 1b	4	0	0	12	2	0
Dougherty, lf	3	0	0	1	0	0
Sullivan, c	3	0	0	5	2	0
Tannehill, ss	3	0	0	1	4	0
Altrock, p	2	0	1	3	3	0
Totals	30	2	4	27	14	1

Cubs (NL)	AB	R	H	O	A	E
Hofman, cf	3	0	0	1	1	0
Sheckard, lf	3	0	0	0	0	0
aMoran	1	0	0	0	0	0
Schulte, rf	4	0	1	1	0	0
Chance, 1b	4	0	1	11	0	0
Steinfeldt, 3b	4	0	0	0	2	0
Tinker, ss	3	0	0	2	3	0
Evers, 2b	3	0	0	1	3	0
Kling, c	2	1	1	9	1	1
Brown, p	2	0	1	1	6	1
Totals	29	1	4	27	16	2

White Sox			0 0 0	0 1 1	0 0 0—2	
Cubs			0 0 0	0 0 1	0 0 0—1	

aFlied out for Sheckard in ninth. Three-base hit—Rohe. Run batted in—Isbell. Sacrifice hits—Hahn, Hofman, Brown. Stolen bases—Isbell, Dougherty. Earned runs—Cubs 1, White Sox 0. Left on bases—Cubs 4, White Sox 3. Struck out—By Brown 7, by Altrock 3. Bases on balls—off Brown 1, off Altrock 1. Wild pitches—Brown, Altrock. Passed balls—Kling 2. Umpires—Johnstone (NL) and O'Loughlin (AL). Time—1:45. Attendance—12,693.

GAME 2

Wednesday, October 10—At South Side Park

White Sox (AL)	AB	R	H	O	A	E
Hahn, rf	3	0	0	0	0	0
Jones, cf	3	0	0	1	0	0
Isbell, 2b	4	0	0	6	2	1
Rohe, 3b	2	0	0	0	3	0
Donahue, 1b	3	0	1	10	1	0
Dougherty, lf	2	1	0	1	0	0
Sullivan, c	4	0	0	8	2	1
Tannehill, ss	3	0	0	0	3	0
White, p	0	0	0	0	1	0
aTowne	1	0	0	0	0	0
Owen, p	2	0	0	1	4	0
Totals	27	1	1	27	16	2

Cubs (NL)	AB	R	H	O	A	E
Hofman, cf	4	0	1	2	0	0
Sheckard, lf	4	0	0	3	1	0
Schulte, rf	4	0	1	1	0	0
Chance, 1b	5	2	1	12	0	0
Steinfeldt, 3b	3	1	3	0	2	0
Tinker, ss	3	3	2	0	3	1
Evers, 2b	4	1	1	4	6	1
Kling, c	2	0	1	5	1	0
Reulbach, p	3	0	0	0	2	0
Totals	32	7	10	27	15	2

```
Cubs ...................................... 0 3 1  0 0 1  0 2 0—7
White Sox ................................. 0 0 0  0 1 0  0 0 0—1
```

aFlied out for White in third. Two-base hit—Kling. Runs batted in—Hofman, Stein-feldt, Tinker, Reulbach. Sacrifice hits—Scheckard, Steinfeldt, Reulbach. Stolen bases—Hofman, Chance 2, Tinker, Evers. Double plays—Sheckard and Kling; Evers and Chance. Earned runs—Cubs 2, White Sox 0. Left on bases—Cubs 6, White Sox 6. Struck out—by Reulbach 3, by White 1, by Owen 2. Bases on balls—off Reulbach 6, off White 2, off Owens 3. Hit by pitcher—by Reulbach (Rohe). Wild pitches—Reulbach, Owens. Hits—off White 4 in 3 innings, off Owens 6 in 6 innings. Losing pitcher—White. Umpires—O'Loughlin (AL) and Johnstone (NL). Time—1:58. Attendance—12,595.

1906 World Series (continued)

GAME 3

Thursday, October 11—At West Side Park

White Sox (AL)	AB	R	H	O	A	E
Hahn, rf	2	0	0	0	0	0
aO'Neill, rf	1	1	0	1	0	0
Jones, cf	4	0	0	1	0	0
Isbell, 2b	4	0	0	1	4	1
Rohe, 3b	3	0	1	0	1	0
Donahue, 1b	3	0	2	14	0	0
Dougherty, lf	4	0	0	0	0	0
Sullivan, c	3	0	0	10	2	0
Tannehill, ss	3	1	1	0	5	0
Walsh, p	2	1	0	0	3	0
Totals	29	3	4	27	15	1

Cubs (NL)	AB	R	H	O	A	E
Hofman, cf	4	0	1	1	0	0
Sheckard, lf	4	0	0	2	0	0
Schulte, rf	4	0	1	1	0	0
Chance, 1b	2	0	0	7	1	0
Steinfeldt, 3b	3	0	0	1	2	0
Tinker, ss	3	0	0	3	2	1
Evers, 2b	3	0	0	1	2	0
Kling, c	3	0	0	11	3	0
Pfiester, p	2	0	0	0	2	1
bGessler	1	0	0	0	0	0
Totals	29	0	2	27	12	2

White Sox	0 0 0	0 0 3	0 0 0—3
Cubs	0 0 0	0 0 0	0 0 0—0

aRan for Hahn in sixth. bReached first on error for Pfiester in ninth. Two-base hit—Schulte. Three-base hits—Donahue, Rohe. Runs batted in—Rohe 3. Sacrifice hits—Donahue, Sullivan. Stolen base—Rohe. Earned runs—White Sox 3, Cubs 0. Left on bases—Cubs 3, White Sox 4. Struck out—By Pfiester 9, by Walsh 12. Bases on balls—Off Pfiester 2, off Walsh 1. Hit by pitcher—By Pfiester (Hahn). Wild pitch—Walsh. Umpires—Johnstone (NL) and O'Loughlin (AL). Time—2:10. Attendance—13,667.

GAME 4

Friday, October 12—South Side Park

Cubs (NL)	AB	R	H	O	A	E
Hofman, cf	4	0	2	1	0	0
Sheckard, lf	3	0	0	1	0	0
Schulte, rf	4	0	0	1	0	0
Chance, 1b	4	1	2	13	1	0
Steinfeldt, 3b	2	0	1	1	1	1
Tinker, ss	1	0	0	1	4	0
Evers, 2b	3	0	1	2	4	0
Kling, c	3	0	0	6	3	0
Brown, p	3	0	1	1	5	0
Totals	27	1	7	27	18	1

White Sox (AL)	AB	R	H	O	A	E
Hahn, rf	4	0	1	1	0	0
Jones, cf	3	0	0	0	0	0
Isbell, 2b	4	0	0	1	3	0
Rohe, 3b	3	0	0	0	4	0
Donahue, 1b	1	0	0	13	2	0
Dougherty, lf	3	0	1	2	0	0
Davis, ss	3	0	0	4	2	1
Sullivan, c	3	0	0	3	1	0
Altrock, p	2	0	0	3	8	0
aMcFarland	1	0	0	0	0	0
Totals	27	0	2	27	20	1

Cubs	0 0 0	0 0 0	1 0 0—1
White Sox	0 0 0	0 0 0	0 0 0—0

aGrounded out for Altrock in ninth. Run batted in—Evers. Two-base hit—Hofman. Sacrifice hits—Donahue, Steinfeldt 2. Tinker 3. Stolen base—Sheckard. Double plays—Kling and Evers; Altrock, Donahue and Sullivan. Earned runs—Cubs 1, White Sox 0. Left on bases—Cubs 5, White Sox 3. Struck out—By Brown 5, by Altrock 2. Bases on balls—Off Brown 2, off Altrock 1. Passed ball—Kling. Umpires—O'Loughlin (AL) and Johnstone (NL). Time—1:36. Attendance—18,385.

GAME 5

Saturday, October 13—At West Side Park

Cubs (NL)	AB	R	H	O	A	E
Hofman, cf	3	2	1	2	0	0
Sheckard, lf	4	0	0	1	0	0
Schulte, rf	5	1	3	2	1	0
Chance, 1b	4	0	1	8	0	0
Steinfeldt, 3b	5	1	1	1	2	0
Tinker, ss	4	1	0	2	2	0
Evers, 2b	3	0	0	2	5	0
aMoran	1	0	0	0	0	0
Kling, c	3	0	0	9	0	0
Reulbach, p	0	0	0	0	2	0
Pfiester, p	0	0	0	0	0	0
Overall, p	2	1	0	0	1	0
Totals	36	6	6	27	13	0

White Sox (AL)	AB	R	H	O	A	E
Hahn, rf	5	2	1	1	0	0
Jones, cf	4	1	1	1	0	0
Isbell, 2b	5	3	4	2	2	2
Davis, ss	5	2	2	2	8	1
Rohe, 3b	4	0	3	0	2	2
Donahue, 1b	3	0	1	15	2	0
Dougherty, lf	5	0	0	0	0	0
Sullivan, c	4	0	0	6	2	0
Walsh, p	2	0	0	0	2	1
White, p	0	0	0	0	0	0
Totals	37	8	12	27	18	6

White Sox	1 0 2	4 0 1	0 0 0—8		
Cubs	3 0 0	1 0 2	0 0 0—6		

aForced runner for Evers in ninth. Two-base hits—Isbell 4, Rohe, Davis 2, Donahue, Chance, Schulte, Steinfeldt. Runs batted in—Schulte 2, Steinfeldt, Davis 3, Isbell 2, Rohe, Donahue. Sacrifice hits—Jones, Sheckard, Reulbach. Stolen bases—Dougherty, Davis, Tinker, Evers. Double play—Schulte, Evers and Kling. Earned runs—White Sox 8, Cubs 3. Left on bases—Cubs 10, White Sox 8. Struck out—By Reulbach 1, by Pfiester 2, by Overall 5, by Walsh 5. Bases on balls—Off Reulbach 2, off Pfiester 1, off Walsh 5, off Overall 1, off White 1. Hit by pitcher—By Pfiester (Donahue), by Walsh (Chance). Wild pitch—Overall. Passed ball—Sullivan. Hits—off Reulbach 5 in 2 innings (pitched to 2 batters in third), off Pfiester 3 in 1⅓ innings (pitched to 5 batters in fourth), off Overall 4 in 5⅔ innings, off Walsh 5 in 6 innings, off White 1 in 3 innings. Winner—Walsh. Loser—Pfiester. Umpires—Johnstone (NL), O'Loughlin (AL), Time—2:40. Attendance—23,257.

GAME 6

Sunday, October 14—At South Side Park

Cubs (NL)	AB	R	H	O	A	E
Hofman, cf	5	1	2	3	0	0
Scheckard, lf	3	0	0	2	0	0
Schulte, rf	5	0	1	0	0	0
Chance, 1b	2	0	0	9	0	0
Steinfeldt, 3b	3	0	0	0	0	0
Tinker, ss	4	0	1	2	6	0
Evers, 2b	4	1	1	2	0	0
Kling, c	4	1	1	6	2	0
Brown, p	1	0	0	0	1	0
Overall, p	2	0	1	0	1	0
aGessler	0	0	0	0	0	0
Totals	33	3	7	24	10	0

White Sox (AL)	AB	R	H	O	A	E
Hahn, rf	5	2	4	0	0	0
Jones, cf	3	2	0	3	0	0
Isbell, 2b	5	1	3	1	4	0
Davis, ss	5	2	2	1	4	0
Rohe, 3b	5	1	2	3	4	1
Donahue, 1b	4	0	2	15	1	1
Dougherty, lf	3	0	1	0	0	1
Sullivan, c	4	0	0	3	1	0
White, p	3	0	0	1	2	0
Totals	37	8	14	27	16	3

```
Cubs ..................................... 1 0 0  0 1 0  0 0 1—3
White Sox ............................. 3 4 0  0 0 0  0 1 *—8
```

aBatted for Overall in ninth. Two-base hits—Schulte, Overall, Evers, Davis, Donahue. Runs batted in—Donahue 3, Davis 3, Isbell, Dougherty, Hoffman, Schulte, Sheckard. Sacrifice hits—Sheckard, Jones. Stolen base—Rohe. Double play—Davis and Donahue. Earned runs—White Sox 8, Cubs 3. Left on bases—White Sox 9, Cubs 9. Struck out—By Overall 3, by White 2. Bases on balls—Off Brown 1, off Overall 2, off White 4. Hit by pitcher—By White (Chance). Hits—Off Brown 8 in 1⅔ innings, off Overall 6 in 6⅓ innings. Loser—Brown. Umpires—O'Loughlin (AL), Johnstone (NL). Time—1:55. Attendance—19,249.

1906 World Series (continued)

Individual Batting

CHICAGO (AL)

	AB	H	2B	3B	HR	R	RBI	BA
F. Isbell, 2b	26	8	4	0	0	4	4	.308
E. Hahn, of	22	6	0	0	0	4	0	.273
B. Sullivan, c	21	0	0	0	0	0	0	.000
G. Rohe, 3b	21	7	1	2	0	2	4	.333
F. Jones, of	21	2	0	0	0	4	0	.095
P. Dougherty, of	20	2	0	0	0	1	1	.100
J. Donahue, 1b	18	6	2	1	0	0	4	.333
G. Davis, ss	13	4	3	0	0	4	6	.308
L. Tannehill, ss	9	1	0	0	0	1	0	.111
E. Walsh, p	4	0	0	0	0	1	0	.000
N. Altrock, p	4	1	0	0	0	0	0	.250
D. White, p	3	0	0	0	0	0	0	.000
F. Owen, p	2	0	0	0	0	0	0	.000
B. O'Neill, of	1	0	0	0	0	1	0	.000
B. Towne	1	0	0	0	0	0	0	.000
E. McFarland	1	0	0	0	0	0	0	.000

Errors: F. Isbell (5), G. Rohe (3), G. Davis (2), P. Dougherty, J. Donahue, E. Walsh, B. Sullivan. Stolen bases: G. Rohe (2), P. Dougherty (2), F. Isbell, G. Davis.

CHICAGO (NL)

	AB	H	2B	3B	HR	R	RBI	BA
W. Schulte, of	26	7	3	0	0	1	3	.269
S. Hofman, of	23	7	1	0	0	3	2	.304
J. Sheckard, of	21	0	0	0	0	0	1	.000
F. Chance, 1b	21	5	1	0	0	3	0	.238
H. Steinfeldt, 3b	20	5	1	0	0	2	2	.250
J. Evers, 2b	20	3	1	0	0	2	1	.150
J. Tinker, ss	18	3	0	0	0	4	1	.167
J. Kling, c	17	3	1	0	0	2	0	.176
T. Brown, p	6	2	0	0	0	0	0	.333
O. Overall, p	4	1	1	0	0	1	0	.250
E. Reulbach, p	3	0	0	0	0	0	1	.000
P. Moran	2	0	0	0	0	0	0	.000
J. Pfiester, p	2	0	0	0	0	0	0	.000
D. Gessler	1	0	0	0	0	0	0	.000

Errors: J. Tinker (2), H. Steinfeldt, J. Pfiester, J. Kling, J. Evers, T. Brown. Stolen bases: J. Tinker (2), J. Evers (2), F. Chance (2), J. Sheckard, S. Hofman.

Individual Pitching

CHICAGO (AL)

	W	L	ERA	IP	H	BB	SO	SV
N. Altrock	1	1	1.00	18	11	2	5	0
D. White	1	1	1.80	15	12	7	3	1
E. Walsh	2	0	1.80	15	7	6	17	0
F. Owen	0	0	3.00	6	6	3	2	0

CHICAGO (NL)

	W	L	ERA	IP	H	BB	SO	SV
T. Brown	1	2	3.66	19.2	14	4	12	0
O. Overall	0	0	1.50	12	10	3	8	0
E. Reulbach	1	0	2.45	11	6	8	4	0
J. Pfiester	0	2	6.10	10.1	7	3	11	0

1917

Roster of 1917 World Champion White Sox (100-54)

Manager: Clarence "Pants" Rowland

	POS.	G.
Benz, Joseph Louis	P	19
Byrne, Robert Mathew	2B	1
Cicotte, Edward Victor	P	49
Collins, Edward Trowbridge	2B	156
Collins, John Francis (Shano)	OF73	82
Danforth, David Chas.	P	50
Faber, Urban Chas. (Red)	P	41
Felsch, Oscar Emil (Happy)	OF	152
Fournier, Jacques Frank		1
Gandil, Chas. Arnold (Chick)	1B	149
Hasbrouck, Robert Lyndon	2B1	2
Jackson, Joseph Jefferson	OF145	146
Jenkins, Joseph Daniel	C	10
Jourdan, Theodore Chas.	1B14	17
Leibold, Harry Loran (Nemo)	OF122	125
Lynn, Byrd	C29	35
Murphy, Joseph Edward	OF	53
McMullin, Frederick Wm.	3B52	59
Risberg, Chas. August (Swede)	SS146	149
Russell, Ewell Albert (Reb)	P35	39
Schalk, Raymond Wm.	C139	140
Scott, James	P	24
Terry, Zebulon Alexander (Zeb)	SS1	2
Weaver, George Davis (Buck) (SS10)	3B107	118
Williams, Claude Preston	P	45
Wolfgang, Meldon John	P	5

1917 World Series Review

The White Sox, behind future Hall of Famers Red Faber and Eddie Collins, defeated Manager John McGraw's New York Giants, four games to two. Faber became the seventh pitcher in history to record three victories in one Series. Collins hit .409 and was credited with three stolen bases. He also played in his 26th World Series game—a new record at the time.

1917 World Series (continued)

GAME 1

Saturday, October 6—At Chicago

Chicago (AL)	AB	R	H	O	A	E
J. Collins, rf	4	1	3	1	0	0
McMullin, 3b	3	0	1	0	3	0
E. Collins, 2b	3	0	0	2	1	0
Jackson, lf	3	0	0	5	0	0
Felsch, cf	3	1	1	4	0	0
Gandil, 1b	3	0	1	10	1	0
Weaver, ss	3	0	0	2	1	1
Schalk, c	3	0	0	3	0	0
Cicotte, p	3	0	1	0	4	0
Totals	28	2	7	27	10	1

New York (NL)	AB	R	H	O	A	E
Burns, lf	3	0	1	2	0	0
Herzog, 2b	4	0	1	3	1	0
Kauff, cf	4	0	0	0	0	0
Zimmerman, 3b	4	0	0	1	3	0
Fletcher, ss	4	0	0	2	3	0
Robertson, rf	4	0	1	0	1	0
Holke, 1b	3	0	2	14	0	0
McCarty, c	3	1	1	2	1	1
Sallee, p	3	0	1	0	6	0
Totals	32	1	7	24	15	1

```
New York .................................. 0 0 0   0 1 0   0 0 0—1
Chicago  .................................. 0 0 0   1 0 0   0 0 *—2
```

Runs batted in—Sallee, McMullin, Felsch. Two-base hits—McMullin, Robertson, J. Collins. Three-base hit—McCarty. Home run—Felsch. Sacrifice hit—McMullin. Stolen bases—Burns, Gandil. Double play—Weaver, E. Collins and Gandil. Left on bases—New York 5, Chicago 3. Earned runs—Chicago 2, New York 1. Struck out—By Cicotte 2, by Sallee 2. Bases on balls—Off Cicotte 1. Umpires—O'Loughlin (AL), Klem (NL), Rigler (NL) and Evans (AL). Time—1:48. Attendance—32,000.

GAME 2

Sunday, October 7—At Chicago

Chicago (AL)	AB	R	H	O	A	E
J. Collins, rf	1	0	0	0	1	0
aLeibold, rf	3	1	1	0	0	0
McMullin, 3b	5	1	1	0	3	0
E. Collins, 2b	4	1	2	4	2	0
Jackson, lf	3	1	3	0	1	0
Felsch, cf	4	1	1	2	1	0
Gandil, 1b	4	0	1	12	1	0
Weaver, ss	4	1	3	7	6	0
Schalk, c	4	1	1	1	2	1
Faber, p	3	0	1	1	4	0
Totals	35	7	14	27	21	1

New York (NL)	AB	R	H	O	A	E
Burns, lf	3	0	1	0	0	0
Herzog, 2b	4	0	0	3	0	0
Kauff, cf	4	0	0	2	0	0
Zimmerman, 3b	4	0	0	4	2	0
Fletcher, ss	4	0	1	2	2	1
Robertson, rf	3	1	2	2	0	0
Holke, 1b	3	1	1	5	0	0
McCarty, c	1	0	1	5	0	0
Rariden, c	2	0	1	1	3	0
Schupp, p	1	0	0	0	1	0
Anderson, p	0	0	0	0	1	0
Perritt, p	1	0	1	0	0	0
bWilhoit	1	0	0	0	0	0
Tesreau, p	0	0	0	0	0	0
Totals	31	2	8	24	9	1

```
New York ..........................  0 2 0   0 0 0   0 0 0—2
Chicago  ..........................  0 2 0   5 0 0   0 0 *—7
```

aStruck out for J. Collins in second. bLined into double play for Perritt in eighth. Runs batted in—McCarty, Jackson 2, E. Collins, McMullin, Leibold, Weaver, Gandil. Stolen bases—E. Collins 2, Jackson. Double plays—Herzog (unassisted); Faber, Weaver and Gandil; Felsch, E. Collins and Weaver; Weaver and Gandil. Left on bases—Chicago 7, New York 3. Earned runs—Chicago 7, New York 2. Struck out—By Schupp 2, by Anderson 3, by Tesreau 1, by Faber 1. Bases on balls—Off Schupp 1, off Perritt 1, off Tesreau 1, off Faber 1. Hits—Off Schupp 4 in 1⅓ innings, off Anderson 5 in 2 innings, off Perritt 5 in 3⅔ innings, off Tesreau 0 in 1 inning. Passed ball—McCarty. Losing pitcher—Anderson. Umpires—Evans (AL), Rigler (NL), Klem (NL) and O'Loughlin (AL). Time—2:13. Attendance—32,000.

GAME 3

Wednesday, October 10—At New York

New York (NL)	AB	R	H	O	A	E
Burns, lf	4	0	1	1	0	0
Herzog, 2b	4	0	1	1	1	0
Kauff, cf	4	0	0	0	0	0
Zimmerman, 3b	4	0	1	0	3	0
Fletcher, ss	4	0	0	1	4	1
Robertson, rf	4	1	3	1	0	0
Holke, 1b	4	1	1	15	0	1
Rariden, c	2	0	1	7	4	0
Benton, p	3	0	0	1	2	0
Totals	33	2	8	27	14	2

Chicago (AL)	AB	R	H	O	A	E
J. Collins, rf	4	0	0	1	0	2
McMullin, 3b	4	0	0	0	1	0
E. Collins, 2b	4	0	2	3	2	0
Jackson, lf	4	0	0	0	0	0
Felsch, cf	3	0	1	5	0	0
Gandil, 1b	3	0	0	6	0	0
Weaver, ss	3	0	2	0	2	0
Schalk, c	3	0	0	9	0	0
Cicotte, p	3	0	0	0	1	1
Totals	31	0	5	24	6	3

```
Chicago ................................. 0 0 0  0 0 0  0 0 0—0
New York ............................... 0 0 0  2 0 0  0 0 *—2
```

Runs batted in—Holke, Burns. Two-base hits—Holke, Weaver. Three-base hit—Robertson. Sacrifice hit—Rariden. Stolen base—Robertson. Double play—Rariden and Herzog. Left on bases—New York 8, Chicago 4. Earned runs—New York 2. Struck out—By Cicotte 8, by Benton 5. Umpires—Klem (NL), O'Loughlin (AL), Evans (AL) and Rigler (NL). Time—1:55. Attendance—33,616.

GAME 4

Thursday, October 11—At New York

Chicago (AL)	AB	R	H	O	A	E
J. Collins, rf	4	0	2	0	0	0
McMullin, 3b	4	0	1	1	2	0
E. Collins, 2b	3	0	1	0	6	0
Jackson, lf	4	0	0	0	0	0
Felsch, cf	4	0	0	2	1	0
Gandil, 1b	4	0	1	15	0	0
Weaver, ss	3	0	0	0	1	0
Schalk, c	3	0	2	6	3	0
Faber, p	2	0	0	0	4	0
aRisberg	1	0	0	0	0	0
Danforth, p	0	0	0	0	1	0
Totals	32	0	7	24	18	0

New York (NL)	AB	R	H	O	A	E
Burns, lf	4	0	1	2	0	0
Herzog, 2b	3	1	1	3	4	1
Kauff, cf	4	2	2	1	0	0
Zimmerman, 3b	4	0	1	2	2	0
Fletcher, ss	4	1	2	1	3	0
Robertson, rf	3	1	1	1	0	0
Holke, 1b	2	0	1	9	0	0
Rariden, c	3	0	0	7	1	0
Schupp, p	3	0	1	1	3	0
Totals	30	5	10	27	13	1

```
Chicago ............................. 0 0 0   0 0 0   0 0 0—0
New York ............................ 0 0 0   1 1 0   1 2 *—5
```

aFlied out for Faber in eighth. Runs batted in—Kauff 3, Schupp, Rariden. two-base hit—E. Collins. Three-base hit—Zimmerman. Home runs—Kauff 2. Sacrifice hit—Herzog. Stolen base—E. Collins. Double plays—Herzog, Fletcher and Holke; Faber, Schalk and Gandil. Left on bases—Chicago 6, New York 3. Earned runs—New York 5. Struck out—By Faber 3, by Danforth 2, by Schupp 7. Bases on balls—Off Schupp 1. Hit by pitcher—By Faber (Holke). Wild pitch—Faber. Hits—Off Faber 7 in 7 innings, off Danforth 3 in 1 inning. Losing pitcher—Faber. Umpires—Rigler (NL), Evans (AL), O'Loughlin (AL) and Klem (NL). Time—2:09. Attendance—27,746.

GAME 5

Saturday, October 13—At Chicago

New York (NL)	AB	R	H	O	A	E
Burns, lf	4	2	1	3	0	0
Herzog, 2b	5	0	1	0	1	1
Kauff, cf	5	0	2	2	0	0
Zimmerman, 3b	5	1	1	1	2	1
Fletcher, ss	5	1	1	2	3	1
Thorpe, rf	0	0	0	0	0	0
Robertson, rf	5	0	3	2	0	0
Holke, 1b	5	0	0	11	0	0
Rariden, c	3	1	3	3	1	0
Sallee, p	3	0	0	0	2	0
Perritt, p	0	0	0	0	0	0
Totals	40	5	12	24	9	3

Chicago (AL)	AB	R	H	O	A	E
J. Collins, rf	5	1	1	1	0	1
McMullin, 3b	3	0	0	1	4	0
E. Collins, 2b	4	2	3	1	4	0
Jackson, lf	5	2	3	3	0	0
Felsch, cf	5	1	3	0	0	0
Gandil, 1b	5	1	1	10	2	1
Weaver, ss	4	1	1	2	2	3
Schalk, c	3	0	1	9	0	0
Russell, p	0	0	0	0	0	0
Cicotte, p	1	0	0	0	2	0
aRisberg	1	0	1	0	0	0
Williams, p	0	0	0	0	0	1
bLynn	1	0	0	0	0	0
Faber, p	0	0	0	0	1	0
Totals	37	8	14	27	15	6

```
New York .............................. 2 0 0  2 0 0  1 0 0—5
Chicago  .............................. 0 0 1  0 0 1  3 3 *—8
```

aSingled for Cicotte in sixth. bFanned for Williams in seventh. Runs batted in—Kauff 2, Robertson, Rariden, Burns, Felsch 2, Gandil 2, Risberg, E. Collins. Two-base hits—Kauff, Felsch, Fletcher, Gandil. Sacrifice hits—Sallee, McMullin. Stolen bases—Kauff, Robertson, Schalk. Double plays—McMullin and Gandil; McMullin, E. Collins and Gandil. Left on bases—New York 11, Chicago 10. Earned runs—Chicago 7, New York 4. Struck out—By Cicotte 3, by Williams 3, by Faber 1, by Sallee 2. Bases on balls—Off Russell 1, off Cicotte 1, off Sallee 4. Hits—Off Russell 2 in 0 innings (pitched to three batters in first inning), off Cicotte 8 in 6 innings, off Williams 2 in 1 inning, off Faber 0 in 2 innings, off Sallee 13 in 7⅓ innings, off Perritt 1 in ⅔ inning. Winning pitcher—Faber. Losing pitcher—Sallee. Umpires—O'Loughlin (AL), Klem (NL), Rigler (NL) and Evans (AL). Time—2:37. Attendance—27,323.

GAME 6

Monday, October 15—At New York

Chicago (AL)	AB	R	H	O	A	E
J. Collins, rf	3	0	0	1	0	0
bLeibold, rf	2	0	1	1	0	0
McMullin, 3b	5	0	0	0	1	0
E. Collins, 2b	4	1	1	1	8	0
Jackson, lf	4	1	1	1	0	0
Felsch, cf	3	1	0	3	0	0
Gandil, 1b	4	0	2	14	0	0
Weaver, ss	4	1	1	2	2	0
Schalk, c	3	0	1	4	1	1
Faber, p	2	0	0	0	0	0
Totals	34	4	7	27	12	1

New York (NL)	AB	R	H	O	A	E
Burns, lf	4	1	0	2	0	0
Herzog, 2b	4	0	2	2	5	0
Kauff, cf	4	0	0	2	0	1
Zimmerman, 3b	4	0	0	1	2	1
Fletcher, ss	4	0	1	1	2	0
Robertson, rf	3	0	1	0	1	1
Holke, 1b	4	0	1	12	0	0
Rariden, c	3	1	0	7	1	0
Benton, p	1	0	0	0	0	0
aWilhoit	0	0	0	0	0	0
Perritt, p	1	0	1	0	1	0
cMcCarty	1	0	0	0	0	0
Totals	33	2	6	27	12	3

```
Chicago  ...............................  0 0 0  3 0 0  0 0 1—4
New York ...............................  0 0 0  0 2 0  0 0 0—2
```

aWalked for Benton in fifth. bPopped up for J. Collins in seventh. cGrounded out for Perritt in ninth. Runs batted in—Herzog 2, Gandil 2, Leibold. Two-base hit—Holke. Three-base hit—Herzog. Sacrifice hit—Faber. Left on bases—Chicago 7, New York 7. Earned runs—New York 2, Chicago 1. Struck out—By Faber 4, by Benton 3, by Perritt 3. Bases on balls—Off Faber 2, off Benton 1, off Perritt 2. Hit by pitcher—By Faber (Robertson). Hits—Off Benton 4 in 5 innings, off Perritt 3 in 4 innings. Passed ball—Schalk. Losing pitcher—Benton. Umpires—Klem (NL), O'Loughlin (AL), Evans (AL) and Rigler (NL). Time—2:18. Attendance—33,969.

1917 World Series (continued)

Individual Batting

CHICAGO (AL)

	AB	H	2B	3B	HR	R	RBI	BA
F. McMullin, 3b	24	3	1	0	0	1	2	.125
J. Jackson, of	23	7	0	0	0	4	2	.304
C. Gandil, 1b	23	6	1	0	0	1	5	.261
H. Felsch, of	22	6	1	0	1	4	3	.273
E. Collins, 2b	22	9	1	0	0	4	2	.409
S. Collins, of	21	6	1	0	0	2	0	.286
B. Weaver, ss	21	7	1	0	0	3	1	.333
R. Schalk, c	19	5	0	0	0	1	0	.263
E. Cicotte, p	7	1	0	0	0	0	0	.143
R. Faber, p	7	1	0	0	0	0	0	.143
N. Leibold, of	5	2	0	0	0	1	2	.400
S. Risberg	2	1	0	0	0	0	1	.500
B. Lynn	1	0	0	0	0	0	0	.000

Errors: B. Weaver (4), S. Collins (3), R. Schalk (2), L. Williams, C. Gandil, E. Cicotte. Stolen bases: E. Collins (3), R. Schalk, C. Gandil, J. Jackson.

NEW YORK (NL)

	AB	H	2B	3B	HR	R	RBI	BA
H. Zimmerman, 3b	25	3	0	1	0	1	0	.120
A. Fletcher, ss	25	5	1	0	0	2	0	.200
B. Kauff, of	25	4	1	0	2	2	5	.160
B. Herzog, 2b	24	6	0	1	0	1	2	.250
D. Robertson, of	22	11	1	1	0	3	1	.500
G. Burns, of	22	5	0	0	0	3	2	.227
W. Holke, 1b	21	6	2	0	0	2	1	.286
B. Rariden, c	13	5	0	0	0	2	2	.385
S. Sallee, p	6	1	0	0	0	0	1	.167
L. McCarty, c	5	2	0	1	0	1	1	.400
F. Schupp, p	4	1	0	0	0	0	1	.250
R. Benton, p	4	0	0	0	0	0	0	.000
P. Perritt, p	2	2	0	0	0	0	0	1,000
J. Wilhoit	1	0	0	0	0	0	0	.000
J. Thorpe, of	0	0	0	0	0	0	—	

Errors: A. Fletcher (3), B. Herzog (2), H. Zimmerman (2), L. McCarty, W. Holke, B. Kauff, D. Robertson. Stolen bases: D. Robertson (2), G. Burns, B. Kauff.

Individual Pitching

CHICAGO (AL)

	W	L	ERA	IP	H	BB	SO	SV
R. Faber	3	1	2.33	27	21	3	9	0
E. Cicotte	1	1	1.96	23	23	2	13	0
D. Danforth	0	0	18.00	1	3	0	2	0
L. Williams	0	0	9.00	1	2	0	3	0
R. Russell	0	0	0.00	0.0	2	1	0	0

NEW YORK (NL)

	W	L	ERA	IP	H	BB	SO	SV
S. Sallee	0	2	4.70	15.1	20	4	4	0
R. Benton	1	1	0.00	14	9	1	8	0
F. Schupp	1	0	1.74	10.1	11	2	9	0
P. Perritt	0	0	2.16	8.1	9	3	3	0
F. Anderson	0	1	18.00	2	5	0	3	0
J. Tesreau	0	0	0.00	1	0	1	1	0

1919

Roster of 1919 American League Champion White Sox (88-52)

Manager: Kid Gleason

	POS.	G.
Benz, Joseph Louis	P	1
Cicotte, Edward Victor	P	40
Collins, Edward Trowbridge	2B	140
Collins, John Francis (Shano)	OF46	63
Danforth, David Chas.	P	15
Faber, Urban Chas. (Red)	P	25
Felsch, Oscar Emil (Happy)	OF	135
Gandil, Chas. Arnold (Chick)	1B	115
Jackson, Joseph Jefferson	OF	139
James, Wm. Henry	P	5
Jenkins, Joseph Daniel	C	11
Kerr, Richard Henry (Dickey)	P	39
Leibold, Harry Loran (Nemo)	OF	122
Lowdermilk, Grover Cleveland	P	20
Lynn, Byrd	C28	29
Mayer, James Erskine	P	6
Murphy, Joseph Edward	OF	30
McClellan, Harvey McDowell	INF	7
McGuire, Thomas Patrick	P	1
McMullin, Frederick Wm.	3B40	60
Noyes, Winfield Chas.	P	1
Ragan, Don Carlos Patrick (Pat)	P	1
Risberg, Chas. August (Swede) (1B22)	SS97	119
Robertson, Chas. Culbertson	P	1
Russell, Ewell Albert (Reb)	P	1
Schalk, Raymond Wm.	C129	131
Shellenback, Frank Victor	P	8
Sullivan, John Jeremiah	P	4
Weaver, George Davis (Buck) (SS43)	3B97	140
Wilkinson, Roy Hamilton	P	4
Williams, Claude Preston	P	41

World Series Review

The 1919 World Series turned out to be the darkest chapter in the game's history. The favored White Sox lost the Series to Cincinnati, five games to three, and it was subsequently charged that eight Sox players had arranged with gamblers to throw games. The eight players were Joe Jackson, Happy Felsch, Chick Gandil, Buck Weaver, Swede Risberg, Fred McMullin, Eddie Cicotte and Claude Williams.

Dickie Kerr, the White Sox star lefthanded pitcher, came out of the Series a hero. He won two of the Sox's three games, including a three-hit shutout.

GAME 1

Wednesday, October 1—At Cincinnati

Chicago (AL)	AB	R	H	O	A	E
J. Collins, rf	4	0	1	0	0	0
E. Collins, rf	4	0	1	3	3	0
Weaver, 3b	4	0	1	0	1	0
Jackson, lf	4	1	0	3	0	0
Felsch, cf	3	0	0	4	0	0
Gandil, 1b	4	0	2	7	0	1
Risberg, ss	2	0	0	5	6	0
Schalk, c	3	0	0	2	2	0
Cicotte, p	1	0	0	0	3	0
Wilkinson, p	1	0	0	0	0	0
aMcMullin	1	0	1	0	0	0
Lowdermilk, p	0	0	0	0	1	0
Totals	31	1	6	24	16	1

Cincinnati (NL)	AB	R	H	O	A	E
Rath, 2b	3	2	1	4	2	0
Daubert, 1b	4	1	3	9	0	0
Groh, 3b	3	1	1	0	3	0
Roush, cf	3	0	0	8	0	0
Duncan, lf	4	0	2	1	0	0
Kopf, ss	4	1	0	1	3	1
Neale, rf	4	2	3	3	0	0
Wingo, c	3	1	1	1	2	0
Ruether, p	3	1	3	0	2	0
Totals	31	9	14	27	12	1

Chicago	0 1 0	0 0 0	0 0 0—1
Cincinnati	1 0 0	5 0 0	2 1 *—9

aSingled for Wilkinson in eighth. Runs batted in—Gandil, Rath, Daubert, Groh 2, Duncan, Wingo, Ruether 3. Two-base hit—Rath. Three-base hits—Ruether 2, Daubert. Sacrifice hits—Felsch, Rath, Roush, Wingo. Sacrifice fly—Groh. Stolen base—Roush. Double plays—Risberg and E. Collins; Risberg, E. Collins and Gandil. Left on bases—Cincinnati 7, Chicago 5. Earned runs—Cincinnati 8, Chicago 0. Struck out—By Cicotte 1, by Wilkinson 1, by Ruether 1. Bases on balls—Off Cicotte 2, off Lowdermilk 1, off Ruether 1. Hit by pitcher—By Cicotte (Rath), by Lowdermilk (Daubert). Hits—Off Cicotte 7 in 3⅔ innings, off Wilkinson 5 in 3⅓ innings, off Lowdermilk 2 in 1 inning. Losing pitcher—Cicotte. Umpires—Rigler (NL), Evans (AL), Nallin (AL) and Quigley (NL). Time—1:42. Attendance—30,511.

GAME 2

Thursday, October 2—At Cincinnati

Cincinnati (NL)	AB	R	H	O	A	E
Rath, 2b	3	1	0	1	2	0
Daubert, 1b	3	0	0	12	2	1
Groh, 3b	2	1	0	0	1	0
Roush, cf	2	1	1	5	0	0
Duncan, lf	1	1	0	1	0	0
Kopf, ss	3	0	1	3	6	0
Neale, rf	3	0	1	1	0	1
Rariden, c	3	0	1	3	0	0
Sallee, p	3	0	0	1	3	0
Totals	23	4	4	27	14	2

Chicago (AL)	AB	R	H	O	A	E
J. Collins, rf	4	0	0	2	0	0
E. Collins, 2b	3	0	0	2	3	0
Weaver, 3b	4	0	2	3	0	0
Jackson, lf	4	0	3	1	0	0
Felsch, cf	2	0	0	5	1	0
Gandil, 1b	4	0	1	7	0	0
Risberg, ss	4	1	1	2	2	1
Schalk, c	4	1	2	2	2	0
Williams, p	3	0	1	0	2	0
aMcMullin	1	0	0	0	0	0
Totals	33	2	10	24	10	1

```
Chicago    ................................ 0 0 0  0 0 0  2 0 0—2
Cincinnati ................................ 0 0 0  3 0 1  0 0 *—4
```

aGrounded out for Williams in ninth. Runs batted in—Roush, Kopf 2, Neale. Two-base hits—Jackson, Weaver. Three base hit—Kopf. Sacrifice hits—Felsch 2, Daubert, Duncan. Stolen base—Gandil. Double plays—Kopf and Daubert; E. Collins and Gandil; Felsch, E. Collins and Gandil; Rath, Kopf and Daubert. Left on bases— Chicago 7, Cincinnati 3. Earned runs—Cincinnati 4, Chicago 0. Struck out—By Williams 1, by Sallee 2. Bases on balls—Off Williams 6, off Sallee 1. Balk—Sallee. Umpires—Evans (AL), Quigley (NL), Nallin (AL) and Rigler (NL). Time—1:42. Attendance—29,690.

GAME 3

Friday, October 3—At Chicago

Cincinnati (NL)	AB	R	H	O	A	E
Rath, 2b	4	0	0	3	3	0
Daubert, 1b	4	0	0	14	1	0
Groh, 3b	3	0	0	2	5	0
Roush, cf	3	0	0	0	0	0
Duncan, lf	3	0	1	0	0	0
Kopf, ss	3	0	1	1	1	0
Neale, rf	3	0	0	1	0	0
Rariden, c	3	0	0	2	3	0
Fisher, p	2	0	1	0	5	1
aMagee	1	0	0	0	0	0
Luque, p	0	0	0	1	0	0
Totals	29	0	3	24	18	1

Chicago (AL)	AB	R	H	O	A	E
Leibold, rf	4	0	0	2	0	0
E. Collins, 2b	4	0	1	1	5	0
Weaver, 3b	4	0	1	0	4	0
Jackson, lf	3	1	2	1	0	0
Felsch, cf	2	1	0	1	0	0
Gandil, 1b	3	0	1	14	1	0
Risberg, ss	2	1	1	4	6	0
Schalk, c	3	0	1	4	0	0
Kerr, p	3	0	0	0	0	0
Totals	28	3	7	27	16	0

Cincinnati	0 0 0	0 0 0	0 0 0—0
Chicago	0 2 0	1 0 0	0 0 *—3

aFlied out for Fisher in eighth. Runs batted in—Gandil 2, Schalk. Three-base hit—Risberg. Double plays—Groh, Rath and Daubert; Risberg and E. Collins. Left on bases—Cincinnati 3, Chicago 3. Earned runs—Chicago 2. Struck out—by Kerr 4, by Fisher 1, by Luque 1. Bases on balls—Off Fisher 2, off Kerr 1. Hits—Off Fisher 7 in 7 innings, off Luque 0 in 1 inning. Losing pitcher—Fisher. Umpires—Quigley (NL), Nallin (AL), Rigler (NL) and Evans (AL). Time—1:30. Attendance—29,126.

GAME 4

Saturday, October 4—At Chicago

Cincinnati (NL)	AB	R	H	O	A	E
Rath, 2b	4	0	1	5	1	1
Daubert, 1b	4	0	0	9	1	0
Groh, 3b	4	0	0	2	3	1
Roush, cf	3	0	0	2	0	0
Duncan, lf	3	1	0	1	0	0
Kopf, ss	3	1	1	1	1	0
Neale, rf	3	0	1	4	0	0
Wingo, c	3	0	2	2	0	0
Ring, p	3	0	0	1	2	0
Totals	30	2	5	27	8	2

Chicago (AL)	AB	R	H	O	A	E
Leibold, rf	5	0	0	0	0	0
E. Collins, 2b	3	0	0	3	5	0
Weaver, 3b	4	0	0	0	3	0
Jackson, lf	4	0	1	3	0	0
Felsch, cf	3	0	1	0	0	0
Gandil, 1b	4	0	1	14	0	0
Risberg, ss	3	0	0	3	4	0
Schalk, c	1	0	0	4	3	0
Cicotte, p	3	0	0	0	2	2
aMurphy	1	0	0	0	0	0
Totals	31	0	3	27	17	2

```
Cincinnati  .............................. 0 0 0  0 2 0  0 0 0—2
Chicago     .............................. 0 0 0  0 0 0  0 0 0—0
```

aFlied out for Cicotte in ninth. Runs batted in—Kopf, Neale. Two-base hits—Jackson, Neale. Sacrifice hit—Felsch. Stolen base—Risberg. Double plays—Cicotte, Risberg and Gandil; E. Collins, Risberg and Gandil. Left on bases—Chicago 10, Cincinnati 1. Earned runs—Cincinnati 0. Struck out—By Cicotte 2, by Ring 2. Bases on balls—Off Ring 3. Hit by pitcher—By Ring (E. Collins, Schalk). Umpires—Nallin (AL), Rigler (NL), Evans (AL) and Quigley (NL). Time—1:37. Attendance—34,363.

1919 World Series (continued)

GAME 5

Monday, October 6—At Chicago

Cincinnati (NL)	AB	R	H	O	A	E
Rath, 2b	3	1	1	0	3	0
Daubert, 1b	2	0	0	11	0	0
Groh, 3b	3	1	0	1	2	0
Roush, cf	4	2	1	2	0	0
Duncan, lf	2	0	0	2	0	0
Kopf, ss	3	0	1	0	4	0
Neale, rf	4	0	0	1	0	0
Rariden, c	4	0	0	10	0	0
Eller, p	3	1	1	0	2	0
Totals	28	5	4	27	11	0

Chicago (AL)	AB	R	H	O	A	E
Leibold, rf	3	0	0	1	0	0
E. Collins, 2b	4	0	0	1	2	1
Weaver, 3b	4	0	2	1	2	0
Jackson, lf	4	0	0	3	0	0
Felsch, cf	3	0	0	7	0	1
Gandil, 1b	3	0	0	8	1	0
Risberg, ss	3	0	0	1	2	1
Schalk, c	2	0	1	3	2	0
Lynn, c	1	0	0	1	0	0
Williams, p	2	0	0	1	0	0
aMurphy	1	0	0	0	0	0
Mayer, p	0	0	0	0	0	0
Totals	30	0	3	27	9	3

Cincinnati	000 004 001—5
Chicago	000 000 000—0

aFanned for Williams in eighth. Runs batted in—Rath, Roush 2, Duncan, Neale. Two-base hit—Eller. Three-base hits—Roush, Weaver. Sacrifice hits—Daubert 2, Kopf. Sacrifice fly—Duncan. Stolen base—Roush. Left on bases—Chicago 4, Cincinnati 3. Earned runs—Cincinnati 4. Struck out—By Williams 3, by Eller 9. Bases on balls—Off Williams 2, off Mayer 1, off Eller 1. Passed ball—Schalk. Hits—Off Williams 4 in 8 innings, off Mayer 0 in 1 inning. Losing pitcher—Williams. Umpires—Rigler (NL), Evans (AL), Quigley (NL) and Nallin (AL). Time—1:45. Attendance—34,379.

GAME 6

Tuesday, October 7—At Cincinnati

Chicago (AL)	AB	R	H	O	A	E
J. Collins, rf	3	0	0	2	0	0
aLeibold, rf	1	0	0	0	0	0
E. Collins, 2b	4	0	0	4	6	0
Weaver, 3b	5	2	3	2	1	0
Jackson, lf	4	1	2	1	1	0
Felsch, cf	5	1	2	2	0	1
Gandil, 1b	4	0	1	11	0	0
Risberg, ss	4	1	0	3	5	2
Schalk, c	2	0	1	4	2	0
Kerr, p	3	0	1	1	4	0
Totals	35	5	10	30	19	3

Cincinnati (NL)	AB	R	H	O	A	E
Rath, 2b	5	0	1	4	1	0
Daubert, 1b	4	1	2	8	0	0
Groh, 3b	4	0	1	2	2	0
Roush, cf	4	1	1	7	2	0
Duncan, lf	5	0	1	2	0	0
Kopf, ss	4	0	0	1	5	0
Neale, rf	4	1	3	3	0	0
Rariden, c	4	0	1	3	0	0
Ruether, p	2	1	1	0	0	0
Ring, p	2	0	0	0	1	0
Totals	38	4	11	30	11	0

```
Chicago ........................... 0 0 0   0 1 3   0 0 0   1—5
Cincinnati ........................ 0 0 2   2 0 0   0 0 0   0—4
```

aGrounded out for J. Collins in seventh. Runs batted in—E. Collins, Jackson, Felsch, Gandil, Schalk, Duncan 2, Ruether. Two-base hits—Groh, Duncan, Ruether, Weaver 2, Felsch. Three-base hit—Neale. Sacrifice hits—Daubert, Kerr. Sacrifice fly—E. Collins. Stolen bases—Leibold, Schalk, Rath, Daubert. Double plays—Jackson and Schalk; Roush and Groh; Risberg, E. Collins and Gandil, Roush and Rath; Kopf and Rath. Left on bases—Cincinnati 8, Chicago 8. Earned runs—Chicago 5, Cincinnati 3. Struck out—By Ring 2, by Kerr 2. Bases on balls—Off Ruether 3, off Ring 3, off Kerr 2. Hit by pitcher—By Kerr (Roush). Hits—Off Ruether 6 in 5 (pitched to three batters in sixth inning), off Ring 4 in 5 innings. Losing pitcher—Ring. Umpires—Evans (AL), Quigley (NL), Nallin (AL) and Rigler (NL). Time—2:06. Attendance—32,006.

GAME 7

Wednesday, October 8—At Cincinnati

Chicago (AL)	AB	R	H	O	A	E
J. Collins, cf-rf	5	2	3	1	0	0
E. Collins, 2b	4	1	2	3	6	1
Weaver, 3b	4	1	0	2	2	0
Jackson, lf	4	0	2	3	0	0
Felsch, rf-cf	4	0	2	2	0	0
Gandil, 1b	4	0	0	9	0	0
Risberg, ss	4	0	0	3	2	0
Schalk, c	4	0	1	4	1	0
Cicotte, p	4	0	0	0	2	0
Totals	37	4	10	27	13	1

Cincinnati (NL)	AB	R	H	O	A	E
Rath, 2b	5	0	1	3	3	1
Daubert, 1b	4	0	0	10	1	1
Groh, 3b	4	1	1	0	2	1
Roush, cf	4	0	0	3	1	1
Duncan, lf	4	0	1	1	1	0
Kopf, ss	4	0	1	2	5	0
Neale, rf	4	0	1	3	0	0
Wingo, c	1	0	1	5	1	0
Sallee, p	1	0	0	0	1	0
Fisher, p	0	0	0	0	1	0
aRuether	1	0	0	0	0	0
Luque, p	1	0	0	0	0	0
bMagee	1	0	1	0	0	0
cSmith	0	0	0	0	0	0
Totals	34	1	7	27	16	4

```
Chicago ............................... 1 0 1  0 2 0  0 0 0—4
Cincinnati ............................. 0 0 0  0 0 1  0 0 0—1
```

aFouled out for Fisher in fifth. bSingled for Luque in ninth. cRan for Magee in ninth. Runs batted in—Jackson 2, Felsch 2, Duncan. Two-base hits—J. Collins, Groh. Sacrifice hits—E. Collins. Double play—Kopf and Daubert. Left on bases—Cincinnati 9, Chicago 7. Earned runs—Chicago 2, Cincinnati 1. Struck out—By Cicotte 4, by Fisher 1, by Luque 5. Bases on balls—Off Cicotte 3. Hits—Off Sallee 9 in 4⅓ innings, off Fisher 0 in ⅔ inning, off Luque 1 in 4 innings. Losing pitcher—Sallee. Umpires—Quigley (NL), Nallin (AL), Rigler (NL) and Evans (AL). Time—1:47. Attendance—13,923.

Thursday, October 9—At Chicago

Cincinnati (NL)	AB	R	H	O	A	E
Rath, 2b	4	1	2	2	2	0
Daubert, 1b	4	2	2	8	0	0
Groh, 3b	6	2	2	1	1	0
Roush, cf	5	2	3	3	0	1
Duncan, lf	4	1	2	1	0	0
Kopf, ss	3	1	1	1	3	0
Neale, rf	3	0	1	4	0	0
Rariden, c	5	0	2	7	0	1
Eller, p	4	1	1	0	0	0
Totals	38	10	16	27	6	2

Chicago (AL)	AB	R	H	O	A	E
Leibold, cf	5	0	1	2	2	0
E. Collins, 2b	5	1	3	4	1	0
Weaver, 3b	5	1	2	1	5	0
Jackson, lf	5	2	2	1	0	0
Felsch, rf	4	0	0	2	0	0
Gandil, 1b	4	1	1	9	0	0
Risberg, ss	3	0	0	2	3	0
Schalk, c	4	0	1	6	3	1
Williams, p	0	0	0	0	0	0
James, p	2	0	0	0	0	0
Wilkinson, p	1	0	0	0	2	0
aMurphy	0	0	0	0	0	0
Totals	38	5	10	27	16	1

```
Cincinnati .............................. 4 1 0  0 1 3  0 1 0—10
Chicago .................................. 0 0 1  0 0 0  0 4 0— 5
```

aHit by pitcher for Wilkinson in ninth. Runs batted in—Roush 4, Duncan 3, Neale, Rariden 2, Jackson 3, Gandil. Two-base hits—Roush 2, E. Collins, Duncan, Weaver, Jackson. Three-base hits—Kopf, Gandil. Home run—Jackson. Sacrifice hits—Duncan, Daubert. Stolen bases—Neale, Rath, Rariden, E. Collins. Left on bases—Cincinnati 12, Chicago 8. Earned runs—Cincinnati 7, Chicago 4. Struck out—By James 2, by Wilkinson 2, by Eller 6. Bases on balls—Off James 3, off Wilkinson 4, off Eller 1. Hit by pitcher—By James (Eller), by Wilkinson (Roush), by Eller (Murphy). Hits—Off Williams 4 in $\frac{1}{3}$ inning, off James 8 in $4\frac{2}{3}$ innings (pitched to two batters in sixth innings), off Wilkinson 4 in 4 innings. Losing pitcher—Williams. Umpires—Quigley (NL), Nallin (AL), Rigler (NL) and Evans (AL). Time—2:27. Attendance—32,930.

1919 World Series (continued)

Individual Batting

CINCINNATI (NL)

	AB	H	2B	3B	HR	R	RBI	BA
M. Rath, 2b	31	7	1	0	0	5	2	.226
J. Daubert, 1b	29	7	0	1	0	4	1	.241
H. Groh, 3b	29	5	2	0	0	6	2	.172
G. Neale, of	28	10	1	1	0	3	4	.357
E. Roush, of	28	6	2	1	0	6	7	.214
L. Kopf, ss	27	6	0	2	0	3	2	.222
P. Duncan, of	26	7	2	0	0	3	8	.269
B. Rariden, c	19	4	0	0	0	0	2	.211
H. Eller, p	7	2	1	0	0	2	0	.286
I. Wingo, c	7	4	0	0	0	1	1	.571
D. Ruether, p	6	4	1	2	0	2	4	.667
J. Ring, p	5	0	0	0	0	0	0	.000
S. Sallee, p	4	0	0	0	0	0	0	.000
S. Magee	2	1	0	0	0	0	0	.500
R. Fisher, p	2	1	0	0	0	0	0	.500
D. Luque, p	1	0	0	0	0	0	0	.000
J. Smith	0	0	0	0	0	0	—	

Errors: M. Rath (2), J. Daubert (2), E. Roush (2), H. Groh (2), R. Fisher, B. Rariden, G. Neale, L. Kopf. Stolen bases: E. Roush (2), M. Rath (2), G. Neale, J. Daubert, B. Rariden.

CHICAGO (AL)

	AB	H	2B	3B	HR	R	RBI	BA
B. Weaver, 3b	34	11	4	1	0	4	0	.324
J. Jackson, of	32	12	3	0	1	5	6	.375
E. Collins, 2b	31	7	1	0	0	2	1	.226
C. Gandil, 1b	30	7	0	1	0	1	5	.233
H. Felsch, of	26	5	1	0	0	2	3	.192
S. Risberg, ss	25	2	0	1	0	3	0	.080
R. Schalk, c	23	7	0	0	0	1	2	.304
N. Leibold, of	18	1	0	0	0	0	0	.056
S. Collins, of	16	4	1	0	0	2	0	.250
E. Cicotte, p	8	0	0	0	0	0	0	.000
D. Kerr, p	6	1	0	0	0	0	0	.167
L. Williams, p	5	1	0	0	0	0	0	.200
R. Wilkinson, p	2	0	0	0	0	0	0	.000
F. McMullin	2	1	0	0	0	0	0	.500
B. James, p	2	0	0	0	0	0	0	.000
E. Murphy	2	0	0	0	0	0	0	.000
B. Lynn, c	1	0	0	0	0	0	0	.000

Errors: S. Risberg (4), E. Cicotte (2), H. Felsch (2), E. Collins (2), C. Gandil, R. Schalk. Stolen bases: E. Collins, N. Leibold, S. Risberg, R. Schalk, C. Gandil.

Individual Pitching

CINCINNATI (NL)

	W	L	ERA	IP	H	BB	SO	SV
H. Eller	2	0	2.00	18	13	2	15	0
D. Ruether	1	0	2.57	14	12	4	1	0
J. Ring	1	1	0.64	14	7	6	4	0
S. Sallee	1	1	1.35	13.1	19	1	2	0
R. Fisher	0	1	2.35	7.2	7	2	2	0
D. Luque	0	0	0.00	5	1	0	6	0

CHICAGO (AL)

	W	L	ERA	IP	H	BB	SO	SV
E. Cicotte	1	2	2.91	21.2	19	5	7	0
D. Kerr	2	0	1.42	19	14	3	6	0
L. Williams	0	3	6.61	16.1	12	8	4	0
R. Wilkinson	0	0	3.68	7.1	9	4	3	0
B. James	0	0	5.79	4.2	8	3	2	0
E. Mayer	0	0	0.00	1	0	1	0	0
G. Lowdermilk	0	0	9.00	1	2	1	0	0

1959

Roster of 1959 American League Champion White Sox (94-60)

Manager: Al Lopez

	POS.	G.
Aparicio, Luis Ernesto	SS	152
Arias, Rodolfo Martinez	P	34
Battey, Earl Jesse	C20	26
Boone, Raymond Otis	1B6	9
Callison, John Wesley	OF41	49
Carreon, Camilo Garcia	C	1
Cash, Norman Dalton	1B31	58
Doby, Lawrence Eugene (1B2)	OF12	21
Donovan, Richard Edward	P	31
Ennis, Delmer	OF25	26
Esposito, Samuel (2B2 SS14)	3B45	69
Fox, Jacob Nelson	2B	156
Goodman, Wm. Dale (2B3)	3B74	104
Hicks, Wm. Joseph	OF4	6
Jackson, Ronald Allen	1B5	10
Kluszewski, Theodore Bernard	1B29	31
Landis, James Henry	OF148	149
Latman, Arnold Barry	P	37
Lollar, John Sherman (1B24)	C122	140
Lown, Omar Joseph	P	60
Martin, Joseph Clifton	3B2	3
McAnany, James	OF	67
McBride, Kenneth Faye	P	11
Moore, Raymond LeRoy	P	29
Mueller, Donald Frederick	OF	4

1959 World Series (continued)

Peters, Gary Chas.	P	2
Phillips, John Melvin (OF23)	3B100	117
Pierce, Walter Wm.	P	34
Raymond, Joseph Claude Marc	P	3
Rivera, Manuel Joseph	OF69	80
Romano, John Anthony	C38	53
Rudolph, Frederick Donald	P	4
Shaw, Robert John	P	47
Simpson, Harry Leon (1B1)	OF12	38
Skizas, Louis Peter	OF6	8
Smith, Alphonse Eugene (3B1)	OF128	129
Staley, Gerald Lee	P	67
Stanka, Joe Donald	P	2
Torgeson, Clifford Earl	1B103	127
Wynn, Early	P	37

1959 World Series Review

Participating in their first World Series in 40 years, the "Go Go Sox," whose pitching speed and defense enabled them to win the AL flag, were defeated four games to two in the fall classic.

Ted Kluszewski, acquired from Pittsburgh in August, was the batting star with a .391 average, three home runs and 10 runs batted in. He clubbed two homers in the opening game, which saw the Sox win, 11–0, behind Early Wynn's standout pitching.

Larry Sherry, the Dodgers' bullpen ace, was the key to the Dodgers' success. He won two games and saved two others.

Playing in the huge Los Angeles Coliseum, the Series set numerous Series attendance records, including a single-game mark of 92,706 in Game 5.

GAME 1

Thursday, October 1—At Chicago

Los Angeles (NL)	AB	R	H	O	A	E
Gilliam, 3b	4	0	1	0	1	0
Neal, 2b	4	0	2	0	3	1
Moon, lf	4	0	1	2	0	0
Snider, cf	2	0	0	2	0	2
Demeter, cf	1	0	0	0	0	0
Larker, rf	4	0	1	4	0	0
Hodges, 1b	4	0	2	10	0	0
Roseboro, c	4	0	0	5	0	0
Wills, ss	3	0	1	1	2	0
cFurillo	1	0	0	0	0	0
Craig, p	1	0	0	0	1	0
Churn, p	0	0	0	0	1	0
Labine, p	0	0	0	0	0	0
aEssegian	1	0	0	0	0	0
Koufax, p	0	0	0	0	0	0
bFairly	1	0	0	0	0	0
Klippstein, p	0	0	0	0	1	0
Totals	34	0	8	24	9	3

Chicago (AL)	AB	R	H	O	A	E
Aparicio, ss	5	0	0	3	3	0
Fox, 2b	4	2	1	2	2	0
Landis, cf	4	3	3	1	0	0
Kluszewski, 1b	4	2	3	8	2	0
Lollar, c	3	1	0	7	0	0
Goodman, 3b	2	1	1	0	0	0
Esposito, 3b	2	0	0	1	0	0
Smith, lf	4	1	2	2	0	0
Rivera, rf	4	1	0	2	0	0
Wynn, p	3	0	1	1	1	0
Staley, p	1	0	0	0	1	0
Totals	36	11	11	27	9	0

```
Los Angeles ............................ 0 0 0  0 0 0  0 0 0— 0
Chicago     ............................ 2 0 7  2 0 0  0 0 *—11
```

aStruck out for Labine in fifth. bGrounded out for Koufax in seventh. cFlied out for Wills in ninth. Runs batted in—Landis, Kluszewski 5, Lollar, Goodman, Wynn. Two-base hits—Fox, Smith 2, Wynn. Home runs—Kluszewski 2. Stolen base—Neal. Sacrifice fly—Lollar. Double play—Aparicio, Fox and Kluszewski. Left on bases—Los Angeles 8, Chicago 3. Earned runs—Chicago 7, Los Angeles 0. Bases on balls—Off Wynn 1, off Craig 1. Struck out—By Wynn 6, by Staley 1, by Craig 1, by Labine 1, by Koufax 1, by Klippstein 2. Pitching records—Off Wynn 6 hits, 0 runs in 7 innings (pitched to one batter in eighth); off Staley 2 hits, 0 runs in 2 innings; off Craig 5 hits, 5 runs in 2⅓ innings; off Churn 5 hits, 6 runs in ⅔ inning (pitched to two batters in fourth); off Labine 0 hits, 0 runs in 1 inning; off Koufax 0 hits, 0 runs in 2 innings; off Klippstein 1 hit, 0 runs in 2 innings; off Klippstein 1 hit, 0 runs in 2 innings. Winner— Wynn. Loser—Craig. Umpires—Summers (AL), Dascoli (NL), Hurley (AL), Secory (NL), Rice (AL), Dixon (NL). Time—2:35. Attendance—48,013.

GAME 2

Friday, October 2—At Chicago

Los Angeles (NL)	AB	R	H	O	A	E
Gilliam, 3b	4	1	1	1	1	0
Neal, 2b	5	2	2	2	4	0
Moon, lf	3	0	1	1	1	0
Snider, cf	4	0	1	1	0	0
Demeter, cf	0	0	0	0	0	0
Larker, rf	3	0	0	4	0	0
Sherry, p	1	0	0	1	1	0
Hodges, 1b	4	0	0	10	1	0
Roseboro, c	4	0	1	6	0	0
Wills, ss	4	0	1	1	6	1
Podres, p	2	0	1	0	0	0
aEssegian	1	1	1	0	0	0
Fairly, rf	1	0	0	0	0	0
Totals	36	4	9	27	14	1

Chicago (AL)	AB	R	H	O	A	E
Aparicio, ss	5	1	2	3	1	0
Fox, 2b	4	0	0	0	5	0
Landis, cf	3	1	0	2	0	0
Kluszewski, 1b	4	0	1	9	0	0
bTorgeson, 1b	0	1	0	0	0	0
Lollar, c	4	0	2	4	0	0
Smith, lf	3	0	1	2	0	0
Phillips, 3b	3	0	1	2	0	0
cGoodman, 3b	1	0	0	0	0	0
McAnany, rf	3	0	0	3	0	0
Rivera, rf	1	0	0	2	0	0
Shaw, p	3	0	1	0	1	0
Lown, p	0	0	0	0	0	0
dCash	1	0	0	0	0	0
Totals	35	3	8	27	7	0

```
Los Angeles ............................. 0 0 0  0 1 0  3 0 0—4
Chicago ................................. 2 0 0  0 0 0  0 1 0—3
```

aHit home run for Podres in seventh. bRan for Kluszewski in eighth. cStruck out for Phillips in eighth. dGrounded out for Lown in ninth. Runs batted in—Neal 3, Essegian, Kluszewski, Lollar, Smith. Two-base hits—Aparicio, Phillips, Smith. Home runs—Neal 2, Essegian. Stolen bases—Moon, Gilliam. Left on bases—Chicago 8, Los Angeles 7. Earned runs—Los Angeles 4, Chicago 3. Bases on balls—Off Podres 3, off Shaw 1, off Lown 1. Struck out—By Podres 3, by Sherry 1, by Shaw 1, by Lown 3. Pitching records—Off Podres 5 hits, 2 runs in 6 innings; off Sherry 3 hits, 1 run in 3 innings; off Shaw 8 hits, 4 runs in 6⅔ innings; off Lown 1 hit, 0 runs in 2⅓ innings. Winner—Podres. Loser—Shaw. Umpires—Dascoli (NL), Hurley (AL), Secory (NL), Summers (AL), Rice (AL) and Dixon (NL). Time—2:21. Attendance—47,368.

GAME 3

Sunday, October 4—At Los Angeles

Chicago (AL)	AB	R	H	O	A	E
Aparicio, ss	4	0	2	0	3	0
Fox, 2b	4	0	3	3	6	0
Landis, cf	5	0	1	2	0	0
Kluszewski, 1b	3	1	1	11	1	0
Lollar, c	4	0	2	5	1	0
Goodman, 3b	3	0	2	1	1	0
cEsposito, 3b	0	0	0	0	0	0
Smith, lf	4	0	0	0	0	0
Rivera, rf	3	0	0	1	0	0
Donovan, p	3	0	1	1	1	0
Staley, p	0	0	0	0	0	0
dCash	1	0	0	0	0	0
Totals	34	1	12	24	13	0

Los Angeles (NL)	AB	R	H	O	A	E
Gilliam, 3b	4	0	0	3	2	0
Neal, 2b	4	1	2	3	2	0
Moon, rf	4	0	0	1	0	0
Larker, lf	2	1	0	1	0	0
Hodges, 1b	2	0	1	6	1	0
Demeter, cf	2	0	0	0	0	0
aFurillo	1	0	1	0	0	0
bFairly, cf	0	0	0	0	0	0
Roseboro, c	3	0	0	9	3	0
Wills, ss	3	1	1	3	2	0
Drysdale, p	2	0	0	1	1	0
Sherry, p	0	0	0	0	0	0
Totals	27	3	5	27	11	0

Chicago	0 0 0	0 0 0	0 1 0—1			
Los Angeles	0 0 0	0 0 0	2 1 *—3			

aSingled for Demeter in seventh. bRan for Furillo in seventh. cRan for Goodman in eighth. dStruck out for Staley in ninth. Runs batted in—Furillo 2, Neal. Two-base hit—Neal. Stolen base—Landis. Sacrifice hit—Sherry. Double plays—Aparicio, Fox and Kluszewski; Roseboro and Neal; Gilliam, Neal and Hodges; Wills, Neal and Hodges. Left on bases—Chicago 11. Los Angeles 3. Earned runs—Chicago 1, Los Angeles 3. Bases on balls—Off Drysdale 4, off Donovan 2. Struck out—By Drysdale 5, by Sherry 3, by Donovan 5. Pitching records—Off Drysdale 11 hits, 1 run in 7 innings (pitched to two batters in eighth); off Sherry 1 hit, 0 runs in 2 innings; off Donovan 2 hits, 2 runs in 6⅔ innings; off Staley 3 hits 1 run in 1⅓ innings. Hit by pitcher—By Sherry (Goodman). Winner—Drysdale. Loser—Donovan. Umpires—Hurley (AL), Secory (NL), Summers (AL), Dascoli (NL), Dixon (NL) and Rice (AL). Time—2:33. Attendance—92,394.

GAME 4

Monday, October 5—At Los Angeles

Chicago (AL)	AB	R	H	O	A	E
Landis, cf	5	1	1	0	0	1
Aparicio, ss	3	0	1	0	2	1
Fox, 2b	5	1	3	3	4	0
Kluszewski, 1b	4	1	2	9	0	0
Lollar, c	4	1	1	6	2	0
Goodman, 3b	4	0	0	0	0	0
Smith, lf	3	0	2	3	0	0
Rivera, rf	3	0	0	3	1	0
Wynn, p	1	0	0	0	1	0
Lown, p	0	0	0	0	0	0
aCash	1	0	0	0	0	0
Pierce, p	0	0	0	0	0	0
cTorgeson	1	0	0	0	0	0
Staley, p	0	0	0	0	0	0
Totals	34	4	10	24	10	3

Los Angeles (NL)	AB	R	H	O	A	E
Gilliam, 3b	4	0	0	0	1	0
Neal, 2b	4	0	0	4	4	0
Moon, rf-lf	4	1	2	3	0	0
Larker, lf	2	1	1	0	0	0
bFurillo, rf	1	0	0	0	0	0
Fairly, rf	1	0	0	0	0	0
Hodges, 1b	4	2	2	10	0	0
Demeter, cf	3	1	2	1	0	0
Roseboro, c	3	0	1	7	0	0
Wills, ss	4	0	1	2	6	0
Craig, p	2	0	0	0	1	0
Sherry, p	0	0	0	0	0	0
Totals	32	5	9	27	12	0

Chicago	0 0 0	0 0 0	4 0 0—4
Los Angeles	0 0 4	0 0 0	0 1 *—5

aStruck out for Lown in fourth. bStruck out for Larker in fifth. cGrounded out for Pierce in seventh. Runs batted in—Kluszewski, Lollar 3, Hodges 2, Roseboro. Two-base hit—Fox. Home runs—Lollar, Hodges. Stolen bases—Aparicio, Wills. Sacrifice hits—Roseboro, Craig, Aparicio. double plays—Wills, Neal and Hodges; Neal, Wills and Hodges. Left on bases—Chicago 9, Los Angeles 6. Earned runs—Los Angeles 4, Chicago 4. Bases on balls—Off Craig 4, off Sherry 1, off Pierce 1. Struck out—By Craig 7, by Wynn 2, by Pierce 2, by Staley 2. Pitching records—Off Craig 10 hits, 4 runs in 7 innings; off Sherry 0 hits, 0 runs in 2 innings; off Wynn 8 hits, 4 runs in 2⅔ innings; off Lown 0 hits, 0 runs in ⅓ inning; off Pierce 0 hits, 0 runs in 3 innings; off Staley 1 hit, 1 run in 2 innings. Passed ball—Lollar. Winner—Sherry. Loser—Staley. Umpires—Secory (NL), Summers (AL), Dascoli (NL), Hurley (AL), Dixon (NL) and Rice (AL). Time—2:30. Attendance—92,650.

GAME 5

Tuesday, October 6—At Los Angeles

Chicago (AL)	AB	R	H	O	A	E
Aparicio, ss	4	0	2	3	5	0
Fox, 2b	3	1	1	4	4	0
Landis, cf	4	0	1	2	0	0
Lollar, c	4	0	0	1	0	0
Kluszewski, 1b	4	0	0	12	0	0
Smith, rf-lf	4	0	0	1	0	0
Phillips, 3b	3	0	1	1	2	0
McAnany, lf	1	0	0	1	0	0
Rivera, rf	0	0	0	2	0	0
Shaw, p	1	0	0	0	3	0
Pierce, p	0	0	0	0	0	0
Donovan, p	0	0	0	0	0	0
Totals	28	1	5	27	14	0

Los Angeles (NL)	AB	R	H	O	A	E
Gilliam, 3b	5	0	4	0	3	0
Neal, 2b	5	0	1	5	2	0
Moon, rf-cf	4	0	1	0	0	0
Larker, lf	4	0	0	3	1	0
Hodges, 1b	4	0	3	7	1	0
Demeter, cf	3	0	0	4	0	0
eFairly	0	0	0	0	0	0
fRepulski, rf	0	0	0	0	0	0
Roseboro, c	3	0	0	6	1	0
gFurillo	1	0	0	0	0	0
Pignatano, c	0	0	0	1	0	0
Wills, ss	2	0	0	1	2	0
aEssegian	0	0	0	0	0	0
bZimmer, ss	1	0	0	0	1	0
Koufax, p	2	0	0	0	0	0
cSnider	1	0	0	0	0	0
dPodres	0	0	0	0	0	0
Williams, p	0	0	0	0	0	0
hSherry	1	0	0	0	0	0
Totals	36	0	9	27	11	0

```
Chicago ................................. 0 0 0   1 0 0   0 0 0—1
Los Angeles ............................. 0 0 0   0 0 0   0 0 0—0
```

aWalked for Wills in seventh. bRan for Essegian in seventh. cHit into force play for Koufax in seventh. dRan for Snider in seventh. eAnnounced as batter for Demeter in eighth. fWalked intentionally for Fairly in eighth. gPopped out for Roseboro in eighth. hGrounded out for Williams in ninth. Runs batted in—None (run scored on Lollar's double play). Three-base hit—Hodges. Stolen base—Gilliam. Sacrifice hits—Shaw 2. Double play—Neal and Hodges. Left on bases—Chicago 5, Los Angeles 11. Earned runs—Chicago 1, Los Angeles 0. Bases on balls—Off Koufax 1, off Williams 2, off Shaw 1, off Pierce 1. Struck out—By Koufax 6, by Williams 1, by Shaw 1. Pitching records—Off Koufax 5 hits, 1 run in 7 innings; off Williams 0 hits, 0 runs in 2 innings; off Shaw 9 hits, 0 runs in 7⅓ innings; off Pierce 0 hits, 0 runs in 0 innings (pitched to one batter in eighth); off Donovan 0 hits, 0 runs in 1⅔ innings. Wild pitch—Shaw. Winner—Shaw. Loser—Koufax. Umpires—Summers (AL), Dascoli (NL), Hurley (AL), Secory (NL), Dixon (NL) and Rice (AL). Time—2:28. Attendance—92,706.

GAME 6

Thursday, October 8—At Chicago

Los Angeles (NL)	AB	R	H	O	A	E
Gilliam, 3b	4	1	0	0	2	0
Neal, 2b	5	1	3	4	4	0
Moon, lf	4	2	1	3	0	0
Snider, cf-rf	3	1	1	2	0	0
eEssegian	1	1	1	0	0	0
Fairly, rf	0	0	0	0	0	0
Hodges, 1b	5	0	1	10	0	0
Larker, rf	1	0	1	0	0	0
aDemeter, cf	3	1	1	4	0	0
Roseboro, c	4	0	0	2	0	0
Wills, ss	4	1	1	2	3	0
Podres, p	2	1	1	0	1	0
Sherry, p	2	0	2	0	2	0
Totals	38	9	13	27	12	0

Chicago (AL)	AB	R	H	O	A	E
Aparicio, ss	5	0	1	1	2	1
Fox, 2b	4	0	1	2	2	0
Landis, cf	3	1	1	2	0	0
Lollar, c	3	1	0	5	2	0
Kluszewski, 1b	4	1	2	10	0	0
Smith, lf	2	0	0	2	0	0
Phillips, 3b-rf	4	0	1	3	1	0
McAnany, rf	1	0	0	1	0	0
bGoodman, 3b	3	0	0	0	1	0
Wynn, p	1	0	0	0	1	0
Donovan, p	0	0	0	0	0	0
Lown, p	0	0	0	0	0	0
cTorgeson	0	0	0	0	0	0
Staley, p	0	0	0	1	0	0
dRomano	1	0	0	0	0	0
Pierce, p	0	0	0	0	0	0
Moore, p	0	0	0	0	0	0
fCash	1	0	0	0	0	0
Totals	32	3	6	27	9	1

```
Los Angeles ...........................  0 0 2  6 0 0  0 0 1—9
Chicago ...............................  0 0 0  3 0 0  0 0 0—3
```

aRan for Larker in fourth. bStruck out for McAnany in fourth. cWalked for Lown in fourth. dGrounded out for Staley in seventh. eHomered for Snider in ninth. fFlied out for Moore in ninth. Runs batted in—Neal 2, Moon 2, Snider 2, Essegian, Wills, Podres, Kluszewski 3. Two-base hits—Podres, Neal, Fox, Kluszewski. Home runs—Snider, Moon, Kluszewski, Essegian. Sacrifice hit—Roseboro. Double play—Podres, Neal and Hodges. Left on bases—Los Angeles 7, Chicago 7. Earned runs—Los Angeles 9,

Chicago 3. Bases on balls—Off Wynn 3, off Donovan 1, off Podres 3, off Sherry 1. Struck out—By Wynn 2, by Pierce 1, by Moore 1, by Podres 1, by Sherry 1. Pitching records—Off Wynn 5 hits, 5 runs in 3⅓ innings; off Donovan 2 hits, 3 runs in 0 innings (pitched to three batters in fourth); off Lown 1 hit, 0 runs in ⅔ innings; off Staley 2 hits, 0 runs in 3 innings; off Pierce 2 hits, 0 runs in 1 inning; off Moore 1 hit, 1 run in 1 inning; off Podres 2 hits, 3 runs in 3⅓ innings; off Sherry 4 hits, 0 runs in 5⅔ innings. Hit by pitcher—by Podres (Landis). Winner—Sherry. Loser—Wynn. Umpires—Dascoli (N.L.), Hurley (A.L.), Secory (N.L.), Summers (A.L.), Rice (A.L.) and Dixon (N.L.). Time—2:33. Attendance—47,653.

Individual Batting

LOS ANGELES (NL)

	AB	H	2B	3B	HR	R	RBI	BA
C. Neal, 2b	27	10	2	0	2	4	6	.370
J. Gilliam, 3b	25	6	0	0	0	2	0	.240
W. Moon, of	23	6	0	0	1	3	2	.261
G. Hodges, 1b	23	9	0	1	1	2	2	.391
J. Roseboro, c	21	2	0	0	0	0	1	.095
M. Wills, ss	20	5	0	0	0	2	1	.250
N. Larker, of	16	3	0	0	0	2	0	.188
D. Demeter, of	12	3	0	0	0	2	0	.250
D. Snider, of	10	2	0	0	1	1	2	.200
C. Furillo, of	4	1	0	0	0	0	2	.250
L. Sherry, p	4	2	0	0	0	0	0	.500
J. Podres, p	4	2	1	0	0	1	1	.500
C. Essegian	3	2	0	0	2	2	2	.667
R. Fairly, of	3	0	0	0	0	0	0	.000
R. Craig, p	3	0	0	0	0	0	0	.000
S. Koufax, p	2	0	0	0	0	0	0	.000
D. Drysdale, p	2	0	0	0	0	0	0	.000
D. Zimmer, ss	1	0	0	0	0	0	0	.000
J. Pignatano, c	0	0	0	0	0	0	0	—
R. Repulski, of	0	0	0	0	0	0	0	—

Errors: D. Snider (2), M. Wills, C. Neal. Stolen bases: J. Gilliam (2), W. Moon, C. Neal, M. Wills.

CHICAGO (AL)

	AB	H	2B	3B	HR	R	RBI	BA
L. Aparicio, ss	26	8	1	0	0	1	0	.308
J. Landis, of	24	7	0	0	0	6	1	.292
N. Fox, 2b	24	9	3	0	0	4	0	.375
T. Kluszewski, 1b	23	9	1	0	3	5	10	.391
S. Lollar, c	22	5	0	0	1	3	5	.227
A. Smith, of	20	5	3	0	0	1	1	.250
B. Goodman, 3b	13	3	0	0	0	1	1	.231
J. Rivera, of	11	0	0	0	0	1	0	.000
B. Phillips, 3b, of	10	3	1	0	0	0	0	.300
J. McAnany, of	5	0	0	0	0	0	0	.000
E. Wynn, p	5	1	1	0	0	0	1	.200
N. Cash	4	0	0	0	0	0	0	.000
B. Shaw, p	4	1	0	0	0	0	0	.250
D. Donovan, p	3	1	0	0	0	0	0	.333
S. Esposito, 3b	2	0	0	0	0	0	0	.000
J. Romano	1	0	0	0	0	0	0	.000
E. Torgeson, 1b	1	0	0	0	0	1	0	.000
G. Staley, p	1	0	0	0	0	0	0	.000

171

1959 World Series (continued)

Errors: L. Aparicio (2), J. Landis, B. Pierce. Stolen bases: J. Landis, L. Aparicio.

Individual Pitching

LOS ANGELES (NL)

	W	L	ERA	IP	H	BB	SO	SV
L. Sherry	2	0	0.71	12.2	8	2	5	2
S. Koufax	0	1	1.00	9	5	1	7	0
J. Podres	1	0	4.82	9.1	7	6	4	0
R. Craig	0	1	8.68	9.1	15	5	8	0
D. Drysdale	1	0	1.29	7	11	4	5	0
J. Klippstein	0	0	0.00	2	1	0	2	0
S. Williams	0	0	0.00	2	0	2	1	0
C. Labine	0	0	0.00	1	0	0	1	0
C. Churn	0	0	27.00	0.2	5	0	0	0

CHICAGO (AL)

	W	L	ERA	IP	H	BB	SO	SV
B. Shaw	1	1	2.57	14	17	2	2	0
E. Wynn	1	1	5.54	13	19	4	10	0
G. Staley	0	1	2.16	8.1	8	0	3	1
D. Donovan	0	1	5.40	8.1	4	3	5	1
B. Pierce	0	0	0.00	4	2	2	3	0
T. Lown	0	0	0.00	3.1	2	1	3	0
R. Moore	0	0	9.00	1	1	0	1	0

SOX-CELLANEOUS

White Sox Presidents

Charles A. Comiskey 1901–31
J. Louis Comiskey 1932–39
Harry Grabiner (VP) 1940
Mrs. Grace Comiskey 1941–56
None 1957–58
William L. Veeck, Jr. 1959-61
Arthur C. Allyn, Jr. 1961–69
John W. Allyn 1970–75
William L. Veeck, Jr. 1976–80
Edward Einhorn 1981–

White Sox in Baseball Hall of Fame

Luke Appling, 1930–43, 1945–50
Chief Bender, 1925
Eddie Collins, 1915–26
Charles Comiskey (manager, owner), 1900–31
Johnny Evers, 1922
Red Faber, 1914–33
Clark Griffith (player, manager), 1901–02
Harry Hooper, 1921–25
Al Lopez (manager), 1957–65, 1968–69
Ted Lyons, 1923–42, 1946
Edd Roush, 1913
Red Ruffing, 1947
Ray Schalk, 1912–28
Al Simmons, 1933–35
Ed Walsh, 1904–16
Early Wynn, 1958–62

(Note: White Sox outfielder Jocko Conlan (1934–35) was inducted as an umpire; Hall of Fame outfielder Hugh Duffy managed the Sox (1910–11); Hall of Fame pitcher Bob Lemon was the White Sox skipper (1977–78); Hall of Fame first baseman Frank Chance was the Sox manager (1924); and Hall of Fame slugger Hank Greenberg was a Sox executive (1959–63).

Uniform Numbers Retired by Sox

2—Nellie Fox
4—Luke Appling

White Sox vs. Cubs in City Series

From 1903 to 1942, Chicago's two major league clubs competed in a postseason series, designed after the World Series itself.

During that time, the White Sox dominated, winning 19 series to the Cubs' six, with the inaugural matchup ending in a tie. A total of 161 games were played, with the Sox victorious in 95, the Cubs 62. Four ended in ties.

In 1949, the Sox-Cubs rivalry resumed with a midsummer benefit game for the Chicago Park District's boys baseball program. During that series, which ended in 1972, the Cubs won 13 and the Sox 10.

The most historic meeting of all was in 1906, when the White Sox and Cubs met in the World Series. The Sox were upset winners over the Cubs, four games to two.

The Sox and Cubs played a pair of games in 1981 as part of the reconditioning before resumption of play after the players' strike (Aug. 7). The teams fought to a 0–0 tie in the first contest at Comiskey Park. The Cubs emerged victorious, 4–3, at Wrigley Field the following day.

No-Hit Games by White Sox

			Sox-Opp.
+1902	(Sept. 20)	James Callahan vs. Detroit	3-0
1905	(Sept. 6)	Frank Smith vs. Detroit	15-0
+1908	(Sept. 20)	Frank Smith vs. Philadelphia	1-0
+1911	(Aug. 27)	Edward Walsh vs. Boston	5-0
1914	(May 14)	James Scott vs. Washington	0-1
		(Pitched 9 hitless innings before Chick Gandil singled; lost on 2 hits in 10 innings)	
+1914	(May 31)	Joseph Benz vs. Cleveland	6-1
1917	(Apr. 14)	Edward Cicotte vs. St. Louis	11-0
*1922	(Apr. 30)	Charles Robertson vs. Detroit	2-0
1926	(Aug. 21)	Theodore Lyons vs. Boston	6-0
+1935	(Aug. 31)	Vernon Kennedy vs. Cleveland	5-0
+1937	(June 1)	William Dietrich vs. St. Louis	8-0
+1957	(Aug. 20)	Robert Keegan vs. Washington (night)	6-0
+1967	(Sept. 10)	Joel Horlen vs. Detroit	6-0
1976	(July 28)	John Odom & Francisco Barrios vs. Oakland	2-1

No-Hit Games Against White Sox

			Sox-Opp.
+1901	(May 9)	Earl Moore, Cleveland	4-2
		(Pitched 9 hitless innings, before Samuel B. Mertes singled; lost on 2 hits in 10 innings)	
1904	(Aug. 17)	Jesse Tannehill, Boston	0-6
	(Sept. 27)	William Dinneen, Boston	0-2
*1908	(Oct. 2)	Adrian Joss, Cleveland	0-1
+1910	(Apr. 20)	Adrian Joss, Cleveland	0-1
1917	(May 5)	Ernest Koob, St. Louis	0-1
+1917	(May 6)	Robert Groom, St. Louis (2nd G)	0-3
+1940	(Apr. 16)	Bob Feller, Cleveland (Opening Day)	0-1
1956	(July 14)	Melvin Parnell Boston	0-4
+1962	(Aug. 1)	William Monbouquette, Boston (night)	0-1

Attendance Records

Day Game: 51,560 (vs. Milwaukee, April 14, 1981)
Night Game: 53,940 (vs. New York, June 8, 1951)
Doubleheader: 55,555 (vs. Minnesota, May 20, 1976)
Opening Day: 51,560 (vs. Milwaukee, April 14, 1981)
Season, Home: 1,657,135 (1977)
Season, Road: 1,444,296 (1977)

+At Chicago
*Perfect Game

Spring Training Sites

1901–2	Excelsior Springs, Mo.	1924	Winter Haven, Fla.
1903	Mobile, Ala.	1925–28	Shreveport, La.
1904	Marlin Springs, Tex.	1929	Dallas, Tex.
1905–6	New Orleans, La.	1930–32	San Antonio, Tex.
1907	Mexico City, Mexico	1933–42	Pasadena, Calif.
1908	Los Angeles, Calif.	1943–44*	French Lick, Ind.
1909–10	San Francisco, Calif.	1945*	Terre Haute, Ind.
1911	Mineral Wells, Tex.	1946–50	Pasadena, Calif.
1912	Waco, Tex.	1951	Pasadena & Palm Springs, Calif.
1913–15	Paso Robles, Calif.	1952	Pasadena & El Centro, Calif.
1916–19	Mineral Wells, Texas	1953	El Centro, Calif.
1920	Waco, Tex.	1954–59	Tampa, Fla.
1921	Waxahachie, Texas	1960–Present	Sarasota, Fla.
1922–23	Seguin, Texas		

White Sox in Annual Hall of Fame Game

1943 — Brooklyn 7, *Sox* 5
1953 — Cincinnati 16, *Sox* 6
1957 — *Sox* 13, St. Louis 4
1970 — Montreal 10, *Sox* 6
1974 — Atlanta 12, *Sox* 9
1980 — Pittsburgh 11, *Sox* 8

SOX TIDBITS

Did you know that . . . ?

Luke Appling set a major league record for most walks by a righthanded batter in one season with 122 in 153 games in 1935.

★   ★   ★

The Sox' Charlie Lindstrom (son of Hall of Famer Fred Lindstrom) had one major league at-bat and it was a triple.

★   ★   ★

Carlos May is believed to be the only professional athlete to wear his birthday on the back of his uniform (MAY 17)

★   ★   ★

In his final full season, Hall of Famer Ted Lyons completed all 20 of his starts, hurled 180⅓ innings, compiled a league-leading 2.10 ERA, and had a 14–6 won-lost record.

★   ★   ★

Carl Reynolds became the first Sox player to hit 20 or more home runs with 22 in 1930.

★   ★   ★

The baseball-playing Roth brothers were involved in an intriguing set of circumstances. Frank, who was a catcher for the Sox in 1926, was born in Chicago and died in Burlington, Wis. Robert, a Sox outfielder in 1914 and 1915, was born in Burlington, Wis., and died in Chicago.

*War Years

*   *   *

Sox players Nick Altrock and Minnie Minoso hold a distinction. One or the other played in every decade between the 1890s and 1980s (not all with the White Sox, however).

*   *   *

The 1920 White Sox became the first major league club to boast as many as four 20-game winners (Red Faber, 23–13, Lefty Williams, 22–14, Dickie Kerr, 21–9, and Ed Cicotte, 21–10). The feat has been matched just once—by the 1971 Orioles.

*   *   *

In 1907 Jiggs Donahue set major league records for putouts (1,846) and total chances (1,998) by a first baseman. He previously held both records, set the year before.

*   *   *

The Sox' Willie Kamm set the modern major league record for putouts by a third baseman, with 243 in 1928. He held the previous mark of 236, set the year before. Kamm also led AL third basemen in fielding percentage six straight years (1924–29).

*   *   *

Chet Lemon, Sox centerfielder, set AL marks for putouts (512) and total chances (536) for outfielders in 1977. He broke Dom DiMaggio's marks of 503 and 526, respectively.

*   *   *

Ed Walsh set major league records for a pitcher with 227 assists and 266 total chances in 1907.

*   *   *

Only three players have played with four AL clubs in one season; all made stops in Chicago: Frank Huelsman, 1904 (started season with Sox); Paul Lehner, 1951; Ted Gray, 1955 (started season with Sox).

*   *   *

Sam Mertes played all nine positions in the field during the 1902 season. Only four have done it, plus two players in one-day stunts. Mertes also set an AL record of 35 outfield assists that season.

*   *   *

Nellie Fox led the American League in singles in 1952 and from 1954–60 (most league—8; most consecutive league, 7). He also led the major leagues in 1952, 1954–57, and 1959 (most consecutive, 4; tied with Ty Cobb for total seasons leading the majors, 6). Fox also led AL in fewest times striking out, 11 times (1952–62), and led AL second basemen in chances accepted nine times (1952–60), putouts 10 times (1952–61), and double plays, five—all league records.

*   *   *

The Sox' Rollie Zeider holds AL rookie record for most steals, with 49 in 1910.

*   *   *

Luis Aparicio led the American League in chances accepted and assists seven times (a record) from 1956–61 and 1968—all with Chicago. Luke Appling also led AL seven times in assists: 1933, 1935, 1937, 1939, 1941, 1943, and 1946.

*   *   *

Ray Schalk led AL catchers in fielding percentage eight times (1913–17, 20–22), chances accepted eight times (1913–17, 19–20, 22) and most putouts nine times (1913–20, 22)—all league records. Had most assists of any catcher in AL history with 1810, just 25 short of Deacon McGuire's major league mark.

*   *   *

The Sox Smoky Burgess led the AL in pinch-hits with 20 in 1965 and 21 in 1966.

*   *   *

The White Sox' Harry McCurdy had 10 straight hits for the club in 1926.

*   *   *

Clark Griffith in 1901 and Ted Lyons in 1930 were the only two White Sox pitchers to win 20 games and hit .300 in the same season.

★　　★　　★

Lefty hurler Jack Harshman hit six home runs in 1956—a Sox record for pitchers.

★　　★　　★

Ted Lyons (21 years), Luke Appling (20), and Red Faber (20) played their entire major league careers with the White Sox. Both Hall of Famers, Lyons and Appling never got into a World Series. Lyons played the longest of any major leaguer without seeing Series action.

★　　★　　★

The 1924 and 1937 White Sox teams each had three .300 hitters. In '24 it was Bibb Falk (.352), Johnny Mostil (.325), and Harry Hooper (.328). In '37 Rip Radcliff (.325), Mike Kreevich (.302), and Dixie Walker (.302) all hit the .300 plateau.

★　　★　　★

The Sox won 15 doubleheaders in 1961 and played in 34—both AL records.

★　　★　　★

The White Sox beat Philadelphia 37 times over the 1915 and 1916 seasons, without a loss in '15. The Sox also beat St. Louis 12 times at home without a loss during the 1915 season.

★　　★　　★

The White Sox won seven doubleheaders from the Athletics during the 1943 season.

★　　★　　★

The Sox used 41 players in a doubleheader vs. Oakland on Sept. 7, 1980.

★　　★　　★

The Sox have led the league in steals more than any other AL club (29), including a league record 11 consecutive years (1951–61). The White Sox also hold the league record for steals of home in one season—15.

★　　★　　★

Ed Walsh (1910–12) and Wilbur Wood (1968–70) each led American league pitchers in games pitched three years in succession. Wood also led the AL in games started, from 1972–74.

★　　★　　★

During Ed Walsh's 40-win season in 1908, he beat both New York and Boston nine times for a league record. He also set an AL record for innings pitched (464).

The Sox' Reb Russell set a league record for most innings pitched by a rookie pitcher with 316 in 1913.

★　　★　　★

The Sox set a league mark for hit batsmen in 1956 (75).

★　　★　　★

Catcher Ray Schalk had the distinction of catching a major league record four no-hitters in a Sox uniform. The pitchers? Jim Scott, Joe Benz, Ed Cicotte, Charlie Robertson (perfect game).

177